EMBODYING ARGENTINA

EMBODYING ARGENTINA

Body, Space and Nation in 19th Century Narrative

by Nancy Hanway

McFarland & Company, Inc., Publishers
Jefferson, North Carolina, and London

For
David and Griffin
and
In memoriam
Liliana Zucotti

LIBRARY OF CONGRESS CATALOGUING-IN-PUBLICATION DATA

Hanway, Nancy, 1959–
    Embodying Argentina : body, space and nation in 19th century
narrative / by Nancy Hanway.
        p.   cm.
    Includes bibliographical references and index.

    ISBN 0-7864-1457-X (softcover: 50# alkaline paper)

    1. Argentine prose literature — 19th century — Criticism
and interpretation.   2. National characteristics, Argentine,
in literature.   I. Title.
PQ7707.N37H36   2003
868'.50809358 — dc21   2002155760

British Library cataloguing data are available

Front cover: Prilidiano Pueyrredón, *Manuela de Rosas y
Ezcurra*, 1851, Museo Nacional de Bellas Artes, Buenos Aires

Manufactured in the United States of America

*McFarland & Company, Inc., Publishers
    Box 611, Jefferson, North Carolina 28640
    www.mcfarlandpub.com*

Acknowledgments

To Steven Ungar and Kathleen Newman, at the University of Iowa, I offer heartfelt thanks for their help and encouragement over many years. For his insightful reading of several drafts, I would like to thank Jeremy Adelman, Director of Latin American Studies at Princeton. At Princeton I was also fortunate to have the gracious assistance of Ricardo Piglia, who commented upon several of my chapters.

I owe an intellectual debt to Kathleen Newman whose teaching and research sparked my fascination with Argentine culture. She has been a trusted mentor and friend. Cristina Iglesia at the Universidad de Buenos Aires has not only informed my readings of nineteenth century Argentine literature, but provided me with a circle of ready-made readers during my time in Buenos Aires.

The Seashore Dissertation Fellowship from the University of Iowa enabled me to spend a year writing without the demands of teaching. The Fulbright International Dissertation Fellowship gave me the ability to research in Argentina.

In Buenos Aires, countless people assisted me in my work: Anita Barrenechea, Silvia Delfino, Laura Malosetti Costa, Jorge Meyer, Lia Munilla, Marcela Nari, Lily Sosa de Newton, Regina Root, Claudia Torre, and Liliana Zucotti were among them. And I owe the wonderful librarians at the Sala de Reservados at the Biblioteca Nacional many thanks. Special thanks go to my friends Ana Von Rebeur and family, Jorge and Fanny Bekerman, Graciela Batticuore, Channing Henry, and Ruth, Horacio and Sol Aguiar.

To my colleagues at Gustavus Adolphus College I owe gratitude for their understanding of the time involved in a project of this kind. Two summer grants and a semester leave during my fourth year were instrumental in helping me finish the book.

David William Foster generously read and commented on Chapter Three. I thank him for his support at a pivotal moment.

My parents, Jim and Betty Hanway, have given me years of their love and support. Nancy Nicol volunteered for childcare during her vacations. Will and Judy Hancock sent us plane tickets and care packages. My entire extended family put up with forgotten birthdays and neglected holidays during the final drafts of this project.

Finally I would like to thank my husband W. David Hancock for his support over many years. Besides enduring bad plumbing karma in Buenos Aires, he gave me constant encouragement during the writing of this book. And, of course, I want to thank my son Griffin, who—like this book— was conceived in Buenos Aires.

Table of Contents

Introduction

In 2001 Argentina faced its most serious national crisis in years: the collapse of the nation's economy that led to widespread unemployment, mass riots, and the loss of thousands of jobs. The fall of the peso in 2002 has provoked fears that the government will be destabilized. A formalized barter system has sprung up, with citizens using coupons to replace the national currency. Argentineans line up in front of European embassies in the nation's capital, seeking repatriation to the countries of their grandparents.

In response to the crisis, the performance group Noche en Vela remounted its production of *Ganado en pie* (*Live Cattle*), a comic work from 2000 that explored the symbols of *argentinidad*, or Argentine-ness. Based on the 1948 essay *Muerte y resurrección del Martín Fierro*, by literary critic Martínez Estrada, the work questions and parodies nineteenth century icons. As one example of its carnivalesque humor, the piece presents a gaucho—the prototypical national symbol—being created in a laboratory. As in the nineteenth century works it mocks, *Ganado en pie* blends fiction with historical reality. The interconnected scenes show actual statesman-authors such as Domingo F. Sarmiento appearing alongside fictional military leaders facing identity crises. With contemporary journalists declaring that the nation is at the point of collapse, it is not surprising that critical response to *Ganado en pie* in 2001 was much less positive than a year earlier. In times of national crisis the symbols of nation and citizenship are held sacred.

At a moment in history when Argentineans are being forced to change their nationality in order to survive, the question "What is *argentinidad*?" becomes more significant than ever. The symbols of Argentine national culture that are now revered came about during another era of intense political and economic crisis. In the second half of the nineteenth century, Argentina endured a tumultuous period of national consolidation, framed by the disintegration of the Federalist government (which fell in 1852) and the liberal revolution of 1880. During these three decades, the country saw the fall of a dictatorship, national schism and reconciliation, several outbreaks of civil war, war with Paraguay, massive immigration, brutal epidemics of yellow fever and cholera, national expansion into the pampas, a war against the indigenous people of the southern pampas, and abrupt economic gains and losses. The crises of this era were reflected in the literature, which produced many of the symbols of *argentinidad* still revered today. Some of the most significant works of Argentine literary history come from the period between 1850 and 1880, among them four narratives that have emerged as classics for twentieth century readers: *Amalia* (1851) by José Mármol, *Recuerdos de provincia* (1850) by Domingo Faustino Sarmiento, *Una excursión a los indios ranqueles* (1870) by Lucio V. Mansilla, and *Martín Fierro* (1872, 1879) by José Hernández.

José Mármol's *Amalia* is considered to be the paradigm of romantic fiction in Argentina. The novelistic action takes place in the Buenos Aires of 1840 during the dictatorship of Juan Manuel de Rosas. The novel involves the forces of civilization (the anti–Rosas *unitarios*) pitted against the agents of barbarism (the pro–Rosas *federalistas*).* Literary critics agree that Amalia is designed to represent the nation of Argentina. Domingo Faustino Sarmiento's *Recuerdos de provincia* mixes fiction and autobiography while promoting the future president's views on education, national progress, and the nature of the nation-family. Lucio V. Mansilla's *Una excursión a los indios ranqueles* is Argentina's most famous domestic travelogue, and was written about Mansilla's journey across the pampas into indigenous territory to re-negotiate a treaty with the Ranquel leaders. Mansilla's literary excursion was a forerunner of the elite, charming, testimonial style of the gentlemen-writers of Argentina's "Generation of 1880."

José Hernández's narrative poem *Martín Fierro* describes the sufferings of a gaucho (horseman of the pampas) who is taken from his home and forced by new laws into the army. Written to protest the unjust treatment of the free gauchos of the pampas by the Argentine government, the poem has become emblematic of Argentine national culture and

---

Rosas represented the Federalist Party, which advocated a federal style republic, with a group of semi-autonomous states. Opposed to Rosas's party were the unitarios (Unitarists), who fought for a centralized rule, with Buenos Aires as the seat of political and economic power.

identity. In 1924, Ricardo Rojas remarked that while Argentina does not have a *Chanson de Roland* or a *Cantar del Mio Cid*, "el *Martín Fierro* llega, por su unidad y por su asunto, a ser para la nación argentina algo muy análago" ("*Martín Fierro*, through its unity and its subject matter, is something very analogous to the Argentine nation") (Rojas qtd. in Isaacson 9).

Along with these canonical texts, the work of two women authors of the period — Rosa Guerra and Eduarda Mansilla de García — should be considered in any analysis of nineteenth century literature of Argentina. The writings of both Guerra and Mansilla de García were published regularly in *porteño* (Buenos Aires) journals. The thematic concerns of their work serve as an indicator of cultural obsessions. The two novels entitled *Lucía Miranda* by Guerra and Mansilla de García were published in the same year (1860) and dealt with the colonial-era myth of the first white woman held captive by indigenous tribes, a theme which was popular in mid-nineteenth century Argentine culture. Mansilla de García's *El médico de San Luis* (also published in 1860) was hailed during its time by Juan María Gutiérrez as an elegant novel of national manners and morals. The novel concerns the details of provincial life and the corrupt system of provincial justice. "El ramito de romero," a short story from 1868, represents a take on *lo nacional* that presents women as the spiritual bridge to full citizenship for men.

What makes all these works of literature significant to a discussion of national culture is that, like their contemporaries in other Latin American nations, authors in Argentina in the nineteenth century understood authorship as a political business. Not only did male authors such as Sarmiento and Hernández seek and gain political office, but they conceived of the novel as both a history-making and nation-building enterprise. As in other parts of Latin America, the emergence of the Argentine nation coincided with the appearance of the romantic novel in Europe; however, the European romantic tradition taken up by Argentine writers was shaped with specific nationalistic goals in mind. As Doris Sommer has noted, these works inscribed national and social ideals within the figure of their feminine protagonists. The central characters were usually women, and the titles of the novels often reflected this feminine presence.

As well as coinciding with the popularity of the romantic novel, the taking on of a feminine voice by Argentine writers occurred at a time when women's bodies were viewed as symbolic of the nation. This was a phenomenon that was not limited to Argentina, or to Latin America. Mary Louise Pratt notes in "Women, Literature and National Brotherhood" that what she calls the "uneasy coexistence of nationhood and womanhood" was played out in the use of female icons as national symbols, such as the

Statue of Liberty in the United States or Marianne in France (53). In this capacity, women acquired new symbolic value in building the nation. Yet symbolic women rarely corresponded to actual women. The noble female figure of nation and the imagined ideal citizen were feminine but not female, gendered but not sexual.

Pratt's idea that these icons had nothing to do with real women was what first sparked my interest in analyzing the works of nineteenth century Argentina. I started with the novel *Amalia*, often referred to as one of the most important manifestations of Hispanic Romanticism, and conceived of primarily by its author as a political and historical treatise. When I began examining the figure of Amalia as representative of the nation, I discovered that the question that haunts the narrative is not, "What is Argentina?" but, "Who is Argentinean?" Instead of trying to define the nation, Mármol, through the character Amalia, presents an *emblematic citizen*: a figure who embodies ideas about both the imagined nation and citizenship. As I began to look at other narratives from nineteenth century Argentina, I saw that the figure of an emblematic citizen appears in each of the literary narratives written during the nearly thirty years between the fall of dictator Juan Manuel Rosas in 1852 and the establishment of the modern Argentinean republic in 1880. Most perplexing was the realization that there was a shift in the gender and racial identification of the body of the emblematic citizen during this period, accompanied by shifts in class identification and regionality: the body of the emblematic citizen is represented as female, civilized, elite, white and urban in 1850 (*Amalia*), and male semi-barbaric, lower-class, rural, racially uncertain, and masculine by 1880 (*Martín Fierro*).

In order to understand both the diversity of emblematic citizens and the rapid shift in subjectivity, I had to remember that the emblematic citizen does not represent those citizens envisioned by nineteenth century Argentine intellectuals as the ideal national subjects. The people who would fit that category were white, educated, Europeanized men of economic means, like the writers themselves. In contrast, the emblematic citizens of literary narratives are often women and racially mixed, lower class men. An examination of earlier nineteenth century literary history provided the answer as to *why* writers chose these diverse subjects. For writers in mid-nineteenth century Argentina, the image of contest to the reign of the paternalistic dictator Juan Manuel de Rosas was a feminine one. Women — white, Europeanized, upper-class women, that is— were deployed fictionally as a means of casting off the "barbarous" ways of leader Rosas and "civilizing" a country which the liberal party would remake in its image. This was particularly true of the famed writers of the "Generation of 1837," the young intellectuals who formed a literary salon in the bookstore owned by Marcos Sastre in Buenos Aires. This short-lived but highly influential literary circle was soon disbanded by Rosas's interdiction, but included the founders of the Romantic Movement in Argentina: Esteban Echeverría, Juan Bautista Alberdi, and Juan María Gutiérrez, among others. In Alberdi's journal *La Moda*, this future statesman and founder of the constitution used the language of fashion and a feminine identity to discuss the future of the nation.

In *Between Civilization and Barbarism*, Masiello has argued that the use of metaphors of femininity by Argentine liberal male writers during the rule of Rosas constructed an idealized feminine citizen. The idealized woman subject served as a guardian of civic honor, morality, and virtue, but this does not mean that the authors ascribed these characteristics to real women. Instead, as Masiello asserts, they "defined the idea of resistance identified in the idealized site of the feminine" (33). Like Masiello's idealized woman subject, the emblematic citizen may stand for and embody the virtues of the ideal citizen. Since there were specific cultural and historical reasons for using particular emblematic citizens, the next issue became why the figure of the emblematic citizen underwent such a dramatic turnaround of gender, race, regionality, and degree of urbanization in such a short period of time. The answer to that inquiry had to do with changes in the meanings attached to physical space during those thirty years. In the texts I analyze, the way in which emblematic citizens interact with their physical environment is always highlighted. There is always at least one scene — and usually repeated scenes— where the body of the emblematic citizen is placed in a physical space that has special significance to the idea of nation in Argentina.

In each of the texts I have identified scenes or sections of chapters in which certain fictional spaces are represented as *literary nation-spaces*: the spaces, lands, or territories where struggles over national identity are represented. Literary nation-space does not refer only to that land mapped out and imagined by the white Argentine government as belonging to the nation. I have devised the term in order to insist upon the changeable and ideological nature of national territory in these texts.

Nation-space can be the interior of a Buenos Aires boudoir, the vast lands of the pampas, the circle around a campfire, or a provincial parlor: the scenes in which nation-spaces appear as literary sites of nation. These scenes are symptomatic sites for reading the literary national ideology of the texts. They are where the authors' beliefs about the race, ethnicity, politics, and gender of the emblematic Argentine citizen are manifested, and are the places where the texts' ideological contradictions can be seen most clearly. Moreover, the spaces that appear as nation-spaces in these literary narratives are always themselves sites of national political debate in the period in which the narratives were written.

It is useful to remember that the actual space of the nation — both the territory that is defined as belonging to the nation and the discursive space of *argentinidad*— is as invented as the community itself. Like those national readers of Benedict Anderson's *Imagined Communities* who call themselves citizens, there is real land that corresponds to nation-space. And like the idea of the nation itself, the character and attributes of nation-space itself are constructed and talked about as "something to which one is naturally tied" (Anderson 143). In the process of nation consolidation in Argentina, the occupation of space involves struggles that are borne out in literature: what territory is defined as national and what is not, what specific spaces are to be occupied by specific citizens, how previously open spaces (whose meanings are not fixed) become national properties.

Literary nation-space is always occupied by emblematic citizens. Their bodies occupy space in a way that is privileged: they have a special relationship to nation-space that is not shared by other characters in the same narrative. The interrelation between the gendered body and space in these scenes is also involved in the construction of nation-space. Nation-space encloses and excludes different kinds of bodies. Within nation-space, however, the bodies of emblematic citizens often experience displacement or fragmentation: the emblematic citizen always seems to be in movement. This movement characterizes the trope itself (the changeable, temporal nature of the emblematic citizen) as well as serving as a metaphor for the shifting nature of territorial boundaries and concepts of national territory.

All categories for inclusion and exclusion within nation-space — gender, race, class, sexuality, education, degree of Europeanization, and regionality — were unstable during this period, but categories of gender are unusually unstable in Argentine literature from 1850–1880. The female body in *Amalia* (1850) is not always feminine during a time when femininity is a marker of white, elite male writers. Male bodies (such as those of immigrant men in *Martín Fierro* [1872, 1880]) are feminized at a time when femininity has become a mark of powerlessness. The shifting nature of gender itself in the period also means that the relationship between gendered and sexualized bodies and the space of the nation is changeable.

While there were continued representations of the nation as a woman in national iconography in the late nineteenth century, there was a change in literary representations of the emblematic citizen. Post 1860s, white women were no longer represented clearly as holders of the virtues of national citizenry. The female body in these texts often demonstrates a partial representation of emblematic citizenship. The change in the projection of the emblematic citizen was accompanied by a change in the ways in which nation-space was represented. Early in the period, with *Amalia*, nation-space appears as a domestic interior, a space where the virtuous "Angel in the House" or the useful republican mother could be found. Later in the period, in *Una excursión a los indios ranqueles* and *Martín Fierro*, nation-space is represented on the pampas, or within a circle of men who tell stories in which women are the troublemakers, their bodies the sites of lust.

The notion of a gendered body brings out the differences in the representation of the body of female citizens in these narratives. In "Gendering Nationhood: A Feminist Engagement with National Identity," Joanne Sharp discusses Benedict Anderson's imagined citizen as a gendered one. Sharp refers to Anderson's contention that the Unknown Soldier is the perfect representation of a citizen, as the dead soldier "could be any member in the fraternity of the imagined community" (99). Pointing out that we can be fairly sure that the anonymous soldier was not a woman, Sharp demonstrates that in their role as good citizens, men protect women at times of war to prevent their violation by non-nationals, since "foreign penetration of the motherland [...] is at the very heart of national security" (100). The notion that women are constructed as being vulnerable citizens through sexuality is only part of what happens in the narratives I examine: the white female body is constructed as a vulnerable object and a seductive one that inspires lust in "barbarians."

Fundamental tensions occur in nineteenth-century texts when dealing with the bodies of women. For nineteenth century writers, the good woman is a spiritual one, who ignores her own sexuality. The idea of the sanctified domestic woman, the Angel in the House of Coventry Patmore's poem of the same name, does not include any concept of female eroticism because a sexual woman in the nineteenth century was conceived of as a prostitute. The normalizing function of sexual discourse in the nineteenth century worked against any positive acknowledgment of women's bodies. When discussing the bodies of women (as in the stories of the *cautivas*, where fears about rape drive the narrative) women are positioned as the cause of trouble. If women characters are emblematic of citizenship in the nineteenth century how is this fear of their sexuality borne out in narrative? How did these repressive beliefs about women's sexuality make themselves felt at the level of national discourse in Argentina?

Foucault has established that the putting into play of repressive sexuality in public discourse has had special reference to nation building.

Referring to the eighteenth century science of population studies in France, Foucault comments that the measures used to analyze and change the sexual conduct of couples became more and more interventionist in the nineteenth century (26). Foucault refers to sexuality as a discourse that oppresses through its very public function. Under the disciplinary discourse of sexuality, women's bodies became targets of control and repression. Women's eroticism is characterized as a dangerous presence, and the idea that women might experience sexual pleasure disturbs this homogenizing project of the nation.

In fact, as the nation became more cohesive in the nineteenth century, Argentine laws curtailed the freedom of women and put more strictures on the bodies of women. Donna Guy comments that

> The civil code enforced after 1871 severely restricted women's civil rights, especially if they were married or had not attained majority. Considered minors, they were completely under the control of husbands or fathers and technically could not manage their own money or property; nor could they work without patriarchal permission [44].

Noting that restrictions against prostitutes were instituted as early as the 1850s and that "prostitution laws were among the first type of labor legislation to challenge the basic civil rights of working women," Guy asserts that "by linking inappropriate female labor with cash wages, politicians declared that lower-class women were as dangerous as prostitutes to the imagined national community" (3). Women's sexuality, when unpoliced, was evidently considered to be a threat to the national community.

In the nineteenth century imaginings of the nation and its citizens, female sexuality also signified the possibility (considered a threat by nineteenth century whites in Argentina) of interracial unions. More so than in other Latin American countries, Argentine intellectuals conceived of the country as one that should be white and Europeanized. Indeed, there are significant differences in the representation of the body — and in particular between the sexualized and racially marked female body — between Argentine works and other Latin American texts of the same period. Argentina had no founding novel of interracial love, such as Cuba's *Cecilia Valdés* (1839, 1882) by Cirilio Villaverde. While Cuba's symbolic woman Cecilia Valdés is an Afro-Cuban prostitute, Argentina's symbolic woman is Amalia, a white, sexually pure, Europeanized figure. Although *Cecilia Valdés* (1867) ends tragically, cutting off the possibility of interracial union, it does acknowledge the presence of Afro-Cubans in nineteenth century Cuba on the one hand, and present a sexualized female on the other.

For a critic examining nineteenth century Argentine literature and history, another question that comes to mind is why there is such a scarce representation of African-Argentines in the nation's literature when historical evidence shows that they represented a large portion of the population of Buenos Aires in mid-century. George Reid Andrews in *The Afro-Argentines of Buenos Aires* (1980) has established that although both census documents and historians have reported a sharp decline in the African-Argentine population in the mid to late nineteenth century, other evidence demonstrates that the African-Argentine community thrived during that time. In describing the racial/ethnic mix of the population, French travel writer Xavier Marmier wrote in 1850:

> Cuentan en primer lugar los habitantes de raza española, descendientes de los conquistadores que impusieron su lengua, sus costumbres y la mayoría de sus nombres; vienen luego los europeos: ingleses, alemanes, franceses, sardos, vascos y bearneses; después los negros, libertos por una ley que no provocó ningún disturbio; los mulatos, los indios, y los gauchos.
>
> (In the first rank are the inhabitants of Spanish race, descendents of the conquerors that imposed their language, customs, and the majority of their names; then come the Europeans: English, German, French, Sardinian, Basque and Béarnaise; after that are the blacks, freed by a law that provoked not one disturbance; the mulattos, the Indians, and the gauchos) [27].*

Andrews believes that African-Argentines in the nineteenth century "were quietly written out of the record by census takers and statisticians, by writers and historians cultivating the myth of a white Argentina" (112). The African-Argentine community gained some political leverage in the early mid-nineteenth century because Juan Manuel de Rosas had recognized the advantages of courting the black community (Andrews 96). In portraying the excesses of the Rosas years, national writers such as José Mármol and Esteban Echeverría directed their anti–Rosas rhetoric against African-Argentines. To *unitarios*, African-Argentines were barbarians, and spies for Rosas.

The gaucho is another example of the contradictions concerning race in nineteenth century Argentine literature. As early as the 1820s, visitors to the pampas recorded the fact that the gaucho's racial status varied. In *Gauchos and the Vanishing Frontier*, Richard Slatta cites Sir Francis Bond Head, a British mine owner, who described gauchos as "'all colors, black, white and red [*sic*]'" (15). While historically, the gaucho was a person of

---

The laws freeing blacks did not create a disturbance because there was almost no use of slavery for agricultural purposes.

mixed-race descent, the representation of the gaucho's racial categorization changed during the nineteenth century. In the 1850s the gauchos are
represented in literature as *mestizos* and therefore, in the views of Mármol and many others, undesirable figures. The projection of the gaucho
as a *mestizo* (considered to be a negative racial category in the nineteenth
century) may relate to the gauchos' perceived status as allies of Rosas and
the *caudillos*: as such they represented a threat to the white, urban elite
who favored the Unitarist cause. But by the 1870s, when the gauchos
were actually being removed from the pampas—forced into military
service or forcibly resettled to work for large landowners—the poem
Martín Fierro counterpoises the gaucho Fierro as a *blanco* (white) against
the blacks, indigenous people, *and* immigrants he meets in his travels. At
a time when the gaucho was still a marginalized figure, the gaucho in literature was being whitened for the purposes of representing the emblematic citizen. Slatta writes that by the end of the nineteenth and beginning
of the twentieth century, nationalists such as Leopoldo Lugones and Juan
José de Lezica were bemoaning — in highly racist terms— the demise of
the gaucho through what they viewed as the "debasing mixture of Indian
and black blood that weakened the 'true creole, descendants of the
Spaniards'" (Lezica qtd. in Slatta, *Gauchos* 14).* Therefore, while the gauchos were generally mixed-race, the perception of their racial status
depended upon the political use to which they were being put. The
nostalgia for the old-time true creole (white) gaucho was based on political fiction.

The representation of indigenous people was much clearer, while still
serving racist ideological ends. In nineteenth century Argentine literature, indigenous people are generally portrayed as the cruel attackers of
peaceful white settlers. The representation of the indigenous people as vil-
lainous destroyers of national harmony can be found in the relationship
between the emblematic citizen and nation-space. This is most evident
from the *cautiva* tales, which appeared regularly in the nineteenth century,
in which the captive white female body is cast as the national victim of the
indigenous population of the pampas, the vast prairie that begins outside
of Buenos Aires. While the pampas itself forms part of the separation of
urban and rural spheres in these narratives, the pampas is divided in nineteenth century literature by the imaginary frontier between white and
native territory. As a threat to economic growth in the pampas, the native
people (in the eyes of nineteenth century whites) represented an obstacle

---

*"Creole" or criollo *refers to a white person of Spanish descent born in Spanish colonial
territory, in what is now Latin America.*

to the economic prosperity of the nation, which became, by definition, exclusive of its indigenous population.

In reading narratives through issues of gender, questions emerge about the the contestatory tone of the works written by women. As the author of articles supporting women's education, Rosa Guerra argued in favor of the idea that well-educated women make better wives and mothers. While Guerra was more radical in her views than many other nineteenth century women writers, her progressive views do not make themselves present when it comes to the sexualized body. Lucía Miranda, Guerra's quasi-historical heroine, suffers in the novel because her body is seen to inspire lust in the indigenous leaders. In the work of Eduarda Mansilla de García, Lucía Miranda is seen as being overeducated: her love of education and narrative represents epic hubris. However, it must be said that these intelligent heroines represent a great advance over the infantile and sentimental *señoritas* who appeared in the stories of most literary journals of the period.

There are other observable differences between the works of the male and female writers I analyze, although not all have to do with the gender of the authors. I discovered that the work of Eduarda Mansilla de García often served as a useful counterpoint to texts by other Argentine authors: as such, I use her work in three of the five chapters of this book. The niece of Juan Manuel de Rosas, Mansilla de García learned to speak French at an early age and acted as her uncle's interpreter during his negotiations with the French envoy while she was just an adolescent. Mansilla de García married an anti–Rosas diplomat and moved to Paris, living in Europe for much of her adult life. As the result of her European residence — and the elegant *salon* she held in her home in Paris — Mansilla de García was influenced by European literary currents much more than were her compatriots residing in Argentina. When comparing her work with that of resident Argentine writers, the differences between nineteenth century Argentine and European literature become more distinct on some issues: most notably the question of women and spiritualism, a common theme in nineteenth century literature in Europe.

The structure of the book is chronological, in that I begin in 1851 and end in 1879. However, the text with the earliest publication date, *Recuerdos de provincia*, from 1850, demonstrates a fairly complex and transitional representation of the emblematic citizen, and reflects some of the ideas about the nation and citizenship that would emerge later in the work of other writers. As a result, I have begun with *Amalia* (1851, 1855), a text that — through the figure of Amalia — demonstrates the characteristics of the emblematic citizen quite clearly.

In Chapter One, I examine the question of nation-space and the emblematic citizen in light of the politicization of interior space during the Rosas era as it appears in *Amalia*. The body of the emblematic citizen is white, elite, educated, and Europeanized. In *Amalia*, the site of nation-space is Amalia's boudoir: a place where each object is politically coded, referring to debates over political and party beliefs and reflecting Mármol's vision of Argentina's future citizens. Mármol refers to Amalia's boudoir as a "museo de delicadezas feminiles" ("museum of feminine delicate things"). The nation-space being constructed is a museum of femininity, in which Amalia's body appears as just another coded object. In having to deal with the eroticism of his lead character, Mármol creates Amalia as a split body: a pure, virtuous body that refers to the nation and citizenship, and an erotic body, useful in creating the desire necessary to further the plot. When referring to Amalia's sexuality, Mármol often employs the spatial language of painting as a means of containing her potentially troublesome sexuality.

The change over several decades in the imagination of the sexualized female body and nation-space is dramatic when contrasting the boudoir scene in *Amalia* with a painting from 1865 by Prilidiano Pueyrredón, titled *La Siesta*. While political space in *Amalia* is imagined as a closed, interior space, the painting *La Siesta* presents two voluptuous female bodies whose sexualized bodies suggest metaphors of possession, and whose physicality appears territorial in shape and size. The paintings of Pueyrredón and the novel *Amalia* promote bonds between elite men. These homosocial bonds are made around and against the sexualized bodies of women, and are related to the idea of nation-space. The discourse surrounding the erotic works of Prilidiano Pueyrredón and of *La Siesta* demonstrates that the feminization of national discourse becomes unstable when confronted with the eroticized female body. Pueyrredón's doubled woman, when considered in the context of how these images circulated, represents as much an erasure of women in the context of nationhood as did the disappearing body of Mármol's character Amalia.

In Chapter Two Sarmiento's *Recuerdos de provincia* from 1850 demonstrates once again the privileging of the white female body. However, Sarmiento introduces the maternal body in order to displace it within the nation-space of his mother's house. In the two chapters dealing with his mother's house, this feminized domestic sphere becomes a battleground for ideas about modernization, national leadership, and the national future. Degrading the maternal place within the domestic sphere, Sarmiento relegates his mother to an antiquated colonial rule which — while giving him the ancestry necessary to produce a clear line into a *criollo* past — must be displaced for more modernizing ways. In the case of Sarmiento, the emblematic citizen is split between male and female, passed from Sarmiento's mother to himself. And while Sarmiento clearly sees himself as the successor to his mother's place at the head of the household, he shows his sisters as controlling the use of domestic space. The responsibility for the displacement of the maternal body belongs to them, and Sarmiento remains a supposedly impartial observer.

The text I use as a counterpoint to *Recuerdos de provincia*, Eduarda Mansilla de García's *El médico de San Luis* (1860), presents another kind of maternal figure: a spiritual head of the household whose body has ceased to exist even before the novel begins. As in *Recuerdos de provincia*, nation-space occurs in the domestic sphere. The degraded mother in Mansilla's text is tied to antiquated colonial ways, which, in Mansilla's view, must make way for newer, more Europeanized traditions. In *El médico de San Luis*, the highly feminized nation-space of the household is changed when highly masculinized figures emerge from the pampas. After a macho *caudillo* and a murderous gaucho penetrate the family, the novel ends with the lessening of maternal power and the strengthening of the patriarchal order. The notion of emblematic citizenship is projected on the sons-in-law: an entrepreneurial Englishman and an honest young judge. For Mansilla de García, the pampas seems to appear as a vague, overdetermined space: an extra-legal space from which trouble can emerge or into which potential troublemakers in the nation can escape. The question of nation-space becomes particularly significant to the function of the maternal in both texts. Both *Recuerdos de provincia* and *El médico de San Luis* present families whose sons must separate from their mothers in order to regain the masculinized order seen as necessary for a strong nation-family.

Chapter Three reveals how the pampas, conceived of as an extra-legal territory in nineteenth century national discourse, is converted into nation-space through the tales of the *cautivas* and by the appearance of the sexualized body of Lucía Miranda. These stories provide an excuse for the appropriation of lands belonging to indigenous tribes. The contrast between the two versions of *Lucía Miranda*, the novels concerning the legend about the first *cautiva* in the Río de la Plata, demonstrates the difference in how space is viewed. In the theme of the *cautiva* at work in nineteenth century Argentina the discourse is one of revenge, in which the fear of the rape and imprisonment of white female bodies by what nineteenth century thinkers considered to be savage native bodies is used to justify the conquest and possession of lands occupied by indigenous tribes.

In both novels, Lucía's body functions as a symbol for the national body (which is under attack), and as a metaphor for national property (territory). In addition, Lucía presents many of the qualities of the emblematic citizen, particularly in her relationship to nation-space. For Guerra, the territory on which the Timbúe people live is potentially useful as nation-space; but it is being squandered by the indigenous population. Guerra's novel reflects the political and economic concerns at play in late 1850s and early 1860s Argentina. Mansilla de García's pampas recalls the dramatic pampas of Echeverría more than the potentially fruitful lands traversed by the indigenous tribes in Guerra's novel. While both texts raise the possibility of intermarriage, this is a short-lived prospect, and the novels make it clear that the writers believe this prospect was ruined by indigenous violence and not by colonial refusal. The inversion of the reality of colonial exploitation of Indian women, as Cristina Iglesia has observed, forms part of the violence of this discourse (*Cautivas* 30).

During the period between 1850 and 1880, the other inhabitants of the pampas, the gauchos, were subjected to regulation and control that meant their bodies were physically resettled to be used as laborers for large ranchers, as soldiers for the seemingly unending series of military engagements throughout the 1860s, or in the long war against the indigenous population. In Chapter Four, I discuss the ways in which Lucio V. Mansilla, in *Una excursión a los indios ranqueles*, recreates the elite space of a gentleman's club on the pampas. In the pampas of *Una excursión a los indios ranqueles*, a series of closed male spaces are constructed in which narratives about the nation are produced: the pampas itself as *tierra adentro* (interior land), the male domain of the military campfire, and finally the interior lives of the men themselves. These closed spaces are represented as producing knowledge about the nation.

For Mansilla the military campfire in particular provides a pseudo-utopian space where men of all classes tell national narratives. These narratives—often in the voice of the loyal gaucho, a newly emerging emblem of national identity—are used by Mansilla the journalist for his own rhetorical ends. In the newspaper, Mansilla is able to assume the voice of the gaucho, a move that allows him to recreate the utopic campfire in the pages of *La Tribuna*: employing the gaucho voice while retaining control of the dissemination and direction of the narrative. The narrative suggests that bonds between men of all classes can cement a national family, although it is doubtful that Mansilla's gaucho soldiers, many forced into service, had the same utopian experience around the campfire as did their elite leader. The figure of the emblematic citizen here is shared between the figure of the loyal gaucho and the elite white *porteño* represented by

Mansilla himself. This precursor/participant in the Generation of 1880 reproduces the atmosphere of the literary salon on the pampas. In this way Mansilla is able to traverse all possible spaces of what will be the nation. The fact that these lands will become nation-spaces through the genocide of indigenous people is virtually ignored.

For a textual, experiential, and even familial counterpoint to Lucio V. Mansilla's text, *Una excursión a los indios ranqueles* is followed by an analysis of the story, "El ramito de romero" by Lucio's sister, Eduarda Mansilla de García. "El ramito de romero" involves the spiritual vision experienced by a young French doctor after he touches a female corpse he finds in the empty surgical amphitheater at his Parisian medical school. I will examine the story in light of concerns with the body and nation-space in *Una excursión a los indios ranqueles*: how knowledge about the nation is produced, how bodies occupy the space of knowledge, and how a sense of the national is tied to gendered, class-identified bodies.

Chapter Five analyzes the relationship between citizenship and space in *Martín Fierro* by identifying those bodies that are feminized (the marginalized bodies of lower class white women, indigenous people, African-Argentines and immigrants) in the narrative. The fragmentation and destruction of feminized bodies that is seen in *Martín Fierro*, a text that privileges the construction of a masculinist discourse of national identity, is echoed in the discourse of public hygiene. The national poem and the regulating discourse of public health both concern the interaction between space and citizenship that was so vital to national discourse in nineteenth century Argentina. The use and abuse of the gaucho body during the 1860s is referenced by Hernández's poem at the same time that the gaucho body is made emblematic of Argentine citizenship. As a discourse that has to do with the control of bodies in public and private spaces in the service of public interest, the discourse of public health categorizes certain bodies as bringing disease and corruption to the city. The destruction of (lower-class) female, immigrant, indigenous, and African-Argentine bodies in the pampas of *Martín Fierro* mirrors the marginalization of those same bodies in the city described in public hygiene texts. In *Martín Fierro* the pampas is being constructed as a nation-space from which certain kinds of bodies will be excluded. In the discourse of public hygiene, the occupation of urban areas by those same marginalized bodies requires control and surveillance by public hygiene officials. The emblematic citizen in the public hygiene discourse is what the controlled bodies are *not*: white, *criollo*, bourgeois, educated, and male.

In his essay "Sarmiento the Writer," Ricardo Piglia comments that

the history of Argentine fiction begins twice. Or perhaps it is better
to say that the history of Argentine fiction begins with the same twice-
told scene of terror and violence. Initially, on the first page of *Facundo*,
which is to say the first page of Argentine literature, and at the same
time (but in a displaced fashion) in "El matadero" by Echeverría [131].

By referring to *Facundo*, Domingo Sarmiento's 1845 purported biography of the great *caudillo* (provincial military leader) Facundo Quiroga,
as the first page of Argentine literature, Piglia does not mean that this is
the first text of literary quality to appear in Argentina. What Piglia signals
by this remark is that Sarmiento's text defines the parameters of Argentine literature for several generations, both before and after its appearance. Subtitled *Civilización y barbarie* (*Civilization and Barbarism*),
Sarmiento's work popularized this dichotomy as the defining theme of
Argentine cultural discourse. For Sarmiento, civilization referred to white,
Europeanized culture, and to the inhabitants of the great cities. Barbarism
referred to non-white, indigenous, African-Argentine, and gaucho culture, and to the rural inhabitants of the pampas. Racial and ethnic categories, therefore, are inscribed in this originating moment of Argentine
culture. The twice-told tale of horror to which Piglia refers has to do with
the violence done in both texts to the bodies of the civilized by barbarians, a theme which appears and reappears throughout the pages of nineteenth century Argentine narrative.

The issue of violence in a text brings up the question of violence done
to a text: i.e. the translations from Spanish to English in this book. Generally, I have done my own translations and am therefore responsible for
any injury done to the originals. There are two notable exceptions: sections from Sarmiento's *Recurdos de provincia* translated in 1948 by Stuart
Grummon for *A Sarmiento Anthology* and Mansilla's *Una excursión a los
indios ranqueles,* translated in 1997 by Mark McCaffrey as *An Expedition
to the Ranquel Indians.*

In the coming years, it will be fascinating to see which markers of
argentinidad that had their roots in nineteenth century culture still remain.
How will future Argentineans understand their country after reverse
immigration has robbed the nation not only of many of its citizens but
also of the myth of Argentina as a place where immigrants come to find
success? As global economic crises and health fears savage the cattle sec-
tor, what will become of the myth of the gaucho? In a recent on-line forum,
the *Clarín.com* asked readers to identify what the recent demonstrations
in the streets of Buenos Aires meant to the nation. Citing Italian philoso-
pher Paolo Virno, the newspaper's editorial staff opined that the demonstrations reflected what Virno calls "multitude in action" and associated

the revolts with "las intensas rebeliones contra la globalización que estallaron en los últimos años en Seattle y Génova. Todas ellas, en [la opinión de Virno], constituyen una forma de contestación frente a la democracia representativa" ("the intense rebellions against globalization that broke out in the last few years in Seattle and Geneva. All of these, in [Virno's] opinion, constitute a form of contentional response to representative democracy") (*Foro de Cultura*). A reader responded that the demonstrations made him afraid:

> Me contaron que en las asambleas barriales que se están realizando ahora en Capital hay opiniones de bastante xenofobia, antisemitismo e intolerancia a las diferencias en general, ya sean raciales, religiosas, de clase y de género. Saben los argentinos ¿qué ideas tiene su vecino? Aparte de compartir las penurias de la argentinidad, ¿que otras cosas compartimos? No sé y la verdad es que me da un poco de miedo.
>
> (I've heard that in the local demonstrations that are going on now in the capital there is quite a bit of xenophobia, antisemitism and intolerance to difference in general — be it racial, religious, difference of class and gender. Do Argentineans know what their neighbor thinks? Apart from the shared poverty of *argentinidad*, what other things do we share? I don't know, and the truth is that it makes me a little afraid) [Manuel Frisa].

History tells us that there is reason for fear. In the recent history of Argentina — the bombing of the AMIA Jewish Community Center in 1994 is only one such example — discrimination and intolerance have had tragic consequences. The idea of *argentinidad* as a shared poverty underscores the discrimination inherent in many nationalist agendas — discrimination that was part of the positivist agenda of Argentina's nation builders. As global economic concerns begin to unravel the work of nineteenth century nations, understanding the roots of nationalist culture is key to knowing what it is that we share as citizens.

ONE

The Body in the Museum: *Amalia* and Pueyrredón

In Argentina, the early and mid nineteenth century represented years of political conflict and social disorder. After the initial emancipation from Spain in 1810, and the brief presidency of Rivadavia, there followed decades of civil war. In 1829, a wealthy *caudillo* (provincial political leader) Juan Manuel de Rosas became Governor of Buenos Aires. Aside from a respite during 1832–1835, he would rule with increasingly autocratic powers until 1852. Controlling the inhabitants of Buenos Aires by the installation of a secret police force known as the *mazorca*, Rosas forced an increasing number of Argentineans into exile, many of them writers and intellectuals whose liberalizing ideas were seen as a threat to the unity of the state.

One of these outcasts was writer José Mármol (1817–1871) who, while exiled in Montevideo, wrote the novel *Amalia* (1851), considered to be the paradigm of romantic prose fiction in Argentina. *Amalia* has received recent attention because, like other nation-building narratives of nineteenth century Latin America, the work inscribes national and social ideals within the figure of a feminine protagonist.*

In early 1850s Argentina, many national politicians and writers dreamed of a land that was white, Europeanized, and civilized, a feat which would be accomplished in their view by European immigration. In *Bases* (1852), the text that served as the foundation of the Argentine constitution,

---

The novel first appeared serialized in the literary supplement of La Semana (Montevideo) in 1851. After the defeat of Rosas early in 1852, Mármol moved to Buenos Aires, interrupting the novel's serialization in chapter twelve of the fifth and final part (Fernández 26). As a result, the novel remained unfinished until Mármol published it in its final form in 1855.

Juan Bautista Alberdi laid down some of the deeply racist beliefs that would determine the future composition of the Argentine population. His slogan "gobernar es poblar" ("to govern is to populate") characterized the conviction of Argentine founders that "if one were to populate a given region or country with Europeans and their descendants, European modes of 'progress' would inevitably follow" (Andrews 102). This belief, inherited from scientific racism, was reflected in Mármol's novel. When representing his emblematic citizen, Mármol used a white, Europeanized, upper-class woman: the figure of Amalia.*

If the nation is located in the *idealized* site of the feminine, then what nation-space does the body of the protagonist Amalia occupy, and how does her construction as an emblematic citizen correspond to her physical body, and to the racial and ethnic categories suggested by her body? While Amalia's physical presence does become increasingly dispersed, her body is the nexus for desire and eroticism in the novel. In fact, Amalia has a split body: an erotic body that is desired and an idealized disappearing body which represents the emblematic citizen.†

Nation-space appears in the second section of the novel as Amalia's boudoir. While Amalia's body is described in luxurious detail, her body is fragmented in space by reflection. The body does not define its own space as much as it is organized within space: in what Mármol calls a "museo de delicadezas feminiles" ("museum of feminine delicate things") in which categories of femaleness are both sensual and yet carefully controlled. Both museum and boudoir, nation-space in *Amalia* is a politically coded storehouse of feminine leisure, occupied by objects that suggest European refinement, Unitarist sensibility, and feminine pleasure. Within this space Amalia's body is fragmented, framed as a work of art, and then projected back into the past as a static, historical object.

Most recent criticism on *Amalia* notes that while the character of Amalia is obviously intended to represent an idealized citizen, she lacks physicality and emotional depth.§ Francine Masiello comments that in contrast with the increasingly present masculine body, the women of the Unitarist cause become gradually less physically visible in the novel,

---

*This is in contrast with what occurred in other Latin American countries. A discussion of this phenomenon can be found in the Introduction.

†By "erotic" I mean that Amalia's body serves to excite sexual desire and is the focus of a scene in which she appears to experience erotic pleasure.

§Remarking on the lack of characterization of Amalia, Doris Sommer argues that— as natives of the port city of Buenos Aires and the old colonial capitol Tucumán, respectively— the novel's lovers Eduardo and Amalia represent a potential reconciliation between Buenos Aires and the interior (100).

effecting political change through acts of idealism and verbal magic (*Between Civilization* 31–32). Not only do women become less visible, but also men become more feminine. Masiello suggests that Mármol's male characters—as did liberal intellectuals of Mármol's generation — usurp the feminine as part of a contentional discourse with the Rosas regime: "the feminine, or invisibility of spirit, is assigned to the sphere of the *unitarios*, while the masculine, or paternal authority, is equated with the crass materialism of the federalists" (*Between Civilization* 31).

Within nation-space Amalia is presented in a position of abandoned pleasure, an erotic pose suggesting bodily pleasure for Amalia, and relating to her desire for Eduardo. Mármol constructs a separate space that will house his protagonist's erotic body: the space of painting. By describing Amalia's body in painterly ways and by referring openly to her "Titianlike" form, Mármol signals her desirability and even her eroticism at the same time that he contains any danger of transgression. The containment of female eroticism in the novel points up the fact that while "femininity" was a category used by elite male writers, female expressions of sexual pleasure might be considered threatening.*

An example of how threatening feminine pleasure could be to nineteenth century culture can be found in the erotic work of Argentine artist Prilidiano Pueyrredón. Still considered to be one of the masters of early Argentine art, Pueyrredón (1823–1870) was heir to a prominent political and military family, and was commissioned in 1851, early in his career, to paint the portrait of Manuela Rosas, daughter of the dictator (see photograph next page). Pueyrredón's paintings include respectable portraits and romantic landscapes that often borrowed from European tradition. However, at the same time that he was painting these more conventional works, Pueyrredón set up a studio life that shocked upper-class Buenos Aires— it was known that he lived with his mistress who was also his housekeeper and who served as his model for nude paintings that were sold privately to gentlemen of leisure. Although Pueyrredón's erotic art was never exhibited in the nineteenth century, the existence of these images, which circulated privately among a group of elite men, was public knowledge because of Pueyrredón's elite status.†

In *La Siesta* (see photograph page 23) two women are shown lying naked, beside one another, on a bed in a luxurious room. One woman is

---

*On this topic, art historian Lynda Nead has observed: "Through the procedures of art, woman can become culture; [...] she becomes image and the wanton matter of the female body and female sexuality may be regulated and contained" (11).

†See Laura Malosetti's "Los desnudos de Prilidiano Pueyrredón como punto de tensión entre lo público y lo privado."

Prilidiano Pueyrredón. *Manuela de Rosas y Ezcurra*. 1851. Museo Nacional de Bellas Artes, Buenos Aires.

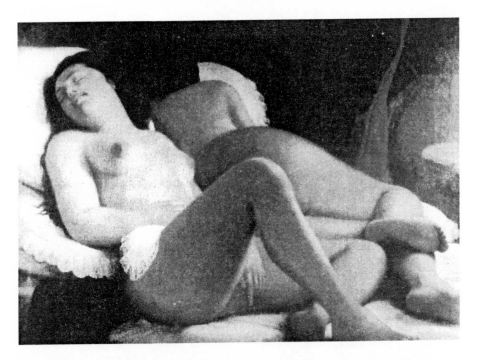

Prilidiano Pueyrredón. *La Siesta*. 1865. Colección Blanquier Buenos Aires.

half-asleep, her face turned towards the imagined viewer, while the other woman can be seen only from the back. The model for Pueyrredón's nudes was known to be his housekeeper, and, indeed, the painting suggests a doubling of the same voluptuous body. Depicting a woman who would "expose" her body in such a way, the painting suggest an excess of eroticism at the same time as it contains and presents the sexuality of this doubled "public" woman for the private pleasure of a man's boudoir. In the private/public tension created by Pueyrredón's painting exists another inverted museum: in this case, the museum suggested is a private space of erotic knowledge about the female body, which is possessed by public men.

La Siesta demonstrates a changed relationship between interior space and the female body. The politicization of domestic space had been replaced by the focus on expansionism. In the huge white sexualized bodies of the women in *La Siesta*, I read two metaphors of possession: of women's bodies and of land; the novel suggests the connections between men of Pueyrredón's class, who really did "own" national territory. These homosocial bonds are made around and against the eroticized bodies of women. Pueyrredón's doubled woman, when considered in the context of how these images circulated, represents as much an erasure of women in the context of nationhood as did the disappearing body of Amalia represented by Mármol: both construct the nation by privileging bonds between upper-class men.

If anyone ever doubted that Mármol considered the act of novel writing to be one of nation building, there is his famous preface to the novel:

> La mayor parte de los personajes históricos de esta novela existen aún, y ocupan la misma posición política o social que en la época en que ocurrieron los sucesos que van a leerse. Pero el autor, por una ficción calculada, supone que escribe su obra con algunas generaciones de por medio entre él y aquellos. Y es ésta la razón por qué el lector no hallará nunca en presente los tiempos empleados al hablar de Rosas, de su familia, de sus ministros, etc.
>
> El autor ha creído que tal sistema convenía tanto a la mayor claridad de la narración cuanto al porvenir de la obra, destinada a ser leída, como todo lo que se escriba, bueno o malo, relativo a la época dramática de la dictadura argentina, por las generaciones venideras, con quienes entonces se armonizará perfectamente el sistema, aquí adoptado, de describir en forma retrospectiva personajes que viven en la actualidad.
>
> (The majority of the historical figures of this novel still exist, and occupy the same social and political positions as in the era in which the events read about in the novel occurred. But the author, by a calculated fiction, supposes that he writes with a few generations between him and his words. And this is the reason why the reader will never find the present tense employed to speak about Rosas, his family, his ministers, etc.
>
> (The author believes that such a system was appropriate as much for the clarity of the narration as for the future of the work, which is destined to be read, like everything that is written, good or bad, relative to the dramatic era of the Argentina dictatorship, by generations to come, with whom the system here adopted — that of describing in a retrospective form people who are still living — will harmonize perfectly.)

Mármol's introduction tells us that he meant his narrative to have the weight of historical truth and that he evidently wanted his contemporary readers to read the novel as if it were a historical text. The dictatorship of Manuel de Rosas is the fiction (the "dramatic era") and Mármol's novel is compared not to other novels but to "everything that is written." In a neat twist of categories, Mármol has fictionalized history and made fiction into historical truth.

Like many nineteenth century Argentine narratives, *Amalia* does read as part historical text and part political treatise. Actual historical figures such as Rosas or his daughter Manuelita rub elbows with the fictional characters of the novel, who themselves often resemble historical figures. Yet in his introduction Mármol turns the work itself into a historical object: he projects the writing of the novel into an imagined and static future, creating Rosas and company as worthy of history before historiographers have had the chance to do so. This formulation of the text gives Mármol's project the curious air of an inverted museum. While a museum often attempts to give the past the flavor of immediacy, by allowing present-day spectators to "witness" the past, Mármol creates the precedent of an imaginary set of future readers who can best understand the past precisely by its *lack* of immediacy, as if those future readers will have a homogeneous and unchanging view of the Rosas era.

The novel is evidently to be read in this imagined future in a different kind of Argentina by a different kind of Argentine citizen. In his reference to the generations to come, Mármol is constructing an imagined community of Argentine reader-citizens. The fact that his text is meant to "harmonize" with these readers also indicates an unwritten bit of circular logic: Mármol evidently intends that *Amalia* will have a part in shaping the historical sense of these reader-citizens. However, since Mármol finished the novel post–1852 — and as Mármol and other *unitarios* were among the victors and the writers of histories from which those future readers would take their impressions— it should come as no surprise that future readers might agree with his vision of the nation.

Amalia takes place in Buenos Aires of 1840. As the novel begins the young and wealthy Eduardo Belgrano is fleeing to Montevideo, with eight other *unitarios* of means, to escape persecution. Their guide to the port turns out to be their betrayer. The men are ambushed and all are killed except Eduardo, who is saved by his best friend, Daniel Bello. Risking his life, Daniel brings Eduardo to the home of his (Daniel's) beautiful cousin, Amalia. Daniel is the novel's real hero. A Unitarist at heart, he comes from a well-respected Federalist family on his father's side. With his family history as his cover, Daniel poses as a loyal Federalist while he works to advance the Unitarist cause. Eduardo stays at Amalia's house during most of the novel, while Daniel — with the assistance of friends and some reluctant allies he has blackmailed into assisting him — spies on Federalists, attends balls, negotiates with exiled *unitarios* in Montevideo, and carries on a spirited romance with his half–French fiancée, Florencia. Eduardo and Amalia fall in love and eventually marry. Federalist soldiers track them down only hours after their wedding. Both Daniel and Eduardo die in the fighting, leaving Amalia to be saved by Daniel's father.

We are first introduced to Amalia through a detailed description that contains valuable information about her status both as an emblematic citizen and tragic heroine. The following scene takes place after Daniel rescues Eduardo from Rosas's savage henchmen and takes Eduardo— injured and weak — to Amalia's home.

> En aquel momento Amalia estaba excesivamente pálida, efecto de las impresiones inesperadas que estaba recibiendo, y los rizos de su cabello castaño claro, echados atrás de la oreja pocos momentos antes, no estorbaron a Eduardo descubrir, en una mujer de veinte años, una fisonomía encantadora, una frente majestuosa y bella, unos ojos pardos llenos de expresión y sentimiento, y una figura hermosa, cuyo traje negro parecería escogido para hacer resaltar la reluciente blancura del seno y de los hombros, si su tela no revelase que era un vestido de duelo.
>
> (At that moment Amalia was very pale because of the shock she had received, and she had tucked the curls of her light brown hair behind her ears a few moments before. This did not prevent Eduardo from noticing that this twenty-year-old woman had an enchanting face, a majestic and beautiful forehead, brown eyes full of expression and sentiment, and a beautiful figure. Her black outfit would appear to have been chosen to make the luminescent whiteness of her chest and shoulders stand out, if the cloth had not revealed that this was a dress of mourning) [71].

Significantly, this first view of Amalia is through Eduardo's eyes: we see her not via the male gaze but a specific male gaze. As will be typical of the rest of the novel, we are given detailed fashion notes: Amalia's grief (the recent deaths of both her husband and mother) is secondary to how her black dress shows off her white chest and shoulders. The paleness of Amalia's skin is also to be seen as a sign of her cultivation. Mármol mentions Eduardo "cuya palidez y expresión dolorida del semblante le daba un no sé qué de más impresionable, noble y varonil" ("whose paleness and sorrowful expression gave him a certain air of sensitivity, nobility and masculinity") (73). This is not only part of the nineteenth century Romantics' obsession with paleness, but also a significant marker of national identity. In a society that was assigning racial, ethnic and class characteristics to the terms "civilization and barbarism," Mármol made his ideal woman and her man white, upper class and of European origin.

Mármol's attitude towards race is clearly deterministic: the language used to describe African-Argentines shows that Mármol — like many of his countrymen — did not consider African-Argentines to be part of a future national family. The very first request that Daniel has for Amalia, when he asks her to risk her life by hiding Eduardo in her house, is that she fire all her black servants. He considers African-Argentines to be potential agents of Rosas. Whereas Rosas befriended marginalized groups, such as the poor and African-Argentines, this movement of inclusion (however cynical on Rosas's part) was clearly not part of the Unitarist construction of an exemplary citizen. In fact, Daniel passes judgment on the lower classes in general, commenting that

> los negros están ensoberbecidos, los blancos prostituídos, pero los mulatos, por esa propensión que hay en cada raza mezclada a elevarse y dignificarse, son casi todos enemigos de Rosas, porque saben que los unitarios son la gente ilustrada y culta, a que siempre toman ellos por modelo.
>
> (the blacks are arrogant, the whites corrupt, but the mulattos, because of that propensity that there is in every mixed race to elevate and dignify itself, are almost all enemies of Rosas, because they know that the *unitarios* are the great and cultivated people, and always take them as their model) [79].

For Daniel, the lower class is completely without hope, with the exception of the "mulattos" who have supposedly been "elevated and dignified" by the very mixing of races. If we are to believe—as both Sommer and Masiello have suggested—that Daniel Bello represents the author's own political beliefs, then for Mármol, class (with race as a given) is the marker for the ideal citizen. Class position, however, must be tempered by a certain amount of street smarts. Daniel is able to outwit even Rosas's cunning network of secret police on their own terms.

Within the novel, being educated and upper class predetermines a level of nobility, which does not guarantee survival. Sommer remarks that by outwitting Rosas, Daniel showed a level of cunning and compromise that was at odds with Amalia and Eduardo's unyielding partisanship (92). Not only does Mármol give Daniel some of the mental traits of his enemy Rosas, but he contrasts Daniel's physiognomy with that of his cousin.

> Este joven, de veinte y cinco años de edad; de mediano estatura, pero perfectamente bien formado; de tez morena y habitualmente sonrosada; de cabello castaño, y ojos pardos; frente espaciosa, nariz aguileña; labios un poco gruesos, pero de un carmín reluciente que hacía resaltar la blancura de unos lindísimos dientes; este joven, de una fisonomía en que estaba el sello elocuente de la inteligencia, como en sus ojos la expresión de la sensibilidad de su alma [...].
>
> (This young man, twenty five years old; of medium height, but perfectly formed, with brown and habitually tanned skin; with brown hair, brown eyes; a wide forehead, an aquiline nose, lips a bit thick,

but of a deep red that showed off the whiteness of his beautiful teeth;
this young man, whose face displayed the eloquence of intelligence
and from whose eyes shone the sensitivity of his soul [...]) [92].

Is Mármol suggesting a trace of the gaucho in Daniel, with his brown,
sunburned face and lips that are "a bit thick"? These traces of what might
be called "barbaric" in nineteenth century terms are suggestive when we
consider that Amalia is presented as Daniel's female alter ego. Daniel's old
friend Dr. Alcorta remarks to Amalia that

> En la fisonomía de entrambos hay muchos rasgos de familia; y creo
> no equivocarme al asegurar que entre ustedes hay también much
> afinidad de alma, pues observo, señora, que usted sufre en este
> momento porque ve sufrir; y esta impresionabilidad del alma, esta
> propensión simpática, es especial en Daniel.
>   (In the physiognomy of both there are many family traits, and I
> don't believe I am making a mistake in being certain that between you
> there is much affinity of the soul, because I observe, señora, that you
> suffer at this moment because you perceive the suffering of others; and
> this impressionability of the soul, this sympathetic propensity is also
> particular to Daniel) [88].

Amalia's European whiteness, therefore, is shadowed by the traces of potential blackness. This is no doubt indicative of the anxieties surrounding
racial mixing on the part of Mármol.

Mármol's move to hint that Amalia might have a positive alter ego
with elements of the "barbaric" suggests that Mármol believes that those
elements considered to be destructive to the nation could be useful in uni-
fying national identity once they were controlled. In fact, Mármol goes one
step further, by placing Amalia in an erotic context, a potentially subversive move on his part that produces the danger of chaos. Women, or at
least idealized nineteenth century Romantic women, were not supposed
to have erotic impulses. Perhaps this is why, after introducing desire in
Amalia, Mármol reverts to the language of painting — making this move
both for plot reasons (to further the romance between Eduardo and
Amalia) and to suggest that this chaos — like the chaos of the 1840's Argentine nation — can be contained.

After Daniel leaves Eduardo in Amalia's house for safekeeping, Amalia
finally goes to bed. In this passage, Mármol positions Amalia as a desiring woman, looking towards Eduardo's bedroom:

> Amalia, entretanto, no pudo volver a la sala sin echar desde el zaguán
> una mirada hacia el aposento en que reposaba su huésped. En seguida,
> volvióse paso a paso a sus habitaciones a esconder, entre la batista de

su lecho, aquel cuerpo cuyas formas, hubieran podido servir de modelo al Ticiano, y cuyo cutis, luciente como el raso, tenía el colorido de las rosas y parecía tener la suavidad de los jazmines.

(Amalia, meanwhile, could not return to the living room without casting a glance from the hall towards the room in which her guest was resting. At once, she returned step by step to her own rooms, to hide — between the batiste sheets of her bed — a body which could have served as a model for Titian; her rose-colored skin, which was as luminous as satin, appeared to be as soft as jasmine flowers) [91].

Is it Eduardo's implicit castration (his wounded leg) that allows Amalia to gaze longingly towards his bedroom? The idea that this was a forbidden act is signaled by the use of the preterit for "poder." "No pudo" signals that Amalia tried but was unable to resist. The line that follows is even more curious: "At once, she returned step by step to her rooms" (91) as if the act of making the decision to return is a quick one, but the trip itself is painful. The juxtaposition of these lines, with a description of Amalia's voluptuous body and luminescent skin, suggests an association between Eduardo's bedroom and hers. Amalia has been given desire.

This is neither the last time that we will see her as a desiring character nor the last time that Mármol will resolve any disjunction between this pure character and her body through the invocation of painting. Every time that eroticism is configured in the novel, we are brought back to a painterly image. Amalia's body is first seen as in a painting, when we are told that she "could have" served as a model for Titian. Her body is described only on its surface: even when discussing how her skin felt, Mármol says that it "appeared" to be as soft as jasmine. She is all surface and there is no tactile sense in the description, as if Mármol reverts to the language of painting to contain any danger in her desire. By describing her eroticism in the language of painting, there is no threat in the novel that Amalia will act upon her desire. She is trapped, framed by a static historical past.

After leaving Amalia's painterly body hidden under the covers, the next female body that appears in the novel is that of Manuela de Rosas, also in bed, but lying, completely dressed, on top of the covers. We first hear her speak as a disembodied voice:

una joven de veinte y dos a veinte y tres años, alta, algo delgada, de un talle y de unas formas graciosas, y con una fisonomía que podría llamarse bella, si la palabra interesante no fuese más análoga para clasificarla.

El color de su tez era ese pálido oscuro que distingue comunamente a las personas de temperamento nervioso, y en cuyos seres la vida vive más en el espíritu que en el cuerpo. Su frente, poco espaciosa, era, sin embargo, fina, descarnada y redonda; y su cabello castaño oscuro, tirado tras de la oreja, dejaba descubrir los perfiles de una cabeza inteligente y bella. Sus ojos, algo más oscuros que su cabello, eran pequeños pero animados e inquietos. Su nariz recta y perfilada, su boca grande pero fresca y bien rasgada, y por último, una expresión picante en la animada fisonomía de esta joven, hacía de ella una de esas mujeres a cuyo lado los hombres tienen menos prudencia que amor, y más placer que entusiasmo. Se ha observado generalmente, que las mujeres delgadas, pálidas, de formas ligeramente pronunciadas, y de temperamento nervioso, poseen cierto secreto de voluptuosidad instintiva que impresionaba fácilmente la sangre y la imaginación de los hombres [...].

Su vestido de merino color guinda, perfectamente ceñido al cuerpo, le delineaba un talle redondo y fino, y le dejaba descubiertos unos hombros, que sin ser los hombros poetizados de María Stuart, bien pudieran pasar por hombros tan suaves y redondos, que la sien del más altivo unitario no dejaría de aceptarlos para reclinarse en ellos un momento, en horas de aquel tiempo en que la vida era fatigada por tantas y tan diversas impresiones

(a young woman of twenty-two to twenty-three years, tall, somewhat thin, with a gracious form, and with a face that might be called beautiful, if the word interesting were not better suited to classify it.

(The color of her skin was that pale dark shade that is commonly found among people of nervous temperament, and in whose beings the spark of life is found more in the spirit than in the physical body. Her forehead, which was not very wide, was, however, fine, honest, and round; and her dark brown hair, pushed behind her ears, revealed the outlines of a beautiful and intelligent head. Her eyes, a little darker than her hair, were small but animated and nervous. Her straight and fine nose, her mouth which was large but fresh and nicely formed, and lastly, a piquant expression in the animated face of this young woman, made her one of those women at whose side men show less prudence than love, and more pleasure than enthusiasm. It has been generally observed that pale, thin women, of lightly pronounced forms and of a nervous temperament, possess a certain secret of instinctive voluptuousness that easily excites the blood and imagination of men [...].

(Her dress of cherry-colored merino wool, perfectly tailored to her body, showed a round and fine form, and revealed shoulders, that without being the shoulders of Mary Stuart, which have been celebrated in poetry, could pass for shoulders so soft and round, that the most committed *unitario* would not hesitate to recline his temple upon them for a moment, during that era in which life was troubled by so many and such diverse impressions) [115].

While herself a model of decorum and gentleness, Manuelita is—by virtue of her physiognomy—a woman who attracts men. Mármol presents

her as unconsciously producing sexual desire; with an "instinctive voluptuousness" that speaks not to the spirit but, importantly, to the "blood and
imagination of men" (115). Unlike in his description of Amalia, Mármol
has given us a description of a body that is fully imagined. The tactile sense,
which is missing in the description of Amalia, is here for Manuela: the
imaginary (future) reader can project himself back into the past as a patriot
(a *unitario*) to rest his head on those soft shoulders. However, in case we
should invest too much in Manuela as a national treasure, Mármol compares her to Mary Stuart, the tragic pretender to the English throne, suggesting that Manuelita is also a pretender, and a false symbol of nation.

There is a bridge between the two houses (Amalia's and Manuela's)
that represents opposing sides of the Argentine nation: a bridge constructed
from the bodies of the two women. But whereas Amalia's body is described
like a covered painting, a static image waiting until she can serve the nation,
Manuela is fully dressed, on top of her bed, as though she is also waiting
for the nation's call: the nation in her case being embodied in her father.
During the Rosas reign, Manuela acted as the first lady of the nation after
her mother's death in 1838. Masiello reports that "[Manuela's] history was
the subject of wild and passionate investigation by *unitarios*" (28). Masiello
comments:

> In an age when sexuality was increasingly confused with politics, lib-
> eral writers emphasized an image of Manuela as a maiden enslaved
> to her father. Some described her as a victim of incest; others painted
> her as a benevolent figure devoted to helping victims of the regime
> [29].

Manuela was used by *unitarios* to represent the excesses of the *rosistas*. In
particular the question of race (Manuelita attended dances of the African
nations) was used by *unitarios* to attack Rosas. Andrews reports that *La
Gaceta Mercantil* felt compelled to defend Manuela in 1843 against the
attacks of *El Nacional*, a *unitario* paper published in Montevideo.

> General Rosas so appreciates the mulattos and *morenos* that he has no
> objection to seating them at his table and eating with them; for which
> *El Nacional* has attempted to mock him, reproaching him because his
> daughter Doña Manuelita de Rosas y Ezcurra shows no reluctance to
> dance on certain occasions with the honest and hard-working mulat-
> tos, *pardos*, and *morenos* [qtd. in Andrews 97].

Manuela was thus a doubly transgressive figure for the time: both a public woman and a black-identified one.

In *Amalia*, Mármol casts Manuela as the virtuous target of her father's cruel attacks against her feminine modesty. Rosas is seen in exaggerated barbarism: rubbing his naked feet, scratching his chest, "sintiendo con ello un verdadero placer, esa organización en quien predominan admirablemente todos los instintos animales" ("feeling as he did a true sense of pleasure, having that constitution in which all the animal instincts predominate so marvelously") (116). Mármol depicts Rosas as encouraging members of his entourage to humiliate his daughter, forcing her to shake hands with blood-spattered killers. In reaction, she suffers visibly. When she first notices the blood covering the hands and arms of Comandante Cutiño, "estaba pálida como un cadáver" ("she was as pale as a corpse") (90). Manuela's refinement and suffering make her a foil to her father's barbarity.

Since Amalia represents the nation for the *unitarios*, and Manuela is first lady of the *rosistas* during the course of the novel, Manuela should logically be Amalia's opposite. However, while Manuela may represent the government, she does not represent the nation: "True to the educational platforms of liberal thinkers, Mármol believed that women could be saved by a combination of formal instruction and refinement of their inclinations toward justice" (*Between Civilization* 29). In other words, Manuela represents not so much the evils of the current government as the promise of a new regime identified with the feminine: even Rosas's daughter could be capable of reform.

It is clear in the second section of *Amalia* that Mármol wishes to make his heroine represent the ideal *unitario* (and therefore Argentine) woman. The section begins with the chapter titled *Amalia Saenz de Olvarrieta*. The chapter starts with a citation about Amalia's native city, a citation taken from the work of a traveler, "el capitán Andrews en su *Viaje a la América del Sur,*" published in London in 1827. "'Tucumán es el jardín del universo, en cuanto a la grandeza y sublimidad de su naturaleza'" ("'Tucumán is the garden of the universe, in terms of the grandeur and sublime quality of Nature'") (225). The British traveler is used to create a distance from Tucumán and also demonstrate the need in Argentine letters for the mediating European. At the same time, the European cannot be depended upon for truth telling, for Mármol adds that "el viajero no se alejó mucho de la verdad con esa metáfora al parecer tan hiberbólica" ("the traveler did not get far away from the truth with this metaphor which appears so hyperbolic") (225).

Two kinds of distance have been created: the traveler's position as an observer from another place is used to give validity to a hyperbolic claim. The hyperbole adds its own distance, to which Mármol refers when he says that the traveler "did not get far away from the truth." While the

British observer carries weight, the Argentine writer is needed to mediate the distance between European observation and Argentine reality. In this formulation, Argentina becomes a place in which hyperbole becomes truth, and metaphor becomes transparent.

For Mármol, then, the relationship between what is European and what is American becomes one in which truth has to be decoded, unveiled: Argentina can only be understood through its own aesthetic. However, Argentine writers were heavily dependent upon European models; in particular, French and English ones. In Montevideo (where Mármol in exile wrote *Amalia*) and in post–Rosas Argentina, French novels formed the bulk of fictional reading available in bookstores, and the majority of novels translated which appeared serialized in literary journals. Mármol's reference to European authors is common. Even descriptions of Argentina are understood by their connection to European readers.

> Y es entre ese jardín de pájaros y flores [...] que se repite con frecuencia ese fenómeno fisiológico de que los ingleses se ríen y los alemanes dudan, como dice el novelista Bulwer, que acontece bajo el tibio cielo de la Italia, y entre los pueblos más meridionales de la península española; es decir, esas pasiones de amor que nacen, se desenvuelven y dominan en el espacio de algunas horas, decidiendo luego del destino futuro de toda una existencia
>
> (And it is in this garden of birds and flowers [...] that a certain physiological phenomenon often occurs, which the English laugh about and the Germans doubt, as the novelist Bulwer says, a phenomenon that gets played out under the warm skies of Italy, and in the more southerly towns of the Spanish peninsula, that is to say, the passion that is born, unfolds, and commands the soul in the space of a few hours, deciding then the future destiny of an entire existence) [226].

Paradoxically, passion comes from geography: emanating from the land itself. Tucumán, according to Mármol, is a place of natural perfection and harmony. Romantic passion also seems to originate from the place.

> Y entre ese jardín de pájaros y flores [...] nació Amalia, la generosa viuda de Barracas [...] y nació allí como nace una azucena o una rosa, rebosando belleza, lozanía y fragancia.
>
> (And in that garden of birds and flowers [...] Amalia, the generous widow of Barracas, was born [...] and she was born there as the lily or the rose is born, overflowing with beauty, luxuriance, and fragrance) [226].

Amalia emerges as a child of nature: she is synonymous with that passionate garden of a place, Tucumán, and with the passion possible in other "more southerly places in the Spanish peninsula." For Mármol, this passion is not accessible to Anglo-Saxon cultures.

Mármol suggests that Amalia herself has not participated in Tucumán's passion, even after her marriage to an old family friend: "El corazón de la joven no había abierto aún el broche de la purísima flor de sus afectos [...]. Más que un esposo, ella tomó un amigo [...]" ("In the heart of the young woman the locket of the pure flower of her affections had not yet opened [...]. More than a husband, she married a friend [...]") (226). While in Tucumán Amalia remains a virgin. Only when she reaches Buenos Aires can her Tucumanian passion make itself felt: when she falls in love with (and marries) Eduardo. While her passion emanates from the land, it requires a certain distance from the land. (Like the distance that *porteño* property owners had?) Therefore, previous to the scene in which she is lying in her boudoir Amalia has been introduced as a woman of paradoxes and most notably as a woman who has not yet experienced sexual pleasure: she is earthy but unearthly, married but a virgin, a woman associated with nature but defined by her possessions.

Amalia's house and its furnishings are described in great detail, and the *criollo*, high bourgeois luxury is a sign for her politics. The fashion notes and domestic descriptions represent more than a desire for luxurious detail: in 1840 Buenos Aires, one's way of dress, way of decoration, and mode of speech were keys to one's political allegiance. Regina West has remarked that during the Rosas period the metonymy of dress allowed authors and bystanders to "read" a person or group, in the same way a twentieth century North American might read the "suits" on Wall Street (2). The same was true for the decorations, objets d'art, and even the fabrics used in the home. Scarlet red (*punzó*) was the defining color of the Rosas government. Citizens were obligated to wear the "divisa punzó" ("scarlet insignia") of the Federalist government. West comments:

> In theory the obligatory scarlet insignia ordered and unified all Argentines under the pledge of Federal power, regardless of sex, race or class. Different styles or aspects of one's attire identified, through legally enforced dress codes, the politics and position of the wearer [1].

As a result, *porteños* during the Rosas era were subject to a high level of intrusion and surveillance by the control mechanisms of the government. In national discourse, this meant that the bodies of women who symbolized the nation were positioned vis-à-vis the clothing that covered them and the objects surrounding them. Often, the bodies of women in cultural discourse seem to exist only to point up the politically coded message being "transmitted" by their clothing.

This politicization of space and the female body was noted by Mármol in other cultural arenas. The celebrated portrait of Manuela de Rosas by Prilidiano Pueyrredón was apparently painted under strict guidelines that were dictated by the committee of influential men who had commissioned the painting (see Fig. 1). Mármol wrote about the guidelines for the painting in *La Semana*, a weekly paper published in Uruguay. Writing about the negotiations of the committee in a manner that ridiculed the Rosas regime, Mármol's article demonstrated the national implications of color in 1850s Argentina:

> El blanco era la mitad del distintivo unitario.
> El celeste, el azul y todas sus modificaciones eran la otra mitad.
> El color de oro, el amarillo, el ante, eran también colores brasileros.
> El negro era duelo.
> El colorado, superior! El colorado es el color de la patria federal [...].
> (White formed half of the *unitario* badge.
> Light blue, blue and all its variations formed the other half.
> Gold, yellow, pale yellow were also Brazilian colors.
> Black represented mourning.
> Red is the best! Red is the color of the Federal Fatherland [...]) [qtd. in Ribera 336].

The committee, according to Mármol, had strict requirements about the positioning of Manuela's body in relation to the items around her, declaring that:

> Manuela debía aparecer parada, con una expresión risueña en su fisonomía, y en al acto de colocar sobre su mesa de gabinete una solicitud dirigida a su tatita. Representándose de este modo la bondad de la joven, en su sonrisa; y su ocupación de intermediaria entre el pueblo y el Jefe Supremo en la solicitud que colocaba sobre la mesa [...].
> (Manuela should appear standing with a cheerful expression on her physiognomy, and in the act of placing on her desk a request directed to her daddy. In this way the goodness of the young woman would be represented in her smile, while her role as intermediary between the people and the Supreme Chief would be represented in the request that she was placing on the desk [...]) [qtd. in Ribera 336–337].

The portrait of Manuela, like most portraits, is a highly codified work. Within the painting, Manuela's body serves only as it brings credit to her father. Here the body is not symbolizing the nation as much as it is signifying a code of conduct.

Nancy Duncan refers to the way in which space is "subject to various territorializing and deterritorializing processes whereby local control is fixed, claimed, challenged, forfeited and privatized" (129). Duncan claims that "liberal political and legal theory can be seen as a territorializing spatial practice that attempts to differentiate the public and private by erecting a boundary around a private sphere of relative non-interference by civil society or the state" (129). Mármol uses private space to signal his characters' significance to the nation. Nation-space is created by Mármol as a "museum of feminine delicacies," suggesting that the struggle over national identity was both gendered and related to historiography. In the passage from *Amalia* below, every detail of Amalia's physical world can be seen as forming part of her relationship to the nation. In this way, Mármol constructs a nation-space which contains objects that relate to his particular beliefs about the construction of national values and citizens, and the future of the nation.

The passage comes directly after the long discussion of Amalia's melancholy history. The reader is placed firmly in the present time of the novel by the words "Eran las diez de la mañana, y Amalia acababa de salir de un baño perfumado" ("It was ten in the morning and Amalia was just getting out of a perfumed bath") (227). This line brings forth an image of Amalia's body that is both sensory and sensual, and is followed by yet another description of a room in Amalia's house, this time a boudoir noteworthy for its luxury.

> La luz de la mañana entraba al retrete, que los lectores conocen ya, a través de las dobles cortinas de tul celeste y de batista, e iluminaba todos los objetos con ese colorido suave y delicado que se esparce sobre el oriente cuando despunta el día.
>
> La chimenea estaba encendida, y la llama azul que despedía un grueso leño ardía en ella se reflejaba, como sobre el cristal de un espejo, en las láminas de acero de la chimenea; formándose así la única luz brillante que allí había.
>
> Los pebeteros de oro, colocados sobre las rinconeras, exhalaban el perfume suave de las pastillas de Chile que estaban consumiendo; y los jilgueros, saltando en los alambres dorados que los aprisionaban, hacían oír esa música vibrante y caprichosa con que esos tenores de la grande ópera de la Naturaleza hacen alarde del poder pulmonar de su pequeña y sensible organización. En medio de este museo de delicadezas femeniles, donde todo se reproducía al infinito sobre el cristal, sobre el acero, y sobre el oro, Amalia, envuelta en un peindador de batista, estaba sentada sobre un sillón de damasco caña,

delante de uno de los magníficos espejos de su guaradarropas; su seno casi descubierto, sus brazos desnudos, sus ojos cerrados, y su cabeza reclinada sobre el respaldo del sillón, dejando que su espléndida y ondeada caballera fuese sostenida por el brazo izquierdo de una niña de diez años, linda y fresca como un jazmín, que, en vez de peinar aquellos, parecia deleitarse en pasarlos por su desnudo brazo para sentir sobre su cutis la impresión cariñosa de sus sedosas hebras.

(The morning light entered the dressing room, with which the readers are already familiar, through the double curtains of sky blue tulle and batiste, and illuminated all the objects with this soft and delicate color, which scatters to the east as the day begins.

(The chimney was lit and the blue flame that dispatched a fat log burning there was reflected, like the glass of a mirror, in the steel plates of the chimney, forming thus the only bright light that there was.

(The gold incense burners, placed on the corner tables, gave off the smooth perfume from the Chilean pastilles that they were consuming; and the goldfinches jumping in the golden wires that imprisoned them, made heard that vibrant and capricious music with which those tenors of the great opera of Nature display the pulmonary power of their small and sensitive constitutions.

(In the middle of this museum of feminine delicacies, where everything was reproduced into infinity in glass, in steel and in gold, Amalia — wrapped in a peignoir of batiste — was sitting on a seat of Damascus cane before one of the magnificent mirrors of her wardrobe; her breast almost uncovered, her arms naked, her eyes closed, and her head resting on the back of the chair, letting her splendid and wavy head of hair be supported by the left arm of a ten-year-old girl, beautiful and fresh as a jasmine flower, who, instead of combing the hair, appeared to delight in passing it over her naked arm in order to feel on her skin the caressing impression of those silken threads) [227–228].

Among the first impressions from this passage, particularly in the first two paragraphs, is the painterly sense of description. We are told how the light enters the room, and how — mediated by the elegant curtains of tulle and batiste — it illuminates the room in blue. The blue is not just any blue; it is "*celeste*," a word which means both "blue" and "of the sky" or "of heaven" in Spanish. So from the outset, all of what we are seeing is illuminated in this heavenly light, giving an ethereal quality to the scene. *Celeste* also was a color associated with *unitarios*, so that a political dimension is immediately present in the scene. More than a mere political code, Amalia's use of *celeste* demonstrated her willingness to put her life in danger. "Aristocratic *unitarios* showed a predilection for French fashion and risked their lives while donning [...] shades of green and light blue"

(West 3). Adding to the painterly quality and political imagination of the description are the double curtains. We are told not only their color but their material, tulle and batiste, which signal the luxury and European refinement of Amalia's dressing room.

Mármol introduces the room by reminding his reader (who originally read the work in serial form) that we have seen it before. Mármol is referring to the first section of the novel, which contains a two-page description of the room during the tense arrival of Daniel and Eduardo at Amalia's home. In this previous scene, Daniel looks for a towel to wash Eduardo's blood from his hands. Without hesitation, Daniel casually "invadió el tocador, manchando las porcelanas y cristales con la sangre y el lodo de sus manos" ("invaded the dresser, staining the porcelains and crystal with the blood and mud on his hands") (74). In the same chapter, Mármol mentions a second time that Daniel has "desordenado [...] las porcelanas y cristales [del tocador]" ("disordered [...] the porcelains and crystals [of the dresser]") (84). Daniel's presence has invaded, disordered, and stained Amalia's dressing room. While Eduardo is clearly domesticated by the time spent in Amalia's house, Daniel brings the physical evidence of the dangerous streets into her dressing room: the blood from Eduardo's fight with the *mazorca* and the mud from the streets themselves are tangible evidence, both of the male body and of the public sphere.

The entrance of daylight into the dressing room is therefore the third time that Amalia's boudoir has been invaded, but this time the reader is invited to enter slowly and with great preparation. The lingering glance has a sensuous quality all its own: all the objects are illuminated with this light, we are told, and we follow the light as it touches objects in the room and eventually is fragmented in reflection. The entering gaze represents the artist's eye and the eye of the spectator, giving the thrill of invading feminine space.

At the same time that the light mimics the way in which the presumably male narrator is entering this sanctified feminine space, it is also associated with femaleness itself. The light is "soft and delicate," words used to describe Amalia. The blue, celestial quality of the light also makes the room ethereal, perhaps the most clear characteristic of this pure and virtuous heroine. The blue light reappears in the second paragraph in the flame that is consuming the log in the fireplace. No longer fragmented, the light is now focalized to a single point of concentration (the flame) and then fragmented again by being reflected in the chimney. Curiously, the narrator feels compelled to tell us that it was reflected clearly "like the glass of a mirror" in the steel. As in the first paragraph, this play of light repeats the fragmentation of the image of Amalia's body, which is reflected in the mirror of her armoire.

The third paragraph represents another shift in focalization by introducing the senses of smell and hearing. First there is a description of the gold incense burners, functioning as a signifier of Amalia's wealth and refinement. The perfume of the incense refers back to Amalia herself, who has just emerged from a perfumed bath. The incense burners sit upon "rinconeras," a word that means either corner tables or corner armoires; the significance being that we are in a space where every corner is filled with furniture. From the incense we move to the image of the caged birds. Again in the birds can be seen a reference to Amalia: the birds are objects of Nature, like Amalia. One of Amalia's most oft-mentioned traits is her "sensitive constitution," and in this paragraph Mármol refers to the "small and sensitive constitution" of the birds. The caged bird is a cliché of caged femininity: this image was a reassuring reminder that women's "wild" nature had been domesticated.* The reference to the "grand opera" of Nature and the "tenor" again seems to civilize even the real symbols of nature in the room: the birds are not only caged but are references to a European art form that was popular among the upper classes in Buenos Aires.

In the fourth paragraph, we finally reach Amalia herself. The paragraph that positions Amalia begins with a curious line: "In the middle of this museum of feminine delicate things." I would like to draw attention to Mármol's curious expression "delicadezas feminiles." The word "delicadeza" is associated with refinement and elegance. To modify these delicate or refined things, Mármol uses "feminil" which is a word that means "relative to women." In the stereotypes of the twentieth century, "feminine delicacy" or even "womanly delicacy" sounds repetitive. However, first of all, Mármol uses the word "delicadezas," which means "delicate things." ("Delicadezas" does not translate precisely into "delicacies" in the sense that it is used in English. That word would be "delicias.") In the context of 1850's Argentina delicacy was both class-identified and (for Mármol) party and race-identified. To be delicate was not a mark of gender, but of education and virtue. Yet overdetermination does exist at the level of social categories: as I have argued, even "feminine" in nineteenth century Argentina does not necessarily refer to women.

All these feminine, delicate things are reproduced into "infinity" in the reflecting surfaces of the room. By the time we reach Amalia herself in

---

*In her article on nineteenth century artist Rosa Bonheur, Whitney Chadwick notes that "the ideological production of middle-class femininity around notions of control over the instinctual life and the social construction of women as the opposite and other of man, depended on images that symbolically secured femininity as both dependent and needing the control of the dominant social group" (96).

this sentence, she has already been fragmented as an image. In an overde-termination of reflection, we see this fragmented image in the mirrors of her wardrobe. As viewers, we are looking over her shoulder at her reflection, lost in the play of refracted reflections. At the same time, the fact that Már-mol focalizes Amalia in the mirror means that she is saved from infinite reproduction like the "other" objects in the room. She is focalized in the "magnificent" (read civilized/*unitario*) mirrors: as if the danger of chaos from her body can be mediated through this civilizing lens.

In *Literatura argentina y realidad política*, David Viñas discusses a description of Amalia's bedroom, pointing to the links between ideology and decoration:

> La materia y los soportes reales están cubiertos por pudor o distan-ciamiento: Las paredes tapizadas aterciopeladamente, las ventanas cubiertas, el piso acolchado, una "colcha," un "tapafundas," "sobre-puestos." El movimiento aéreo reaparece "entre nubes" disfumán-dose en "una tenue neblina." Todo contribuye a lograr un tono de "leve y vaporosa neblina," de imprecisión e irrealidad, de subréptica y reiterada remisión a "Italia," a lo francés, a "Cambray" y a la India.
>
> (The material and the structures are covered by modesty and distance. The velvet-covered walls, the covered windows, the carpeted floor, a "coverlet," a "blanket cover," "things put upon one another." The airy movement reappears "between clouds," evaporating into a "tenuous mist." Everything contributes to a tone of "light and vaporous mist," or imprecision and unreality, of surreptitious and repeated reference to "Italy," to French things, to "Cambray" and to India) [132].

Viñas's argument points up not only the impression of unreality, but more significantly, he employs the concept of "pudor." While discussing nineteenth century Spanish novels, Elizabeth Scarlett claims that in Span-ish literature "pudor" (a blend of modesty and shame) "is more essential than that of privacy (for which there is no exact Spanish equivalent), espe-cially regarding the female body" (5). Amalia's bedroom, like her body, is characterized by its covered surfaces. All of the objects in Amalia's boudoir, including Amalia's body, could be seen as a representation of feminine delicacy. Yet if her "delicadezas" are a symbol of her refinement, then what is particularly feminine about them? And why does Mármol call the boudoir a museum? What is feminine in the novel is the sensuality of the space: an abandonment to physical pleasure, surrounding oneself with a physical environment that enhances physical pleasure and oneself. The pleasure, however, belongs to the (male) narrator, his voyeurism excused by the displaced witness who is the mark of innocence.

The notion of the museum as a nation-space is essential to understanding the links between Mármol's representation of Amalia's body in her boudoir, and how the female body then functions within national discourse. The objects in Amalia's boudoir have been reconstructed painstakingly as meaningful artifacts which reference an organized historical past for Mármol's reader-citizens and a known political present for Mármol's contemporary readers. The excessive number of objects might represent chaos except that — like the wild birds that become operatic tenors and like Amalia herself — there is a "sensitive constitution" to the boudoir. In the case of the objects arranged by Mármol in Amalia's boudoir, the orderliness asserts a rhetoric of emblematic citizenship. The fact that citizenship, while embodied in a woman, refers to male subjects can be deduced from the fact that within her museum, the body of Amalia always exists as a reflection. Within nation-space, she appears as an object, reflected in a mirror.

For Mármol, Amalia's erotic body is a chaotic, fragmented one: the erotic makes it potentially dangerous, the fragmentation perhaps a reference to the fragmentation of the national body. In *The Body in Pieces*, art historian Linda Nochlin maintains that the omnipresence of the fragment in the visual representation of the French revolution was related to the fact that the French Revolution was "destroying one civilization before creating a new one" (197). Nochlin refers to the imagery of destruction and dismemberment in the French Revolution as reflecting the actual dismemberment of human bodies through the guillotine.

The fragmented and destroyed [white] male body also emerges in *Amalia*. The plot of *Amalia* hinges upon Eduardo's terrible injury, which keeps him trapped in Amalia's house. The signs of violence on the white male body are made evident through the blood that tracks its way through all the houses of the principal characters. Amalia's reaction is one of incomprehension: "tanto Eduardo como Daniel, ofrecían dos figuras como no había imaginádose jamás: eran dos hombres completamente cubiertos de barro y de sangre" ("Eduardo and Daniel presented two figures that she had never even imagined: two men completely covered in mud and blood") (73). The choice of words here is significant: Amalia had never even *imagined* seeing two men covered in blood, in spite of the fact that she lived in a city where people were being killed on a semi-regular basis. Amalia's experience of the violence done to fragmented male bodies is given distance. Their fragmentation represents physical pain and political events: historical events played out on corpses. The fragmentation of Amalia's body, however, occurs within the context of Mármol's "museum of feminine, delicate things." The delicate things, as I have noted above, represent not

Amalia's gender but her class, race, and ethnicity. Her body is not only fragmented within but fragmented *by* the objects surrounding her, just as gender is often subsumed by those same categories of difference that mark national identity for nineteenth century liberals.

Nead has argued that the female body in art "symbolizes the transformation of the base matter of nature into the elevated forms of culture and the spirit. The female nude can thus be understood as a means of containing femininity and female sexuality" (2). Mármol's painterly images of Amalia's body forestall the potentially subversive element of female eroticism by fragmenting and containing Amalia's body. Amalia's erotic body is—significantly—a white, upper-class body. The bodies of non-white women barely appear in the novel, and when they do Mármol does not consider them as objects of desire. This erasure of the non-white female body in the novel mimics the erasure—both actual and textual—of the non-white citizen in post-colonial Argentina. While Amalia's "alter ego," Daniel, negotiates the civilization-barbarity dichotomy in favor of the nation, the normative Argentine citizen remains relentlessly white and, of course, male. A similar operation of erasure of other races and female bodies was present in nineteenth century Argentine painting, complementing the literary construction of the citizen, and contributing to the creation of a new public sphere in the post–Rosas period.

La Siesta and the Doubled Body

Prilidiano Pueyrredón had studied painting in Europe, returning to Argentina where his works showing naked women — such as his 1865 painting *La Siesta*—often circulated privately. Argentine society was not ready for *La Siesta*: as late as 1893, journalists were still having to defend the public exhibition of nudes. Jorge Romero Brest writes that in nineteenth century Argentina "hubieron dos únicas oportunidades para el desarollo de la pintura: hacer paisajes pintorescos y retratos, con predominio de estos" ("there were only two opportunities for the development of painting: to do picturesque landscapes and to do portraits, with the predominance of the latter") (19). Pueyrredón's nudes, however, were not intended for consumption by the wider public that viewed his portraits and landscapes. The elitism of these private erotic images (the expense of obtaining them assured that only a limited number of men could possess them) meant that the nudes registered a hidden world in which erotic images of the female body circulated among a privileged group of men. Representing the chaos of Eros—and the possibility of feminine pleasure—they contain female sexuality by framing and making it static: the representation of female eroticism operates for the benefit of a limited number of the powerful.

The change over several decades in the relationship between the female body and nation-space is dramatic when contrasting the boudoir scene in *Amalia* with *La Siesta*. In *Amalia* nation-space is imagined as a closed, interior womanly space: a boudoir that is also a museum of citizenship. In Amalia's boudoir, every piece of furniture, the color and material of the curtains, and even the fragmented body of Amalia herself correspond to Amalia's status as the emblematic citizen. Pueyrredón's painting suggests another kind of museum: a private space of erotic knowledge about the female body, which is possessed by public men. The elite public men who possessed these paintings were also of the same class who would become large landowners. And in 1865 — the year in which Pueyrredón painted *La Siesta*— the politicization of domestic space had lessened, and the concept of nation-space was focused on the concept of territory. The painting of *La Siesta* presents two voluptuous females whose sexualized bodies suggest metaphors of possession, and whose physicality appears territorial in shape and size.

Pueyrredón encompassed multiple contradictions: he was the son of a revered public figure and part of Buenos Aires' aristocracy. His father, Juan Martín de Pueyrredón, had been one of the early members of the post-independence ruling *junta*, and was elected "Director supremo" (chief executive) from 1816 to 1819. Upon his return from Europe young Prilidiano painted portraits of the Argentina elite, gaining the commission to paint Manuelita Rosas in 1851. While modern art historians consider him one of Argentine's most significant nineteenth century painters, his contemporaries found him a strange and almost embarrassing figure. His talent was acknowledged, but his studio life was considered shocking. Laura Malosetti claims that, as a notorious figure of legend,

> Pueyrredón se habría entregado a la pintura de cuadros de asuntos "obscenos" y "lascivos," debido a las extravagancias y libertadas que le permitía su vida de "señorito" rico [...]. Que era un hombre de costumbres "raras," que se ocultaba en largos encierros en el altillo de su quinta, que la modelo de esos cuadros era su ama de llaves [...].
>
> (Pueyrredón had dedicated himself to painting works with "obscene" and "lascivious" themes, due to the extravagance and freedom allowed by his life as a rich man's son [...]. That he was a man of "strange" habits, that he hid out for long periods behind the high wall of his quinta, that the model for those works was his housekeeper [...]) [129].

Prilidiano Pueyrredón's work had as much to do with a tension between "high" and "low" art as with a tension between public and private. Relating his work to the erotic daguerreotype, Malosetti argues:

> La pintura erótica ha sido patrimonio de las clases altas, de quienes tuvieron el dinero y el poder como para la sofisticación del placer sensual y para mantenerlo oculto, a resguardo de las miradas "vulgares."
>
> (Erotic painting has [always] been the patrimony of the upper classes, of those who had the money and the power to obtain the satisfaction of sensual pleasure and to keep it hidden, safe from the gaze of the "vulgar") [133].

The suggestion here is that what makes the erotic "vulgar" is not its association with sexuality but the gaze of lower-class men.

La Siesta is similar in composition and theme to Courbet's *Sleep* (1862) although Malosetti believes that there is no way in which Pueyrredón could have seen Courbet's painting, which was painted for the French ambassador of Turkey and was only shown in 1872 and to great scandal (132). (Pueyrredón's painting was originally untitled: *La Siesta* was a twentieth century means of identifying the painting in a catalogue.) Never exhibited at all during the nineteenth century, the painting remained for many years in a private collection in Argentina.

In a time when artists were almost obligated to be creating "national" art, Pueyrredón was remarkably decadent. Yet what was most shocking about Pueyrredón's work was that to speak of his paintings was to make public the very machinations of power that occurred in elite groups of men, a bonding between men that occurred around and about the bodies of women. For while Pueyrredón was publicly criticized, or snubbed, in references to the great artists of the day, elite men were buying his erotic works. Malosetti refers to Pueyrredón's work as showing

> [u]n indicio acerca de las imágenes eróticas que circularon entre un círculo de la clase alta porteña, que había estado exiliado en Europa y traía una nueva liberalidad en sus costumbres privadas. Trajeron daguerrotipos eróticos y, al menos Pueyrredón, hizo pinturas de ese tenor. Ellos no pretendieron hacer públicas esas "modas francesas" sino que las guardaron en la intimidad de su círculo de hombres. Allí habrían quedado si no fuera por la trascendencia de la figura pública de Pueyrredón.
>
> ([a]n index of the erotic images that circulated among a circle of the upper-class *porteños*, who had been exiled in Europe and brought a new liberality in their private customs. They brought erotic daguerreotypes and, Pueyrredón at least did paintings in the same vein. They did not care to make these "French fashions" public, but

wanted to keep them safely guarded in the intimacy of the circle of men. There they would have stayed if it were not for the transcendence of the public figure of Pueyrredón) [133].

The model-mistress of an upper-class *porteño* is shown in Pueyrredón's work as enjoying sexual pleasure. This is not the clothed, white, upper-class body that national discourse had constructed as suitable for public circulation in art. Instead the bodies exposed in *La Siesta* are tied to "animal" passion and prostitution.

As the son of a prominent political figure, Pueyrredón's paintings—even without being shown publicly—put sex into cultural discourse in an inescapable fashion. Pueyrredón's erotic works referenced European private customs. Yet to be European in nineteenth century Buenos Aires, was to have a link to "lo civilizado" ("the civilized"). To create art that referenced European norms had also been a goal throughout the nineteenth century of Argentine artists of all kinds. Pueyrredón's work, however, embraced a side of European culture that was not included in Argentinean definitions of "lo civilizado." The breakdown of the categories of civilization and barbarism was therefore threatened by the public knowledge of Pueyrredón's work.

These two disparate cultural expressions *Amalia* and *La Siesta* are linked not only through the positioning of erotically charged female bodies in the boudoir but in the displacement of the body of the emblematic citizen. The displacement of the body of the all-white *criolla* (Amalia) from the boudoir suggests a struggle over the changing discourse surrounding the body that occurred in the fifteen years between the writing of *Amalia* and the painting of *La Siesta*.

In the painting, two women lie naked on a bed, next to one another. One woman is facing the imagined viewer. Her eyes are closed, she has a slight smile on her face, and her hair is somewhat tangled. She has placed one of her hands over her pubic area; the corner of a lace-edged sheet drapes her right hip. The second woman is seen only from the back. The bedclothes are lace-edged and elegant. The first woman cannot be completely asleep: the tension in her bent leg suggests that she is half-awake. Her rumpled hair, the sheet draped over her thigh, and the slight smile on her face give the impression that she has just experienced sexual pleasure. The second woman, who is seen from the back, is mostly seen as a mound of buttock and hip. On close examination it appears to be the same woman: the body shape, hair color, etc. give the impression of a doubled body. In addition, her torso should extend behind the first woman, instead of slightly above her as shown in the painting. The second body, therefore, is split, further disordering the image.

In using the painting as a means of reading the scene in *Amalia*, one of the immediate contrasts is how the body is "mirrored" in both scenes. In *Amalia*, the body of Amalia is fragmented by the mirror, which also distances us as spectators from participating in any direct voyeurism. In *La Siesta* the doubling of almost identical bodies suggests a mirror image which itself is not symmetrical but is instead disordered. The woman whose face we see would, in a true mirror image, be caught with her body in profile. We are not looking at her mirrored reflection. And yet the image of the woman whose back is towards us seems to be the same model: as if the same dark-haired voluptuous woman is caught in two different poses on the same bed. Whereas Amalia's desiring body is destabilized through its fragmentation, the body in *La Siesta* destabilizes through the doubling of the image: what exactly are we seeing? Moreover, the doubling of desire and the lavishness of the bodies in Pueyrredón's painting produce a sense of erotic fulfillment.

However, erotic depictions of women's pleasure have more to do, as John Berger has remarked, with the sexual pleasure of men (55), creating an image of female desire for the consumption of the male spectator. In *La Siesta* the sexualized bodies of the two women have been painted for the erotic pleasure of a wealthy man. The sexual pleasure suggested by the half-smile and the rumpled bedclothes suggests that the woman (and possibly the second woman as well) has had sex with the man viewing the painting. The man positioned as the spectator has access—either as their lover or as a privileged spectator — to these two women who represent an excess of female sexuality. Femininity is not recalled by the painting. Delicacy exists only as a reference to class privilege, in the luxurious bedclothes and in the ability of the spectator to have access to these public women. Femaleness occurs in overdetermination: in fact, the roundness of the hips of the second woman appears as the true center of the painting, along with the draped hand of the first woman which both hides and invites the viewer to gaze at her pubic area.

The luxurious bedclothes are significant to an understanding of the painting. By the mid 1860s in Buenos Aires there was a totally distinct set of meanings attached to household objects and clothing than there was in 1850. The color of one's clothing referred not to the politics but to the personality of the wearer, especially if that wearer was a woman. In *La Primavera*, a weekly *porteño* literary journal from 1863, a column entitled "Observaciones" refers to the properties of women according to the colors they wear: "Las mujeres que gustan vestirse de blanco son generalmente buenas [...]. Las que prefieren el azul son casi siempre celosas [...]. Las partidarias de los colores vivos son de carácter inquieto" ("Women who like to dress in white are generally good [...]. Those who prefer blue are almost always jealous [...]. Those who favor bright colors usually have a restless personality") (31). The dramatic difference in the discussion of color between the Rosas era and a mere decade later is notable. These changes also indicate a revised conception of the private and public spheres in Argentina, one in which the lack of consciously political codification in the domestic interior and clothing meant a greater sense of a distinction between public and private spheres.

In *La Siesta*, the lace border on the sheets and pillows of the bed denotes that the women are sleeping in a place of luxury and refinement: it does *not* represent political opposition as it did in *Amalia*. French fashion and even French lingerie had become desirous to wealthy *porteños* in the 1860s, as private wealth increased. In "Sexo y matrimonio en la sociedad tradicional," Rodríguez Molas discusses the ways in which intimate facts of the body became a symbol of upper-class refinement. Referring to the influx of European fashion in the late 1850s and 1860s, Rodríguez Molas notes:

> Otra consequencia de las mencionadas transformaciones la encontramos en la mayor preocupación por la higiene íntima [...]. También, por entonces, en Buenos Aires las mujeres se preocupan por la estética de la ropa interior que usan y los avisos de los periódicos comienzan a anunciar la venta de lencería importada de Francia.
>
> (Another consequence of the aforementioned transformations can be found in the greater preoccupation with intimate hygiene [...]. Also, as a result, in Buenos Aires women begin to concern themselves with the aesthetics of the undergarments that they wear and the advertisements in the newspapers start to announce the sale of lingerie imported from France) [39].

The lace-bordered sheets and the lingerie effect of the lace across the woman's pubic area might reference the changes occurring in *porteño* high society even as they recall erotic images from Europe. Yet while women might be buying lingerie, and the medical school had the Spanish text *Elementos de higiene privada* (1861) as required reading for its students, the portrayal of details of the body in cultural discourse was not considered to be acceptable.

The elegant refinement of the bed clothes also depicts an intruding figure in the newly intimate space of private life and among the men who might be founding their own families in post–Rosas Argentina. Jean Franco references the increased separation of public and private in nineteenth century Mexico, declaring that it produced something of the same effect on women's sexuality that religious discourse had done, making it either heretical or impossible. For men, on the other hand, the bohemian life allowed them to cross over into the low and forbidden world of sexual promiscuity [95].

However, the fact that upper-class men concealed their visits to Pueyrredón's studio—and, at times, even their association with him — demonstrates that the celebration of the bohemian lifestyle that would become more popular towards the end of the century had not yet become a fact of public admittance. What is at issue in Pueyrredón's painting is, instead, the competition and rivalry between men. The painting recalls that for upper-class *porteño* men the ability to move between "low" and "high" areas of the city meant that there were few spaces that escaped their knowledge. The circulation of elite men among all spaces of the city—and nation — would be repeated again in literature, particularly with the "Generación de '80," the age of the "gentlemen-writer."

In writing about nineteenth century Mexico, Franco refers to "the carving out of a territory of domestic stability and decency from which all

A nineteenth century Buenos Aires portrait of upper-class porteños. Colección Witcomb, Archivo de la Nación, Buenos Aires.

low elements were expelled" (81). In nineteenth century Buenos Aires, the territory of domestic stability also concerned the virtuousness of women of the upper class, who would be producing national leaders. The familiar call from feminists of the day was for women to be "spiritual" leaders unconcerned by issues of corporality. Poems in literary journals generally use language that relates women to heavenly beings. The upper-class women who appear in photographs of the era, on the other hand, are burdened by clothing that appears designed to increase their corporality, and which, through the multiple layers of expensive material, demonstrated their wealth and position. The family portraits from this period show upper-class women positioned as solid figures of bourgeois comfort, seated beside their husbands, surrounded by their children, with a hovering maid, of mixed ethnicity, behind them (see photograph opposite page). In Pueyrredón's painting, the foregrounding of the maid would itself be a shock — as much of a shock as her nakedness.

The sanctified space of the national family in Argentine cultural discourse of the mid to late nineteenth century was perceived as one in which ruling class interests were merged: remember the joining of Amalia's provincial wealth and Eduardo's *porteño* aristocracy. The sexual pleasure of a young housekeeper in the home of one of Argentina's most illustrious families disturbed the illusion of the utopian national family. It also revealed the deception behind the ideal of the republican mother: that the founding of the Argentine national "family" occurred in back rooms, among public men, engaged in private dealings which involved transactions involving women whose bodies might be publicly exposed. The representation of female Eros does not mean that the notion of femaleness has become a possible cultural context: instead, the female body exists in a boudoir-within-a-boudoir in the hidden museum of the male bedroom.

Two

The Degraded Mother:
Recuerdos de provincia and
El médico de San Luis

In *Facundo* (1845) Domingo Sarmiento cast the future of the Argentine nation in terms of a now-famous binary that projected Argentine progress as a struggle between barbarism and civilization. In his 1995 essay "Sarmiento the Writer," Ricardo Piglia recounts the anecdote that opens *Facundo*, where Sarmiento tells of writing "On ne tue point les idées" ("One can never kill ideas") under the nation's coat of arms as he fled Argentina in 1840:

> A fines del año 1840 salía yo de mi patria, desterrado por lástima, estropeado, lleno de cardenales, puntazos y golpes recibidos el día anterior en una de esas bacanales agrientas de soldadesca y mazorqueros. Al pasar por los baños de Zonda, bajo las armas de la patria que en días más alegres había pintado en una sala, escribí con carbón estas palabras: "On ne tue point les idées." El Gobierno, a quien se comunicó el hecho, mandó una comisión encargada de descifrar el jeroglífico, que se decía contener desahogos ignobles, insultos y amenazas. Oída la traducción: "¡Y bien!" dijeron. "¿Qué significa esto?"
>
> (Toward the end of 1840, I left my native land, banished by shame, crippled, full of bruises, jabs and blows received the day before in one of those bloody bacchanalias staged by soldiers and political gangs. Upon passing the baths of Zonda, under the nation's coat of arms—which on happier days I had painted in a salon—I wrote the following words with a piece of coal: "On ne tue point les idées." The officials who received word of the deed sent a commission assigned to decipher the hieroglyphics, which were said to contain

ignoble outbursts, insults, and threats. Once the translation was heard:
"Well!" they said. "What does that mean?") [16].

Piglia comments that

this is the tale of a persecuted man who flees into exile and writes in
another language. He takes his body, marked by the violence of barbarism, but also leaves his mark: he inscribes a hieroglyphic in which
culture is coded, thus creating a microscopic counterpart to the great
enigma that he endeavors to translate by deciphering the life of
Facundo Quiroga [132].

For Piglia, Sarmiento has exchanged a body marked by violence for writing which serves as a code for European culture. The words are in French —
the language of high culture for Argentine letters— and also a language of
resistance in nineteenth century Buenos Aires. To speak or write in French
signaled that Rosas's censorship had failed; it was an act of defiance. The
message itself had to do with bodies; i.e., men and women could be killed
(their bodies destroyed, as Rosas tried to do to Sarmiento) but ideas could
not be destroyed. Sarmiento claims to have written his message beneath
the nation's coat of arms, suggesting by the content of the message that he
conceived of the nation as an abstract rather than as a physical entity: it
is formed not by men and women but by ideas.

Sarmiento did not die in Chile, but returned to Argentina to become
its president many years later. With his ambitious programs for national
education and his desire to "civilize" the pampas, he would attempt to
reform or erase the "barbarians" from the national arena. What Sarmiento
seems to imply in the anecdote is that the barbarians might beat you to
death with the dictionary without understanding that the imagined nation
is the nation itself. Sarmiento concludes the anecdote with

Significa simplemente que venía a Chile, donde la libertad brillaba
aún, y que me proponía hacer proyectar los rayos de las luces de su
prensa hasta el otro lado de los Andes. Los que conocen mi conducta
en Chile, saben si he cumplido aquella protesta.
   (It meant simply that I was coming to Chile, where liberty still
shone, and that I proposed to shine the light of [Chile's] free press on
the other side of the Andes. Those who know of my actions in Chile
know whether I have kept my word) [16].

The barbarians, therefore, are associated with a violently marked physical body while the marginalized intellectuals are associated by implication
with freedom from the body. Sarmiento's story implies that the body
can be exchanged for writing and that — through letters— the exile can be

present in his homeland by "shining" his light across the Andes or, as was often the case, across the Rio de la Plata. The exiled intellectual has now gained the status of an epic hero: writing guarantees his immortality, or as Foucault puts the same idea, "narrative redeemed his acceptance of death" (*Birth of the Clinic* 117).

Introducing *Facundo* with an anecdote that refers to his own near-death (the near-erasure of his own body), Sarmiento sets himself up as a hero. It is significant then that he also introduces the chapter on his mother in his 1850s memoir *Recuerdos de provincia* by referring to a time when he became convinced that she had died, although she was, in fact, alive. Her near-death sets the scene for a description of her life.

> En Nápoles, la noche que descendí del Vesubio, la fiebre de las emociones del día me daba pesadillas horribles [...] y al despertar de entre aquellos sueños que querían despedazarme, una idea sola quedaba tenaz [...]: ¡mi madre había muerto!
>
> (In Naples, the night that I came down from Vesuvius, the fever of emotions from the day gave me horrible nightmares [...] and on waking from amongst those dreams that were trying to tear me apart, one lone idea took hold of me [...]: my mother had died!) [204].

This very dramatic anecdote allows Sarmiento to accomplish several things at once. Primarily, it gives him the right to pronounce his mother's epitaph while she is still alive. His descent from Vesuvius gives a tragic dimension to a life that was (in the terms of traditional narrative, at least) far from dramatic. Sarmiento's mother is given the romantic qualities that her hard-working life might lack for a nineteenth century reader.*

In addition, Doña Paula's imagined death connects her to the past of epic heroes. Referring to a statement by the President of Chile that Sarmiento should not expose his indigent childhood to "los ojos del vulgo" ("the eyes of the vulgar") (218), Sarmiento comments:

> ¡Pobres hombres los favorecidos de la fortuna, que no conciben que la pobreza a la antigua, la pobreza del patricio romano, puede ser llevada como el manto de los Cincinatos, de los Arístides, cuando el sentimiento moral ha dado a sus pliegues la dignidad augusta de una desventaja sufrida sin mengua!
>
> (Poor are those men favored by fortune, who do not know that poverty in the ancient style, the poverty of a Roman patrician, can be

---

*Sarmiento's description contains a great deal of gothic fancy: he mentions the "spewing of the volcano, the darkness of the abysm" as responsible for producing his nightmare (204). Naples was the favorite spot of romantic European travelers, with Lamartine, it should be added, as the most conspicuous member of this group. The vision does not appear in Sarmiento's account of his trip to Italy in his Viajes (1849).

worn like the mantel of the Cincinnatus, of the Aristides, when moral sentiment has given their poverty the august dignity of disadvantage suffered without inferiority!) [218].

Sarmiento's mother now belongs by association to a category of ruined aristocracy — a reference that will become more significant later when Sarmiento describes how she came from the ruined branch of a wealthy colonial family. In addition, numerous classical references tie Doña Paula to an earlier statement of Sarmiento's in a series of articles on women in the Chilean newspaper *El Mercurio* in 1841. Praising the strength of Roman mothers, Sarmiento claims that this "alone perhaps, laid the groundwork for Rome's greatness" (qtd. by Garrels 281). Death has considerably added to Doña Paula's qualities as a heroine. One might, in fact, say that death has redeemed her as acceptable for narrative.*

This movement of erasure is fascinating when considered against the figure of Doña Paula that appears later in the text. Doña Paula Albarracín de Sarmiento ranks among the most visible symbols of national motherhood in nineteenth century Argentine narrative. Yet while Sarmiento's mother has been held as an ideal of republican motherhood — and while Sarmiento produces her at first as a tragic heroine — the figure that appears in *Recuerdos de provincia* is a more complex and less cohesive figure than the symbolic construction that Sarmiento perhaps intended. Doña Paula is linked to a glorified colonial past that is also presented as an obstacle to nineteenth century progress. Furthermore, Sarmiento's projection of his own family as the model national family is complicated by the fact that his mother was the sustaining force of the household. Not only did Doña Paula build "el hogar paterno" ("the paternal home") through money she earned before her marriage, but she, and not her husband, supported her children through her work as a weaver.

In the two chapters devoted to his mother, Sarmiento glorifies the maternal by showing the mother-headed household to be one of virtue, devotion, and industry. The domestic interior appears in the text as nation-space. The fact that Sarmiento projected a maternal-led household at a time when the state was headed by Rosas, the epitome of patriarchal authority, is surely not coincidental. The notion of progress put forth by Sarmiento, however, works against favoring female labor and creates a rhetorical problem which Sarmiento must untangle: he must present his family as a model for the Argentine nation at the same time that he divests

---

Sarmiento often reinvented his life and history for public consumption, casting them with such importance that he was nicknamed "Don Yo" (an approximate translation would be "The Honorable Me").

the maternal figure of power and presents the son as the appropriate leader for the new nation. This is accomplished in the narrative through the reorganization of household space. Doña Paula's power in family life is weakened in the narrative by her daughters, who physically displace Doña Paula's body — and her virtuous but now outmoded ideas—from the center of family life.

Another text from the nineteenth century employs the same move of glorifying the maternal figure at the same time that she is displaced from the center of family life: the novel *El médico de San Luis* by Eduarda Mansilla de García (1838–1892). María, the mother of Mansilla's 1860 novel, differs greatly from Doña Paula in the sense that María's main sphere of influence is spiritual. Almost a non-existent physical entity, María has no need to be displaced by her daughters: she does not function as the center of domestic activity. From the outset, her daughters are seen as the center of family life.

While putting forth his wife as an example of virtue and domestic happiness, the narrator of *El médico de San Luis*, Dr. Wilson, laments her lack of authority, as well as the lack of authority represented by Argentine mothers in general. Not until his son rebels does Wilson recognize what the novel views as his own weak fathering. The novel suggests that an excessive degree of motherly devotion paired with a lack of patriarchal discipline can lead to ruin. As the result of María's overindulgence and Wilson's ineffective fathering, the family's spoiled son, Juan, runs off to loot and plunder with a violent *caudillo*. The narrator cites Juan's feminized upbringing as the almost explicit reason for this need to attach himself to the *caudillo*. The lack of consistent male authority in the novel is compensated for by this introduction of frontier violence and the bonds between the men who live there. Wilson and his son are finally freed through the violent actions of this gaucho soldier.

The idea of the emblematic citizen in this text is shared among several characters. As a feminized patriarch, Wilson cannot heal himself or create the conditions for a new nation. Despite the fact that María and Wilson represent the European/Argentine mix that nineteenth century nationalists felt would better the nation, as parents they are shown to lack the sense of balance of "lo masculino" and "lo feminino" that is presumably needed. Only the marriages between Wilson's daughters and their suitors, a young Englishman, and the honest young man who has just been appointed town judge, reflect hope for the future. The future is seen to be in the alliance not only between the women and their husbands, but between the young men themselves. Emblematic citizenship in the novel is represented by the friendship between the educated European and the self-educated Argentine intellectual: the sons who will lead the nation. Wilson's sons-in-law seem like a match made by Sarmiento himself.

Recuerdos de provincia: Republican Motherhood Displaced

In *Over Her Dead Body: Death, Femininity and the Aesthetic*, Elisabeth Bronfen argues that

> As the outsider per se, Woman can also come to stand for the complete negation of the ruling norm, for the element which disrupts the bonds of normal conventions and the passage through which that threat to the norm is articulated. The construction of Woman-as-Other serves rhetorically to dynamise a social order, while her death marks the end of this period of change. Over her dead body, cultural norms are reconfirmed or secured, whether because the sacrifice of the virtuous, innocent woman serves a social critique and transformation or because a sacrifice of the dangerous woman reestablishes an order that was momentarily suspended due to her presence [181].

Sarmiento's mother does not fit neatly into Bronfen's categories. Yet for Sarmiento she certainly emblematized a notion of noble, martyred republican motherhood and a certain defiance of patriarchy; and her imaginary death allows Sarmiento to construct order in its absence. In "Mothers Alive and Dead: Multiple Concepts of Mothering in Buenos Aires," Donna Guy invokes Bronfen's argument about the symbolic sacrifice of woman, commenting that

> These women were both real and symbolic, and their sacrifice may have served to stabilize society, but as mothers of the future citizenry, they could never fulfill their patriotic duty. Thus new forms of female patriotism had to be envisioned and constructed to both stabilize society as well as protect the future of the State [44].

Sarmiento's decision to temporarily sacrifice his mother in the text of *Recuerdos de provincia* can be traced back to this notion of an absent, pre-republican mother whose strength was necessary to "jump-start" the nation. The defiance of patriarchy was necessary in a society ruled by the patriarchal Rosas. But those very qualities were not required for the republican mothers of a new Argentina.

Between the revolution and the construction of a new state, between revolutionary mothers and republican ones, there is a void, represented by Doña Paula's imagined death. What fills this void is Sarmiento in his capacity as a first-person narrator, as the "*Don Yo*" whose individual experience would symbolize that of the nation. In *Foundational Fictions*, Doris Sommer refers to Sarmiento's admiration of Cooper when she states that Sarmiento reduces "the female to a blank page, the better to bear man's inscription [...]" (57). Sylvia Molloy, in her essay "The Unquiet Self" likewise refers to Sarmiento's "heroic image of himself," and notes, "he himself will be the document, the writing on the blank page" (198). And Sarmiento—as he was writing *Recuerdos*—"was also circulating a photographic portrait with the caption, 'Sarmiento, future president of Argentina'" (Sommer 73), obviously intending to fill that blank page with an image that would stay in his readers'/potential voters' minds.

What seems certain from Sarmiento's writings is that he often constructed his own family history alongside the history of the nation:

> Aquí termina la historia colonial, llamaré así, de mi familia. Lo que sigue es la transición lenta y penosa de un modo de ser a otro; la vida de la república naciente, la lucha de los partidos; la guerra civil, la proscripción y el destierro. A la historia de la familia se sucede, como teatro de acción y atmósfera, la historia de la patria.
>
> (Here ends the colonial history, I'll call it that, of my family. What follows is the slow and difficult transition from one way of being to another; the life of a nascent republic, the fight between different sides; the civil war, the proscription and the displacement. The history of the family is followed, like the theater of action and atmosphere, by the history of the nation) [235].

Sarmiento sees the nation not only in terms of his own family politics but in a curious way, as branching off from his family, as if his family were the emblematic — even original — Argentine family. This discourse on family origins is repeated when he presents his own birth and that of the nation as one — linking his body and that of his mother to the nation's birth. "Yo he nacido en 1811, el noveno mes despúes del 25 de mayo!" ("I was born on in 1811, the ninth month after the 25th of May") (235) he proclaims, as if his cells began their division at the moment Argentina declared independence from Spain. The notion that Sarmiento imagines himself as embodying the Argentine essence has been remarked on by other critics. Molloy suggests, "Sarmiento pictures himself as [...] the Argentine, forming with his country one inseparable body" (198).

Inscribed in Sarmiento's images of the bodily origins of the nation is a maternal politics of nation, a politics through which women are made responsible for society's ills or virtues. This notion comes from Rousseau, who in his *Second Discourse* outlines the duties of the republican mother and promotes the confinement of women to the private sphere of the home. In Rousseau's conception, women rule domestically through their role as the "chaste guardians of morals" (89). Their private function as modest and virtuous mothers will make itself felt "for the glory of the State and public happiness" (89). Elizabeth Garrels has noted the evident borrowing by Sarmiento from both Rousseau and Fénelon, an influence she ascribes to Sarmiento's repeated readings of Louis Aimé Martin's *De l'éducation des mères de famille* (1834). Garrels comments that Sarmiento took on Aimé Martin's belief, that "a woman's role as mother, and thus as transmitter of moral and religious sentiment to future generations, is the most important and sacred of missions" (278). And, in an article in *El Mercurio* in 1841, Sarmiento imparted great power to mothers in shaping their children's lives:

> Nothing is more evident than the way in which a man's character, his habits, likes and inclinations, show signs in adult life of the impressions he has received in his first years, in that age wherein education is confided to the tenderness of mothers [qtd. by Garrels 272–273].

But while Sarmiento ascribes many of his positive qualities to his mother's influence, it is difficult to find a scene in which Sarmiento and his mother interact. While there is nothing to suggest that she was anything other than a completely devoted mother, Sarmiento does not describe her in terms of her devotion to him: his mother is described almost completely in terms of her labor and her place at the head of the household. In fact, the description of tenderness in the education of children so prized by Sarmiento sounds much more like the description of another republican mother, one of the most prominent literary mothers of nineteenth century Europe: the mother of Alphonse de Lamartine.

The figure of Alix de Lamartine comes into play almost immediately in the description of Doña Paula. When writing about his mother, Sarmiento begins by declaring: "La madre es para el hombre la personificación de la Providencia, es la tierra viviente a que se adhiere el corazón, como las raíces al suelo" ("A mother is for man the personification of Providence, she is the living earth to which his heart clings, like roots to the soil") (204). Yet even in these glowing words, there is a sense of unrest. Sarmiento then proceeds to describe Lamartine's mother (and not his own) as

> uno de los más bellos tipos de mujer que ha conocido la historia [...] mujer adorable por su fisonomía y dotada de un corazón que parece insondable abismo de bondad, de amor y de entusiasmo sin dañar a las dotes de su inteligencia suprema que ha engendrado el alma de Lamartine, aquel último vástago de la vieja sociedad aristocrática que

se transforma bajo el ala materna para ser bien luego el ángel de paz
que debía anunciar a la Europa inquieta el advenimiento de la
república.

(one of the most beautiful examples of woman that history has
ever known [...] a physically beautiful woman, possessed of a heart
that appears to have contained unending depths of goodness, love and
enthusiasm without neglecting the gifts of the supreme intelligence
which engendered the soul of Lamartine, that last vestige of the old
aristocratic society, who was transformed under maternal wings to
become an angel of peace that would proclaim the coming of the
republic to a nervous Europe) [204].

According to Sarmiento, this paragon of republican motherhood and womanhood was physically beautiful and emotionally tender, helping develop her son's genius. Following the description of Alix de Lamartine, Sarmiento continues almost apologetically to describe his own mother:

Para los efectos de la corazón no hay madre igual a aquella que nos
ha cabido en suerte; pero cuando se han leído páginas como las de
Lamartine, no todas las madres se prestan a dejar en un libro esculp-
ida su imagen. La mía, empero, Dios lo sabe, es digna de los honores
de la apoteosis, y no hubiera escrito estas páginas si no me diese para
ello aliento el deseo de hacer en los últimos años de su trabajada vida,
esta vinculación contra las injusticias de la suerte. ¡Pobre mi madre!
[200].

(In his own heart every man knows that there never was a mother
like the one given him by fate, but after reading pages like Lamartine's it is clear that not every mother's image lends itself to perpet-
uation in book form. Mine, however, God knows, is worthy of the
honor of the apotheosis, and I should never have written these pages
had I not been encouraged in the task by the desire to make this tardy
reparation for the injustices that fate dealt her during the latter years
of her overburdened life. Poor mother! [*Anthology* 56].

This curious paragraph would seem, logically, to be followed by a description of the injustices that Sarmiento's mother suffered that made her "worthy of all the honors of the apotheosis." Instead of describing her sufferings, Sarmiento launches into his story (cited above) of descending from Vesuvius and imagining the death of his mother. The absence of background concerning his mother — exactly at the moment when her history is waiting to be told — signals a rhetorical shift in the writing, a change in focus from the mother to the son, whose experience of her death is imbued with historical references that make her worthy of narrative. Sarmiento's mother can now exist alongside Lamartine's as deserving the honor that Sarmiento sees in being described in a book written by her son.

The fact that Sarmiento used Lamartine's work as a model for *Recuerdos* is well documented. Tulio Halperín Donghi, among others, has noted that Sarmiento seems to have embarked on the writing of *Recuerdos* with a conscious hope of producing a similar effect as that produced by Lamartine's *Les Confidences*. Likewise, Molloy cites a letter from Sarmiento to Vicente Fidel López in which Sarmiento stated, "I am preparing a fat book entitled *Recuerdos de provincia*, or something like that, in which, with the same candor as Lamartine, I compose my own panegyric" (210).

The comparisons to Lamartine (1790–1869) are particularly significant. For in examining the life of the author of *Méditations* and *Les Confidences*, it is easy to see the appeal that Lamartine held for Sarmiento. Lamartine was a former salon poet turned popular writer, former royalist diplomat turned liberal politician. A generation older than Sarmiento, Lamartine supported the education of women and founded a small school for girls in 1828. (Sarmiento founded a small school for girls in San Juan in 1838.) Like Sarmiento, Lamartine was influenced by Saint-Simonianism with regard to the influence of Christianity in politics, but objected to the revision in family structure, sexual morality, and private property advocated by Saint-Simonians (Fortescue 95). And like Sarmiento, Lamartine based his *Confidences* on another model: Rousseau's *Confessions*.

Also like Sarmiento, Lamartine tended to rewrite history to suit the politics of the moment. He was an unrelenting self-promoter who was connected to nearly everyone of literary and political importance in France. In 1840 Lamartine had protested the re-burial of Napoleon's remains in Paris "arguing that Napoleon had destroyed liberty, established a personal dictatorship and created a new hierarchical élite [...]" (Fortescue 92). The specter of a poet-politician arguing against a tyrant — even a dead one — must have seemed attractive to Sarmiento. In *Histoire des Girondins* (1847) Lamartine celebrated France's revolutionary past and implicitly foretold the Second Republic in which he played a key part. By comparing himself to Lamartine, therefore, Sarmiento is referring to *himself* as an "angel of peace" who is "proclaiming" the coming of a republican Argentina. Sarmiento's own history (*Recuerdos*) then serves two purposes. Like *Les Confidences*, it serves as his own panegyric. Like *Histoire des Girondins* it will proclaim a new republic in its evocation of a historical past (a unified Argentina, a first republic) and a political future (a second republic, with Sarmiento as politician-poet leading the way.) All comparisons to Lamartine by Sarmiento involve this need to project himself onto the national scene, a need that makes itself evident in *Recuerdos*.

There is a great deal of rhetorical tension in the segment where

Sarmiento attempts to re-create his own mother to vie with that of Lamartine. While the two sons may have shared some political and literary experiences, the two mothers seem worlds apart. Alix des Roys de Lamartine was the daughter of the head of finances for the Duke of Orléans. However, while her upbringing may have prepared her for the sophistication of court life, her marriage to Lamartine's father, a provincial landowner and a soldier in the King's guard, placed her in relative penury. Most significant to the use of Lamartine's description for Sarmiento was that Lamartine's mother — while raised among aristocratic privilege — becomes a model of bourgeois motherhood. What appears in depth is the picture of Madame de Lamartine as the familiar "angel in the house" of nineteenth century culture.

In describing how his mother used to sit in the evening in the salon, Lamartine refers to her beauty as being of both the body and of the spirit.

> Cette beauté, bien qu'elle soit pure dans chaque trait si on les contemple en détail, est visible surtout dans l'ensemble par [...] ce rayonnement de tendresse intérieure, véritable beauté qui illumine le corps par dedans, lumière dont le plus beau visage n'est que la manifestation en dehors.
>
> (This beauty, pure in each feature if one contemplates them in detail, is visible above all in the whole by [...] the shining light of interior tenderness, true beauty which illuminates the body from within, light of which the most beautiful face is only an exterior manifestation) [52].

Roddy Reid in *Families in Jeopardy: Regulating the Social Body in France 1750–1910* discusses the pre–1789 revolution discourse surrounding the corrupt female-gendered aristocratic body and the family. Referring to later rhetoric concerning the need for domestic harmony, Reid comments that "Here the aristocratic body of blood, honor, pleasure, and privilege gives way to the virtuous body nurtured by regulated family life and democratic social obligations, the basis of an entirely new imagined community" (45).

In the conception of family promoted by Rousseau, in his *Discourses* and in *Emile*, the new mother was a figure opposed to what Rousseau believed were the immoral ways of women of the Old Regime. Lamartine's mother fits the picture of the "new" mother almost perfectly. Lamartine describes his mother's attention to the physical, moral, and educational needs of her children and the many effective ways in which she managed her household. Reid has commented on how household management becomes a watchword for familial discussion in post–Revolutionary discourse, as there was a greater insistence upon the reorganization of the private sphere.

This new republican familial discourse promoted a breakdown of aristocratic norms: "The new literature of family encouraged the withdrawal of families from Old Regime sociability, which did not observe sharp distinctions between public and private space" (48). Lamartine's family—cut off from many of their aristocratic ties by political and economic events—seems to fit this notion of withdrawal. And *Les Confidences*, written only a few years before Lamartine participated in the Revolution of 1848, shows him constructing what Reid would call a national politics of familial ideology. Reid refers to this new familial discourse as achieving "the invention of a national community based on the new norms of 'family' that potentially includes in its embrace all social groups while in actuality maintaining social distinctions and differences" (50). Lamartine is promoting the same kind of familial discourse when he proclaims,

> quand je dis une bonne famille, je n'entends pas une famille noble de cette noblesse que les hommes honorent et qu'ils enregistrent sur du parchemin. Il y a une noblesse dans toutes les conditions.
>
> (when I say a good family, I do not mean a noble family of that nobility that men honor and register on parchment. There is nobility in all social conditions) [19].

Lamartine's sentiments are echoed by Sarmiento's reference to his family's past glory—as he calls upon Roman nobility to refer to the dignity of poverty and his mother's narrative worth.

Given Sarmiento's dual motive in writing *Recuerdos*, it is not surprising that Sarmiento's mother does indeed measure up to Lamartine's "angel of the house" by the end of *Recuerdos*. In fact Doña Paula surpasses Madame de Lamartine in many significant aspects. The displaced aristocratic body of the mother in Lamartine has emerged from the downward movement from one class to another that robs the female body of freedom (the intellectual court sophisticate turned model of sacrificing bourgeois womanhood). Yet Sarmiento's mother belongs to long-gone colonial grandeur in which women's labor was valued and through which nineteenth century patriarchal norms were upset. Her real sufferings occur in the text because of the institution of modernizations. She is seen to submit to the very changes that rob her of her freedom, displace her body from the center of the house, and take away her power as head of the household.

The rhetorical unease in the chapter and the need for the maternal body to be displaced in Sarmiento's narrative—the need for her to die and be resurrected before we even meet her—can be traced to the fact that in life she upset patriarchal norms. Sarmiento admires her for her strength, but presents her labor as a feature of a lost colonial past and demonstrates that the next generation — while retaining the moral qualities of industriousness that Sarmiento considers proper to women — gives back the space that she occupied in favor of one occupied by Sarmiento himself. This is represented in the text through the presentation of the domestic interior as a space of struggles over ideological issues that are related not only to the personal family life of the Sarmiento family but also to the future of the nation. As the site of struggles over colonial antiquity versus "national" progress, the house becomes nation-space in this text.

Sarmiento uses his mother in *Recuerdos de provincia* to point up his own fitness to lead Argentina and separate himself from a colonial past. Her imagined death creates an immediate feeling of tenderness and admiration for his "filial pity" as well. After informing us that he purchased a requiem mass for his mother in Rome, Sarmiento discusses how he had envisioned returning to Argentina to pay his last respects:

> hice el voto [...] mientras estuve bajo la influencia de aquellas tristes ideas, de presentarme en mi patria un día, y decirle a Benavides, a Rosas, a todos mis verdugos, vosotros también habéis tenido madre: vengo a honrar la memoria de la mía; habed, pues, un paréntesis a las brutalidades de vuestra política, no manchés un acto de piedad filial. ¡Dejadme decir a todos quién era esta pobre mujer que ya no existe!
>
> (I came to the decision [...] while I was under the influence of those sad ideas, of presenting myself in my homeland one day, and saying to Benavides, to Rosas, to all my tormentors, you also had a mother: I come to honor the memory of mine; halt then for a moment the brutalities of our politics, don't taint an act of filial piety. Let me tell everyone the story of this poor woman who is no longer living!) [205].

In this imagined declaration, the brutalities of politics come to a halt so that motherhood can be honored. For the moment, mothers are put above politics. Sarmiento's mother becomes a representative of all mothers, but — more to the point — representative of a certain kind of motherhood. He ends this reverie by claiming, "!Y, vive Dios, que lo hubiera cumplido, como he cumplido tantos otros buenos propósitos, y he de cumplir aún muchos más que me tengo hechos!" ("And as God is living, I would have done it, just as I have fulfilled so many other good intentions, and I must fulfill even many more than I have done!") (205). This dramatic declaration serves to answer attacks on Sarmiento's character by the Rosas government, which had for many years been trying to get him deported from Chile to answer charges of treason. It also points up Sarmiento's unrelenting messianism, giving Sarmiento — like Lamartine — the chance to present himself as a fulfiller of promise. He follows by declaring

Por fortuna, téngola aquí a mi lado, y ella me instruye de cosas de otros tiempos, ignoradas por mí, olvidadas de todos. ¡A los setenta y seis años de edad, mi madre ha atravesado la cordillera de los Andes para despedirse de su hijo, antes de descender a la tumba! Esto sólo bastaría a dar una idea de la energía moral de su carácter.

(Fortunately I have her here by my side, and she instructs me in the things of other times, unknown by me, forgotten by all. At seventy-six years of age, my mother has crossed the Andes to take leave of her son before descending to the tomb! This alone is enough to give an idea of the moral energy of her character) [205].

Note that Sarmiento again refers to her death, which he relates to himself by commenting that she has come to say good-bye to him before she dies.

The house itself is described in minute detail in the two chapters that deal directly with Sarmiento's mother. The first, entitled simply "La historia de mi madre" ("the history of my mother"), encompasses more family history, a biography of the priest who educated his mother, and the very brief story of his father. The almost complete absence of any mention of his father in these chapters inscribes a politics of familial lack characterized by the house. The chapter entitled "El hogar paterno" deals with a description of the building, layout, and living arrangements of Sarmiento's childhood home, although the chapter is mostly about Sarmiento's mother. El hogar "paterno" is shown to be a highly charged battleground in *Recuerdos*. In fact, the title is obviously not intended to be ironic, since Sarmiento begins by stating "La casa de mi madre, la obra de su industria [...]" ("The house of my mother, the work of her industry [...]") (219). For Sarmiento points out that his mother (and not his father) built the house with money she earned from work before her marriage.

La casa de mi madre, la obra de su industria, cuyos adobes y tapias pudieran computarse en varas de lienzo tejidas por sus manos para pagar su construcción, ha recibido en el transcurso de estos últimos años algunas adiciones [...]. Su forma original, empero, es aquella a que se apega la poesía la corazón, la imagen indelable que se presenta porfiadamente a mi espíritu, cuando recuerdo los placeres y pasatiempos infantiles [...].

Hacia la parte del sur del sitio de treinta varas de frente por cuarenta de fondo, estaba la habitación única de la casa, dividida en dos departamentos: uno sirviendo de dormitorio a nuestros padres, y el mayor, de sala de recibo con su estrado alto y cojines, resto de las tradiciones del diván árabe que han conservado los pueblos españoles [...]. Adornando las lisas murallas dos grandes cuadros al óleo de Santo Domingo y San Vicente Ferrer, de malísimo pincel, pero devotísimos, y heredados a causa del hábito dominico. A poca

distancia de la puerta de entrada, elevaba su copa veringera la patri-
arcal higuera que sombreaba aún en mi infancia aquel telar de mi
madre, cuyos golpes y traqueteo de husos, pedales y lanzadera, nos
despertaban antes de salir el sol para anunciarnos que un nuevo día
llegaba, y con él la necesidad de hacer por el trabajo frente a sus necesidades [219–220].

(My mother's house, the product of her own industry, the mud
bricks and walls of which could be computed as so many yards of
linen woven by her hands, has had some additions during the past few
years [...]. Its original form is the one to which the poetry of my heart
clings, the indelible picture that always comes to my mind when I
recall my childhood pleasures and amusements [...].

(On the southern part of our lot, thirty yards wide by forty deep,
stood the single unit of our house, divided into two rooms, one serving as our parents' bedroom and the other and larger one as the living room, with its high couch and cushions, a relic of the traditions
of the Arab divan still retained by the Spanish peoples [...]. Two large
oil paintings of St. Dominic and St. Vicente Ferrer—by an execrable
brush, sacred and inherited because of their Dominican habits—
adorned the smooth walls. A short distance from the front door, the
[patriarchal]* fig tree raised its dark branches, which, during my
childhood, still shaded my mother's loom, the clatter from whose
spindles, pedals, and shuttle awakened us before sunrise to announce
that a new day had begun and with it the need to cope with its problems [*Anthology* 68]).

An essential part of her character, as drawn by her son, is that
Sarmiento's mother saw the feeding and maintenance of the family as her
charge, given that her husband seems to have been an absent or ineffectual
provider. It was Doña Paula who made their marriage possible by building a house for them. And it was Doña Paula who anguished over their
lack of resources. Sarmiento refers to his parents' house as a "Noah's ark"
and his mother as "piloto de la desmantelada nave" ("pilot of the wrecked
boat"). The colonial and nineteenth century Latin American house—often
seen to be a patriarchal enclosure for women, and certainly a symbol of
normative family life—is out of kilter. Sarmiento's mother has displaced
patriarchy, and she has done it through her work.

In fact, work is the defining characteristic of Sra. Sarmiento.
Sarmiento states that "el hábito de trabajo manual es en mi madre parte
integrante de su existencia" ("the habit of manual work is in my mother

*The translator substituted the word "matriarchal." Sarmiento uses the word "patriar-
cal," which can be translated as patriarchal and perhaps also "parental" but not "matriarchal."

the integral part of her existence") (214). At one point, he even refers to her as "la noble obrera" ("the noble working woman") (214), making her an embodiment of a kind of working class woman. This class, however, as he indicates, can no longer exist. Referring to his mother's youth as a hard-working craftswoman, he remarks: "En aquellos tiempos, una mujer industriosa, y lo eran todas, aun aquellas nacidas y criadas en la opulencia, podía contar consigo misma para subvenir a sus necesidades" ("In those times, an industrious woman, and they all were, even those born and raised in opulence, could count on themselves to provide the necessities of life") (213).

The fact that Sarmiento's mother pays the workers building her house by producing and selling cloth gives her a certain freedom, a freedom which is directly related to the absence of modern industrialization: "El comercio no había avanzado sus facturas hasta lo interior de las tierras de América, ni la fabricación europea había abaratado tanto la producción como hoy" ("Commerce had not pushed its productions into the interior of the lands of America, nor had European goods cut into production as much as they have today") (213, *Anthology* 73). Doña Paula's ability to build her own house is therefore related to the nation's lack: the scarcity of nineteenth century modernization. The home has been constructed as the result of Doña Paula's freedom in the colonial era to support herself. The struggle between Doña Paula and her daughters in the text will ultimately affect the interior space of the home and displace the body of Doña Paula from the family parlor. As the house serves as the nation-space in this text, the displacement of the maternal body indicates the future displacement of this kind of economic freedom for women, as well as the rejection of colonial norms.

However, Sarmiento does not present himself as a reformer. In fact, Sarmiento indicates that the modernizing drive in the family came from women—from his sisters—while he appears in this section as a passive spectator of "un drama de familia en que lucharon porfiadamente las ideas coloniales con las nuevas" ("a family drama in which colonial ideas battled relentlessly with new ones") (220):

> hubo una revolución interior que costó dos años de debates y a mi madre gruesas lágrimas al dejarse vencer por un mundo nuevo de ideas, hábitos y gustos que no eran aquellos de la existencia colonial de aquella era el último y más acabado tipo [225]
>
> (a domestic revolution took place that cost two years of arguments and caused my mother to shed many a tear before resigning herself to a new world of ideas, habits and tastes different from those of the colonial period of which she was the last and most final representative [*Anthology* 75]).

By describing the fight from the old to the new, which originates in the domestic sphere as a "domestic revolution" and referring to the "new world of ideas" by which his mother is vanquished, Sarmiento describes the house as a national battleground. The fact that his mother is ultimately beaten by the new order, indicates Sarmiento's approval of the spatial displacements of the maternal body, which are created in the text.

The family drama to which Sarmiento alludes also has to do with the body. Sarmiento's sisters began their changes when they reached "la edad núbil" ("the nubile age") (225). Sarmiento mentions two changes which represent his sisters' mania for change: the first is the replacement of the "tarima" ("divan") for the upright chair. Sarmiento describes the *tarima* as a

> lugar privilegiado en que sólo era permitido sentarse a las mujeres, y en cuyo espacioso ámbito, reclinadas sobre almohadones (palabra árabe), trataban visitas y dueños de casa aquella bulliciosa charla que hacía de ellas un almácigo parlante) [227].
>
> (privileged place in which only women were permitted to sit, and in whose spacious precincts, leaning back against the cushions, *almohadones* they received and prattled with their visitors and the lords of the house [*Anthology* 75]).

The space that Sarmiento has described is both consciously exoticized (Sarmiento's text in Spanish contains several linguistic references to the Arabness of the divan) and constructed as a space of feminine conversation and ease. Yet the space he has described does not concur with his description of his mother's habits. His mother had little time to socialize, and the noise associated with her is the clatter of spindle wheels: the noise of her labor. In Sarmiento's description of the use of the *tarima* in the house, the *tarima* serves as a place for his mother's solitude and work: "gustaba sentarse en un extremo a tomar mate por la mañana, o a devanar sus madejas, o bien a llenar sus canillas de noche, para la tela del día siguiente" ("she liked to sit on one end to drink her mate* in the morning, or to unwind her skeins of wool, or even to fill her bobbins at night, for the next day's weaving") (227). There is very little suggestion that Sarmiento's mother ever relaxed, even on this supposed space of feminine ease.

The reasons for the changes enacted by Sarmiento's sisters had to do with a transformation of the domestic space from a place of feminine

---

Mate is a bitter, herbal tea that acts as a stimulant, much like caffeine. The herbs are placed in a hollowed-out gourd, which is filled with boiling water. The tea is drunk through a metal straw that has a strainer on one end.

privacy to a more public arena in which men and women mixed. The divan — which allowed women to relax half-prone — was part of an old tradition (exoticized by Sarmiento) in which women were separated from men:

> ¿Por qué se ha consentido en dejar desaparecer el estrado, aquella poética costumbre oriental, tan cómoda en la manera de sentarse, tan adecuada para la holganza femenil, por sustituirle las sillas en que una a una y en hileras, como soldados en formación, pasa el ojo revista en nuestras salas modernas? Pero aquel estrado revelaba que los hombres no podían acercarse públicamente a las jóvenes, conversar libremente, y mezclarse con ellas, como lo autorizan nuestras nuevas costumbres, y fue sin inconveniente repudiada por las mismas que lo habían aceptado como un privilegio suyo.
>
> (Why was it accepted that the divan, that poetic oriental tradition, so comfortable to sit upon, so adequate for feminine relaxation, be substituted in our modern living rooms by seats, which one by one in rows, look like soldiers in formation, ready for review? Well, the effect of that divan was that men could not publicly approach young women, converse freely, and mix with them, as our new customs authorize, and it was repudiated as inconvenient by the same [women] who had formerly accepted it as their privilege) [227].

The revolution in this paragraph has its generals in his sisters and its soldiers in their chairs. Sarmiento claims at the end of the paragraph that the *tarima* was repudiated by the same women who had formerly accepted it as their privilege. But unless he is referring to his own sisters, it seems clear that the new generation, and not the old, was responsible for the demise of the divan. Earlier in the paragraph, he remarks that "los hombres no podían acercarse públicamente a las jóvenes" ("men could not publicly approach young women") (227), i.e. his sisters and their friends. It seems evident that the change that Sarmiento attributes to Enlightenment ideas is actually born of nineteenth century fashion.

The body of Sarmiento's mother is clearly displaced in this narrative: her former physical rituals are changed until it seems there is no place left for her. She is not mentioned as one of the women who might benefit (i.e. be approached in conversation) by this change. In their nineteenth century fever for modernizations, Sarmiento's sisters have displaced the body of their mother from the center of the salon. This displacement reflects the changes in domestic space in the nineteenth century: the salon is no longer a familial space but a public reception room. The bodies that displace the maternal body of Doña Paula are those of her own daughters— now mature, womanly bodies— and the young men who will be entering the salon.

Sarmiento approves of these changes by pitying his mother and tacitly applauding his sisters. However, when they remove the paintings of saints from the walls, Sarmiento becomes both a victim and a bemused observer. "Protesto que yo no tuve parte en este sacrilegio que ellas cometan, las pobrecitas, obedeciendo al espíritu de la época" ("I protest that I had no part in the sacrilege that they committed, the poor things, obeying the spirit of the era") (228). Sarmiento's sisters, in his formulation, are "obeying" the spirit of the era, obedient to the fashion that holds pictures of saints to be vulgar. By depicting his sisters as unable to resist the call of ideology, Sarmiento places himself outside of ideology. He is positioned as the arbiter of value in the home.

What Sarmiento refers to in the beginning as the "patriarchal fig tree" is also erased from the home by Sarmiento's sisters. The tree, it should be remembered, "shaded the loom"; it is a link to Doña Paula's labor, the reminder that she built the house. Sarmiento indicates that his sisters' wish to get rid of the tree had to do with the etiquette of the era. Sarmiento writes:

> las miradas cayeron en mala hora sobre aquella higuera viviendo en medio del patio, descolorida y nudosa en fuerza de la sequedad y los años. Mirada por este lado la cuestión, la higuera estaba perdida en el concepto público; pecaba contra todas las reglas del decoro y de la decencia [...]) [233].
> (glances unhappily fell upon that fig tree, discolored and knotty from drought and years, that grew in the middle of the patio. If the matter was looked at from this angle the fig tree was lost to public esteem. It sinned against every rule of decorum and decency [...] [Anthology 77]).

Again, the tree is displaced — like Doña Paula herself — because of the public function of the house. There are several comparisons between the tree and Doña Paula in the description of its destruction:

> Los golpes del hacha higuericida sacudieron también el corazón de mi madre, las lágrimas asomaron a sus ojos, como la savia del árbol que se derramaba por la herida, y sus llantos respondieron al estremecimiento de las hojas [...]) [234].
> (The ax strokes, fatally wounding the tree, also racked my mother's heart, tears welled up in her eyes like the sap that dripped from the tree's wound, and their flow increased with the wrenching of its leaves) [Anthology 77].

However, Sarmiento gives us a happy ending to the tragedy of the fig tree, for he himself replaces the tree with an orchard behind the house. He is careful to tell his readers that he built the orchard and the surrounding wall with his own savings. The tree that sheltered the house is replaced by the orchards enclosed space, which, Sarmiento informs us, was "digno de su alta ciencia agrícola" ("worthy of her high agricultural attainments") (235). Sarmiento's modernization is seen as improving and modernizing domestic space.

This action in *Recuerdos de provincia* provides a metaphor for what would happen later in the pampas before and during Sarmiento's presidency, with the fertile space that (for Sarmiento) needed to be modernized requiring the displacement of bodies and the enclosure of outmoded means of expression. The enclosure of lands on the pampas in the 1870s, the forced removal of unemployed gauchos from the lands, and the genocide of indigenous population were all committed in the name of "modernizing" and "improving" the nation. Sarmiento's drive to place European bodies (farmers and sheepherders) on the pampas in place of the indigenous and gaucho bodies involved his wish to create a Europeanized nation, dependent more on the kind of organized agricultural production that he created behind his mother's home. In *Recuerdos de provincia*, while decrying his sisters' destruction of the fig tree, Sarmiento notes that he created something she loved just as well, and which was much more useful: a little orchard upon which the family subsisted. Again, the outmoded ways of the colonial era are replaced by nineteenth century science. The comparison between the fig tree and the body of Doña Paula means that Sarmiento, as well as his sisters, displaces the maternal body, enclosing his mother inside the walls of her perfect little orchard.

El médico de San Luis:
Spiritual Motherhood in Excess

Eduarda Mansilla de García (1838–1892)—the daughter of General Lucio Mansilla and the niece of Juan Manuel de Rosas—appeared in Argentine political life at an early age. She played a part in national politics as an adolescent when she worked as interpreter for her uncle in his negotiations with the French envoy Count Waleski. Following her uncle's fall from power, she married an anti–Rosas diplomat named Manuel García and moved with him throughout his career, which took them mainly to Paris and the United States. As a result of her long residence in France, Eduarda Mansilla sometimes wrote in French (Larraya 6). Her work was then translated by her brother, writer and military officer Lucio V. Mansilla, whose *Una excursión a los indios ranqueles* (which I analyze in

Chapter Four) remains one of the classic texts of nineteenth century Argentine literature.

As Sarmiento did in *Recuerdos de provincia*, Eduarda Mansilla used a foreign model for her 1860 novel *El médico de San Luis* which would resonate within the work itself. Antonio Pagés Larraya, in his biographical introduction to Mansilla's novel, remarks that "*El médico de San Luis* es casi una imitación de *El vicario de Wakefield* de O. Goldsmith, pero tan bien adaptada al medio y las costumbres criollas que resulta un cuadro costumbrista de la ciudad puntana" ("*El médico de San Luis* is almost an imitation of *The Vicar of Wakefield* by O. Goldsmith, but so well adapted to the *criollo* environment and customs that it becomes a folkloric image of the provincial city") (6). However, there is no outright modeling of the mother in Goldsmith's text by Mansilla. The resonance of Goldsmith's novel is found in the voice of the British narrator himself, and the domestic politics—the values of virtuous labor, strong family, and prudent marriage—that the novel espouses.

The novel takes place in San Luis, a small town near Mendoza, in Argentina. The narrator is a Scottish physician named Wilson who married an Argentine woman and settled down to bear three children: Juan, his sickly and spoiled son, and Sara and Lía, two beautiful identical twin daughters. The novel's plot first revolves around the appearance of the young Englishman Jorge Gifford—whose father had jilted Wilson's sister Jane years before—and the romances between the twins and the eligible young men of the town, who represent different strata of *criollo* provincial life. The plot is complicated by two events: when Wilson's son Juan runs away and joins up with the evil *caudillo* Ñato (who serves as a symbol of frontier cruelty and barbarism) and when the corrupt town judge imprisons Wilson and the judge's young secretary, Amancio. When the novel ends, Juan has been returned to the family fold, Gifford and Sara are married, and a possible marriage is projected for Lía and Amancio, who has been appointed as the new judge following the murder of Amancio's corrupt predecessor.

In *El médico de San Luis* the politics of domestic space with regard to the nation are evident. I argue that the home is constructed as nation-space in the text: it is the place where struggles over education, work, religion, and immigration take place, and where Mansilla's narrator expounds at length on the education of Argentine citizens. Francine Masiello refers to *El médico de San Luis* as a novel of manners in which "characters correct the ills of the nation from the vantage point of the home; matters of political conduct and morals are explained through the ethos of domesticity" (75). At the time in which Eduarda Mansilla was writing *El médico de San Luis*, the nation as an entity was in flux. The exemplary family life of the novel presented a future for a chaotic nation, a place in which "the antinomies of civilization and barbarism are to be resolved" (Masiello, 76). Masiello claims very convincingly that the novel's conclusions—in which successful romances produce ties between the European and American children and strengthen bonds between professional classes—"reiterate Mansilla's parallel of family and nation, perhaps echoing the extreme privilege that Mansilla perceived in her own household" (79).

Mansilla is fond of giving her narrator long sermon-like passages in which Wilson comments on the makings of a virtuous home.* In fact, Wilson's soliloquies are directed towards the *Argentine* reader. That reader—sometimes addressed as "you,"—is evidently constructed as an inhabitant of Argentine cities, with access to sites of power. At times, Wilson's directives are in the form of calls to action: to educate the gaucho, to improve the lot of the poor. Often, Wilson's monologues have to do with motherhood, which is a running theme in his musings on the differences between European and Argentine societies.

In *El médico de San Luis*, one of the novel's conflicts has to do with what the narrator considers to be the excessive maternal devotion that his wife gives to their son. This gendered conflict—which María loses at the end of the novel—presents a mother whose tenderness makes her son unfit to be a useful citizen. While María is seen as having failed in her duty towards her son, she has raised twin daughters who eventually attract civic-minded sons-in-law. In Mansilla's novel, ideals of citizenship are shared among many characters, although I will argue that María's sons-in-law (the self-made Argentine intellectual turned lawgiver and the elite European entrepreneur) are the figures that best embody the qualities of the emblematic citizens in the narrative. For the narrative eventually becomes a story about the bonds between sons, who must avoid "excessive" femininity in order to build a strong nation-family.

Like *Recuerdos de provincia*, *El médico de San Luis* presents another retrograde view of mother. Yet in Mansilla de García's novel, maternity itself is presented as a social category that degrades Argentine women. The passage below could be seen as a response to *Recuerdos de provincia*, in that once again daughters are seen to be horrified by their mother's backwardness.

> En la República Argentina la mujer es generalmente muy superior al hombre, con excepción de uno o dos provincias. Las mujeres tienen la rapidez de comprensión notable y sobre todo una extraordinaria

---

This is another echo of The Vicar of Wakefield. *However, since Goldsmith's narrator was a minister, his pronouncements were usually directed towards another character.*

facilidad para asimilarse, si puede así decirse todo lo bueno, todo lo nuevo que ven o escuchan. De aquí proviene la influencia singular de la mujer, en todas las ocasiones y circustancias. Debiendo no obstante observarse que ésta, soberana y dueña absoluta, como esposa, como amante y como hija, pierde, por una aberración inconcebible, su poder y su influencia como madre. La madre europea es el apoyo, el resorte, el eje en que descansa la familia, la sociedad. Aquí, por el contrario, la madre representa el atraso, lo estacionario, lo antiguo, que es a lo que más horror tienen las americanas; y cuanto más civilizados pretenden ser los hijos, que a su turno serán despotizados por sus mujeres y sus hijas, más en menos tienen a la vieja madre, que les habla de otros tiempos y de otras costumbres. Muchas veces me ha lastimado ver una raza inteligente y fuerte, encaminarse por un sendero extraviado, que ha de llevarles a la anarquía social más completa, y reflexionando profundamente sobre un mal cada día creciente he comprendido que el único medio de remediarlo sería robustecer la autoridad maternal como punto de partida, inspirando a los hijos el respeto del pasado y haciendo que los padres no sacrifiquen sus mas caras prerrogativas a un necio movimiento de vanidad) [26–27].

(In the Argentine Republic, woman is generally superior to man, with the exception of one or two provinces. Women are notably swift of comprehension and have an enormous facility to absorb, it might be said, all novelty and goodness. Here, the singular influence of woman becomes apparent on every occasion and circumstance. We should also observe how woman, sovereign and absolute mistress in her role as wife, lover, or daughter, loses, for an inconceivable flaw, her power and influence as mother. The European mother is the sustenance and resource of family and society. Here, on the contrary, motherhood represents backwardness, stasis, and tradition, which always inspire horror in American women. And no matter how civilized their [sons] claim to be, they will always be tyrannized by their wives and daughters, and still have their mother speaking to them about the value of older times and customs. Often I have suffered upon seeing an intelligent and forceful race march on an erroneous path that leads to social anarchy. Reflecting profoundly on this ever growing evil, I have come to understand that the only cure is to be found in strengthening maternal authority as a point of departure for something new [Masiello, *Between Civilization* 77]).

Francine Masiello discusses this passage in terms of family politics, stating "social anarchy may be cured by strengthening the mother's authority" (77). Masiello's point is well taken; the novel is evidently a call for a politics of the home. Or as Masiello argues, "Mansilla proposes a way to order the modern home with emphasis on the united family and the prosperity of domestic life" (76).

It should also be noted that Wilson sees his family as being an exception to the rule in several categories, but most notably in the figure of the mother. The narrator sees his wife as a woman of limited intellect (unlike most Argentine mothers) but insists that his daughters respect her authority (unlike most Argentine daughters.) For Argentine mothers to gain respect, therefore, Argentine fathers need to lead the way. The work of strengthening maternal authority is done for the daughters who will model European mothers in their own marriages. This is only one of several examples of how paternal authority — as the power behind the throne of maternal strength — is seen to be the key to domestic happiness.

In examining the way in which women figure in the novel, the passage cited above is most curious for noting the horror American women feel for their mothers. Here the terms "women" and "mother" are put at opposition. "Women," in Mansilla's passage, stands for the adult daughters who are horrified at the backwardness of their mothers. This brings to mind some interesting parallels between this passage and *Recuerdos de provincia*. Mansilla's reference to the mother speaking about "the value of older times and customs" echoes Sarmiento's statement about his mother's teaching: "she instructs me in the things of other times, unknown by me, forgotten by all" (205). The horror inspired by a mother's backwardness recalls Sarmiento's sisters' distaste for what their mother held dear. In *El médico de San Luis*, however, the conflict between mother and daughters which results in the displacement of the maternal body from the home in *Recuerdos de provincia*, is projected onto other, less idealized, families. Rather than being displaced by her daughter's bodies, the maternal body in Mansilla's novel hardly appears at all.

Despite the insistence on the maternal in the novel, the figure of María never appears much in relation to her household: there are few scenes that discuss her domestic activity. I use the word "activity" instead of labor, because white, Europeanized women do not engage in work in the novel. All labor in *El médico de San Luis* is done by the servants: "Tía" Marica and "Tío" Pedro, the ancient former slaves. Both servants are shown jealously guarding their duties, even in their old age. For domestic bliss, Mansilla de García seems to be saying, the nation-family must include these quasi-family members, whose labor produces domestic plenty. The fact that Mansilla constructs her idealized domestic sphere around the labor of former slaves demonstrates that in her view, the happiness of the nation-family would continue to depend upon the hierarchy of race and class.

Yet even apart from María's separation from household chores and activity, the absence of the maternal body in the novel is notable. María figures physically only in regards to her spirituality or emotion: when she worships at the altar or dabs her eyes with a handkerchief when thinking of her run-away son. Otherwise, she is present almost as a disembodied voice. There are almost no descriptions of her physical appearance.

The absence of the mother's physical body in the text concurs with the novel's association of the maternal with the spiritual. Women, according to Mansilla's narrator, are by definition spiritual beings. A theme that would reoccur in Mansilla's writings, and one that appears often in literary publications in Mansilla's era, is that by their association with love and faith, women bring men closer to God.

> Ellas [...] ofrecen esos modestos dones, como la constante aspiración de sus almas hacia ese infinito a cuyo fin tienden todas las aspiraciones humanas. El sabio por medio de su ciencia, la mujer por sus ofrendas, sus plegarias, su fe; la flor por sus perfume, y la naturaleza toda por sus millones de voces, entonan el himno de amor que unen el creador a sus criaturas y confunde todos los seres con su esencia.
>
> (They [...] offer those modest gifts, which represent the constant aspiration of their souls towards that infinity towards which all human aspirations strive. The wise man through his science, the woman through her offerings, her prayers, her faith; the flower through its perfume, and all nature through millions of voices, intone the hymn of love that unites the creator to His creatures and mingles all beings with His essence) [147].

The narrator refers often to his wife's low intelligence and poor education: "María está muy lejos de tener una inteligencia privilegiada: puede más bien asegurarse que es tardía de comprensión y pobre de imaginación" ("María is very far from having a superior intelligence: it would fairer to say that she is slow in comprehending and has a poor imagination") (17). However, these passages always end by indicating that superior intelligence and education are not the qualities that bring about domestic happiness. In fact, it is suggested that María has the ability to be a good mother solely through her constant devotion to the spiritual life of the home. Religious devotion produces domestic harmony:

> ¡Oh, cuántas veces en las noches de los primeros años de nuestro casamiento la he visto arrodillada delante de una imagen de la Virgen del Rosario [...] mientras que Juan, mi hijo mayor, y dos criados que lo han visto nacer, hacían coro repitiendo la constante invocación a la madre de Dios! Más de una vez el dulce y tranquilo acento de aquella madre rodeada de sus hijas y sus criados, pidiendo el pan de cada día al Padre nuestro, arrancó dulces lágrimas de mis ojos.
>
> (Oh, how many times at night during the first years of our marriage have I seen her kneeling before an image of the Virgin of the

Rosary [...] while Juan, my oldest child, and two servants who had
witnessed his birth, repeated in chorus the constant invocation to the
Mother of God! More than once the sweet and tranquil voice of that
mother surrounded by her children and her servants, asking for daily
bread from our Father, brought sweet tears to my eyes) [17–18].

Despite María's intellectual defects, she holds the key to domestic happiness as the keeper of the spiritual life of the home.

Much more than their mother, Wilson's twin daughters— Lía and
Sara — have a strong physical presence in the novel, in part because of the
confusion between them. Some small points of plot complication result
from the identical twins' amazing physical similarity. As the center of family life, they add to the social comfort of the home. It is their activity that
figures in the novel. But as they are members of a much more comfortable class than were Sarmiento's sisters, the daughters of the Wilson
family involve themselves in domestic activity that does not detract
from their gentility: "Las niñas arreglan la sala, acomodan prolijamente
nuestro cuarto de dormir, y corren con todos los modestos enseres del
comedor" ("The girls arrange the living room, constantly decorate our
bedroom, and take charge of all the modest appointments of the dining
room") (19).

The body that appears in even greater physicality is the handicapped
body of Jane, Wilson's embittered spinster sister. As the result of the acci-
dent that deprived her of the use of her leg and — it is implied — scared
away Charles Gifford, Jane uses crutches to walk. The noise made by her
crutches signals the routines of domestic life: the narrator recognizes it is
mealtime because of the noise made as Jane walks to the table. As a representative of European womanhood, it is significant that Jane lost her
physical strength and her husband because of her courage and willfulness:
riding beside her fiancé in the pampas. Far from being inscribed in the
romantic cult of invalidism, Jane has a wasted, broken body that stops the
production of meaning. Her excessive Protestant fervor is shown to be
unproductive and embittering, suggesting that even spirituality requires
a sense of balance. She also serves as a warning about female hubris: the
text seems to suggest that her superior intelligence and education cannot
serve the family since her willfulness destroyed her chances for happiness.

The nation's future citizens, Mansilla seems to suggest, should be
educated according to the class status of the family and the needs of the
nation. Mansilla's narrator claims that education for both men and women
must be tailored to suit Argentine — and not European — norms. The narrator declares that the fault lies in the original impulse of turning away
from Spain and turning towards France for inspiration, instead of trying

to devise a system of education that would be suitable for America. For that reason, the sons of Argentina "[l]lenanse la cabeza [...] de teorías inaplicables al país en que viven" ("fill their heads with theories which are inapplicable to the country in which they live") (28). Wilson also claims that this "inappropriate" education leads to dissatisfaction among family members with their place in the social formation. Disrespect from the children will be followed by shame among the parents, and—for the narrator—a false projection out of the family's class status:

> y el pobre padre se avergüenza de su profesión, del trabajo con que ha ganado honradamente su pequeña fortuna, y sufre un extraño fenómeno: le parece que sus hijas tienen razón. ¿Y cómo no? ¿acaso no han aprendido más que el...? Es necesario vender la tienda. ¡oh! no, ¡qué idea! Su hijo mayor podría.... ¡Pero que! Si es tan instruido, está estudiando para doctor ... es rabajarlo, y quién sabe ... con el tiempo, llegará a escribir un diario, será convencional y de ahí a ministro [...]. ¡Oh! es cosa hecha.
>
> (and the poor father becomes ashamed of his profession, of the work with which he has honorably made his little fortune, and he suffers a strange fate: it seems to him that his daughters are right. And why not? Don't they know more than him...? He must sell the store. Oh, no! What an idea! His oldest son could.... And so what! As he is so well-educated, he's studying to be a doctor ... that would be lowering him, and who knows ... with time, he will get to write for a newspaper, he will be a conventionary, and from there a minister [...]. Oh! it's a done deal) [28–29].

Mansilla sees the inappropriate education given to Argentine youth as provoking disrespect for parents.

> Las niñas [...] educadas para muñecas, saben comprender que mamá y papá no hablan ni entienden el francés; pero no llegan a descubrir que su pobre madre es una honrada señora que se sacrifica por ellas, y por su piano y por su inglés y su francés, al grado de remendarse sus medias ella misma [...] mientras las niñas duermen, tranquilas y confiadas, el sueño de su juventud.
>
> (The girls [...] educated like dolls, know enough to comprehend that Mama and Papa neither speak nor understand French; but they never realize that their poor mother is an honorable lady who has sacrificed for them, and for their piano and English and French lessons, to the point of mending their stockings by herself [...] while the girls sleep, tranquil and confident, the sleep of youth) [28].

Respect for parental authority has been sacrificed in this passage for education. The narrative suggests that the accomplishments that lead to a well-ordered household have been replaced by knowledge that is superfluous to domestic bliss.

Oddly enough for an intellectual whose brilliant salon was a focus of elegant Parisian life, the novel does not advocate educating women to be the equals of men. The narrator more or less refuses to educate his daughters beyond teaching them to speak English, even though his wife has begged him to teach his girls "todo cuanto es costumbre sepan las niñas bien educadas en Inglaterra" ("everything it's customary for well-educated girls in England to know") (26). In fact, the doctor sees the cultivation of knowledge that would be more appropriate to "una señorita destinada a vivir en Grosvenor Square" ("a young lady destined to live in Grosvenor Square") (26) as a luxury that his daughters cannot afford. To his wife's request he responds that "lo poco que ella sabía había de ser mucho más provechoso a nuestras queridas hijas, que cuanto yo pudiese enseñarles" ("the little that she knew would be much more beneficial to our dear daughters, than everything I could teach them") (26). As a result of the narrator's educational program for his daughters, his girls

> están acostumbradas a mirar a su madre como a la imagen de cuanto hay de más noble y santo sobre la tierra, saben que en la vida la felicidad no se encuentra sino limitada, y que para ser dichosos basta la calma de una conciencia tranquila y la fe en nuestros deberes.
>
> (are accustomed to looking at their mother as the image of everything that is most noble and saintly on earth, they know that in this life happiness is only found briefly, and that to be satisfied one needs to have a tranquil conscience and faith in our obligations) [29].

For Mansilla, the danger of overeducation seems to be that women of a certain class will be unable to produce happiness in their homes either as wives, mothers, or daughters.* The dissatisfaction with their origins that (the text suggests) necessarily comes with the acquisition of knowledge threatens the social order. The novel seems to imply that only upper-class women (like the mythical woman in London's Grosvenor Square and like Mansilla herself) are justified in gaining a complete education. Otherwise, such knowledge is a luxury.

The novel's suggestion that maternal love and spirituality be the

---

*In an article published in La Nación, in July of 1883, Mansilla wrote, "I am not in favor of the emancipation of woman in the sense of believing that she can compete with man in the sciences and professional development [...]. I believe that nature has disposed of things differently and that woman is destined to carry on her breast the child who will become a man" (qtd. in Masiello, "Lost in Translation" 78n).

watchword for the national family is complicated by implicit warnings again investing too much power in the mother. For Mansilla, mother love must be balanced by patriarchal discipline, especially where sons are concerned. For despite the narrator's good intentions towards his children, his Argentine-born son Juan is a weak, spoiled child who becomes an undereducated and "overemotional" young man. The overindulgence of his mother is seen to be the root of his problems, as is the emphasis on emotion in his upbringing that has made him (in his father's eyes) excessively sensitive. The novel implies that this "excess" of mother love has also made Juan disinterested in work, and in particular, disinterested in the affairs of the family's little estate.

> En vano traté de dedicarle al cultivo de mi pequeña chacra, pintándole la agricultura como la más noble de todas las ocupaciones, como la más independiente, sujeta sólo a las mudanzas del tiempo. No me gusta, fue su respuesta: prefiero mi caballo.
> (In vain, I tried to interest him in the cultivation of my little farm, describing agriculture to him as the most noble of all occupations, as the most independent, only subject to the movements of time. I don't like it, was his response: I prefer my horse) [31].

This passage suggests that as the result of his feminized upbringing, Juan cannot stand work: like his mothers and sisters, he does not labor.

Juan's interest in horses and his distaste for agriculture link him to the pampas and the "savage" life of the gaucho. Before long, he runs off to become a soldier. Soon the family hears word that he has taken up with a cruel *caudillo* Ñato, who, it is reported, lived with the indigenous people and "sabe ganarse la gente y poner ley a los indios; a fe que lo respetan" ("knows how to win over people and force the Indians to obey him; so that they respect him") (36). While Masiello has stated that "the maternal figure is destined to cure the ills of barbarism," (77), it appears from the novel's conclusion that excessive maternal tenderness breaks down the organized and prosperous national family, and produces not only a weak son but one who turns towards the "savage." The *caudillo*, in the context of Mansilla's novel, functions as an example of lawlessness that the strong family can combat as long as the feminine is not allowed to run amuck. In this way, the novel devalues the feminine and creates a distinction between civilized and barbaric men. The *caudillo* also takes the place of a strong father figure. In his quest for a strong father, Juancito turns towards this mythologized figure of masculinity. Yet the figures who will resolve this problem are — as in Sarmiento— not the fathers but the sons.

After Wilson loses his son, several quasi son figures appear in the

novel. The first such figure is that of Amancio, the secretary to the corrupt town judge. In some respects Amancio could be Juan's alter ego.
Recalling members of the Generation of 1837, Amancio reads Rousseau and
loses himself in his books to romantic excess, becoming pale and fever-
ish. Wilson attributes Amancio's excitable temperament to this excessive
study. Here — unlike in Sarmiento— books are another mark of feminine
excess. Amancio's "excessive" bookishness is shown to be the result of his
mother's weakness: allowing him to keep the books she actually needed
to sell in order to live, and in allowing him to study until he became dan-
gerously ill. Sharing a trait that seems endemic to all Argentine-born,
upper-class white men in novels, Amancio hates doing manual labor. The
doctor remarks that "su organización delicada y eminente nerviosa no se
prestaba a ningún trabajo grosero y puramente mecánico" ("his delicate
and eminently nervous constitution did not lend itself to any purely
mechanical and physical work") (43). Again, the overindulgent mother is
seen to be the cause of a distaste for labor.

The second quasi son figure is that of Jorge Gifford, the son of Carlos
Gifford, who jilted Wilson's sister Jane many years before. Now ruined finan-
cially, Carlos Gifford has sent his son to America to make his fortune. Jorge
Gifford is like Amalia in his lack of emotional depth. Serving to embody the
qualities of British courage, loyalty, and calmness, he also appears as the
"good" son that Wilson needs. Wilson's two future sons-in-law— the passionate self-made Argentine intellectual and the elite, educated English immigrant — are a love match that even Sarmiento would have approved. For the
novel eventually becomes a story about the bonds between men, focusing on
the sons: about Juan's ability to become a man, and to break away from what
the novel constructs as his mother's excessive devotion, Amancio's success
despite his poverty, and Gifford's success in righting the old wrong.

The issues of property and authority that surface when Juancito runs
away to the pampas become crucial to the resolution of the novel as questions of provincial justice determine the fate of Wilson's family. Immediately upon Wilson's imprisonment questions of authority and property are
put into play. In *El médico de San Luis*, the machinations of the corrupt
town judge — Amancio's employer — result in both Wilson and Amancio's
imprisonment. The corrupt nature of provincial justice was a familiar
theme in mid to late nineteenth century Argentine literature. In Mansilla'
novel this justice is feminized: the lack of a strong authority is associated
with a supposedly dangerous reliance on the feminine. The weak-willed
governor, for example, is described as "un hombre débil y sin inteligencia, entregado completamente a su Ministro, el cual a su turno es el esclavo
de su mujer, que según las malas lenguas influye más de lo que debe en

los asuntos del Juzgado" ("a weak man and without intelligence, completely dependent on his Minister, who in his turn is the slave of his wife, who according to gossip influences more than she should in the affairs of Justice") (114). The influence of women in public affairs is in this way demeaned.

The "feminized" provincial structure of justice is combated by ties between men, which are associated with the freedom and masculinity of the pampas. During Wilson's jail sentence, he attempts to heal the wound of an imprisoned gaucho. In a jail scene that again echoes *The Vicar of Wakefield*, Wilson serves as his jail mate's confessor. The gaucho Pascual confesses to two murders: that of his wagon train boss and that of an indigenous man. Murdering an "indio," however, is seen to be justified: the man had taken Pascual's wife captive and refused to sell her "back" to him. This time he shows no remorse in killing, for "aquella muerte era diferente de la del capataz, porque era por cobrar lo que era mío" ("that death was different from that of the captain, because it was to take back what was mine") (101). The space opened by this confession — in which Pascual becomes a man of property defending his rights against the "barbarian" — opens up the bonds between men that are so important to the gaucho code. Pascual's wife is reduced to the status of an object owned by the gaucho. Ludmer and others have signaled the importance that male friendship has in the gaucho genre. This kind of bonding now occurs in *El médico de San Luis* as a means of resolving an over dependence on the feminine. Wilson discovers that Pascual has befriended Wilson's son's Juan, and that his son is in the jail cell beside him.

While Wilson forges ties with the gaucho — the representative of barbarism — Jorge Gifford makes justice work to his advantage by his ties to civilization. He attempts to free Wilson and his son from jail by presenting himself to the most respectable man in San Luis, Don Mauricio. Don Mauricio has never appeared before in the novel, and so his presence is somewhat in the role of a *deus ex machina*. He is also presented as the model of Argentine civilization. Gifford enthuses:

> ¡Cuánto admiré tan espontáneo ofrecimiento sin conocerme, sin más que por mi nombre, que le era totalmente desconocido, y por el aspecto de mi persona! Este es un rasgo muy común en América, que sólo aquí se encuentra, y que nadie aprecia mejor que el europeo
>
> (How I admired such a spontaneous offer, made without his knowing more about me than my name, which was totally unknown to him, and my appearance! This is a very common trait in America, which is only found here, and which no one appreciates better than the European) [113].

While Wilson uses Don Mauricio's intervention to save his son, Wilson himself is finally saved by the actions of the sergeant with whom he shares his cell. Pascual escapes and murders the corrupt judge. While Wilson cannot condone the murder, the frontier justice enacted by Pascual neatly ties up the plot problems: Juancito is no longer a fugitive from justice, Amancio steps into the judge's job and can court Lía, and Wilson is freed and can give away his daughters in marriage to Gifford and Amancio.

The fact that justice is served by this intrusion of so-called barbaric elements from the pampas is curious considering the novel's insistence on the ability of a happy, "civilized" domestic space as the ideal space for producing national harmony. But it must be remembered that — as in Sarmiento's *Recuerdos*— a constant movement of displacement in the novel projects the idealized family forward to the next generation, where sons rather than mothers or fathers rule the day.

The tension between Europe and America is significant to the production of the maternal body in these texts. In *Recuerdos de provincia* the European republican mother (specifically based on the mother in Lamartine's *Les Confidences)* is the originating model for Doña Paula; surpassing that model is also one of the reasons that Sarmiento introduces Doña Paula as the head of the household. In *El médico de San Luis* the European mother is the model for American mothers, but Mansilla places great importance in the power of the father. For Mansilla, patriarchal authority must be in place for respect for mothers to exist. Wilson's daughters, who are shown to have received a very limited education which Mansilla presents as befitting their gender, social class, and nation, are portrayed as especially fit in their future roles as mothers.

In *Recuerdos*, Sarmiento shows his mother to be the founder of their family home, an event he connects to her colonial past and to outmoded forms of industry. Her body is eventually displaced from domestic nation-space by the modernizing tendencies of their daughters: this has implications that reach far outside the privacy of the home. The displacement of the maternal body in Sarmiento's text is referenced to changes in provincial industry, to Enlightenment philosophy, to nineteenth century custom, to religious tradition. The destruction of the fig tree that represents Doña Paula's body is the signal that a new era of progress has begun. While drying his mother's tears, Sarmiento also encloses her in the walls of his progressive little orchard.

In *El médico de San Luis*, the displacement of the maternal body is part of the category of maternity itself which is conceived as spiritual rather than physical. The mother in *El médico de San Luis* does not occupy physical space in the household; her body is associated with spiritual devotion. Women are conceived of as the spiritual and emotional guides of the family, which is seen as the key to public/national happiness. Maternity and even femininity are seen as categories that degrade men: there is a devaluing of femininity in Mansilla de García's novel. For Mansilla de García, motherly devotion should never be produced in excess lest it interfere with male productivity. While the Europeanized sons-in-law represent the future of the nation's citizens, the resolution to the problem of weak paternal authority and excessive maternal devotion comes from the pampas: when the happy little nation-family opens its doors to masculine barbaric violence. This event, however, is dependent upon the sacrifice of the gaucho and the rejection of the perceived excess of mother love: the enclosure of maternal devotion is resolved through the forging of bonds between men.

One of the paradoxes that emerges from reading *Recuerdos de provincia* against *El médico de San Luis* is that education for women as mothers—a crucial question in Mansilla's novel—is not of overriding importance in the chapters on Sarmiento's mother in *Recuerdos de provincia*. While Sarmiento was a champion of women's education, he does not lament his mother's deficiencies in this area. But it is important to remember that Sarmiento's writing was always directed towards a specific end, and that his digressions always have a rhetorical point. In *Recuerdos*, the question of women's education becomes significant only in how it demonstrates Sarmiento's fitness for national politics. Doña Paula was not a well-educated woman; her learning, therefore, did not add to her qualities as the mother of the national leader Sarmiento. Instead, in a comment that Mansilla might have made about the idealized mother in *El médico de San Luis*, Sarmiento comments on the moral instruction his mother gave him, adding that "Aparte de esto, su alma, su conciencia, estaban educadas con una elevación que la más alta ciencia no podría por sí sola producir jamás" ("Notwithstanding her lack of mental training, her soul and her conscience had been better educated than they could have been by the greatest learning") (206, *Anthology* 57).

Entangled with the tropes of nation-space and the emblematic citizen in *Recuerdos de provincia* and *El médico de San Luis* is the figure of a degraded mother. In both texts, nation-space is found in the home: the site where questions concerning the future of the nation and its citizens are played out in the narrative. In *Recuerdos*, the embodiment of emblematic citizenship is held in part by Sarmiento's mother: I have argued that in order to present himself as a national leader, Sarmiento represents his mother as having the qualities of the idealized citizen and a republican mother, at the same time that he displaces her from a role he desires for himself. In *El médico de San Luis*, the qualities of citizenship are shared by several characters, but are most clearly embodied by Wilson's sons-in-law. As in *Recuerdos de provincia*, sons— and not parents— are seen as representing the ideal of citizenship: the nation's future is projected onto a younger generation of men.

THREE

Valuable White Property: Two Versions of the Myth of Lucía Miranda

In post–1852 Buenos Aires, the long struggle in Argentine discourse to define the terms civilization and barbarism found focus in another fictional woman. The mythical figure of Lucía Miranda, in her role as the "first" *cautiva* (white woman held captive by indigenous peoples), emerged as a significant cultural icon in mid-nineteenth century Argentine narrative and art. While the character Amalia may have been the ideal iconic representation of the nation for pre–1852 Argentines, the legend of Lucía Miranda was more suited as a myth of origin to the nation which would take shape in the years between 1852 and 1880, a nation that was shaped in part by the genocide of the indigenous population in the pampas.

Two novels by Eduarda Mansilla de García and Rosa Guerra retell the legend of Lucía Miranda.* Both novels are titled *Lucía Miranda* and both were first published in 1860. The interplay between racially inscribed bodies and territory in the novels addresses some of the major debates of mid-nineteenth century national discourse: the desire of white Argentines to expand into the pampas, the effort to prescribe the relationship between territory and citizenship, and the quest to reconcile a divided nation. As a trope in nineteenth century Argentine literature and culture, the figure of the *cautiva* has the function of constructing indigenous territory as nation-space. Although the novels differ greatly in how interracial unions

---

Mansilla's Lucía Miranda *appeared in* La Tribuna *as a serial between May and July 1860.* Guerra's Lucía Miranda *was published in June of the same year (Lichtblau 93–94).*

and citizenship are constructed, the lands belonging to the indigenous population emerge in both texts as potential national property and as a place where Argentine national identity is represented.

Cristina Iglesia has noted that through the Lucía Miranda story, "los conquistadores definen el espacio americano como propio y al indio como violador de la frontera" ("the conquerors define American space as their own, and the Indian as the violator of the frontier land") (56). It is clear that even in its earliest appearance in Ruy Diaz de Guzmán's *Historia del descubrimiento, conquista y población del Río de la Plata* (1612), the story involves a racist discourse of revenge in which the fear of the rape and possession of white female bodies by indigenous men is used to justify the conquest and possession of native lands. The story of Lucía Miranda takes place during the first colonial expeditions to the Río de la Plata. The legend is based in some historical fact, involving the Spanish settlement of the Fort of Espiritú Santo, which was established along the Paraná River in 1527.* In most nineteenth century versions, Lucía is the beautiful and virtuous young wife of a Spanish captain at the fort. Mangora, the young *cacique* of the Timbúes, falls passionately in love with Lucía and asks her to become his mistress. Because of Lucía's refusal, the Timbúe *cacique* destroys the Spanish fort and kills its inhabitants, dying in the attempt to capture Lucía. Lucía is taken prisoner by Mangora's brother Siripo who— with greater crudeness— proposes the same fate for her. Eventually, Lucía and her husband are put to death at the stake because of her repeated refusals to give in to the sexual demands of the *cacique*.

Lucía stands for the white Argentine nation that is considered to be vulnerable to indigenous attack and as an idealized citizen who has a privileged but troublesome relationship to the land and to its indigenous inhabitants. In the analyses of the novels below, I show how these links between the racially marked female body and space are connected to the desire for expansionism of post–1850s Argentina. Whereas Lucía's body is viewed as stolen and as a site of potential violation, the bodies of indigenous women are offered freely to Lucía's husband Sebastián. This difference between indigenous people and Europeans is mirrored by the differences in the use of space as portrayed in the two novels. In Guerra's novel the supposed carelessness and disorder with which the indigenous people use space is compared to the industrious and ordered habits of the residents of the fort. The controlling metaphor here is one of property: the settlers understand the value of the land they inhabit (and the women possess) as

---

*While the settlement did exist, Martiniano Leguizamón, in his 1919 La leyenda de Lucía Miranda, concluded that the story of Lucía Miranda existed only in the imagination of Ruy Díaz (8).

property, while the indigenous inhabitants are shown to squander the land and its resources. In contrast, Mansilla de García focuses on the pampas as a dangerous and masculinist space that encompasses all contradictions of the nation: a convenient space of marginality that resolves potential national conflicts by serving as an extra-legal space of refuge.

The figure of Lucía Miranda is a particularly complex one to decode because in the nineteenth century the myth of the *cautiva* occupied several cultural realms concurrently — appearing in painting, poetry, drama, and novels — and blends historical truth and national rhetoric. The long narrative poem *La Cautiva* (1837) by Esteban Echeverría is the best known nineteenth century work in which the connection between a white captive woman and the white nation is made. The quasi-historical figure of Lucía Miranda seems to have obsessed nineteenth century Argentine writers. In *Between Civilization and Barbarism: Women, Nation and Literary Culture in Modern Argentina*, Francine Masiello notes that as a literary topic the story of Lucía Miranda grew in popularity over the course of the nineteenth century, until several fictionalized versions appeared in the latter half of the century, coinciding with a period of national expansion (37). The appearance of the Lucía Miranda myth as the subject of two novels in 1860 by Rosa Guerra and Eduarda Mansilla de García was followed by its appearance in 1863 in *El Charrúa* by Pedro Bermúdez, in 1864 in *Lucía Miranda* by Miguel Ortega, and also in 1864 in Alejandro Magariños Cervantes's *Mangora* (Masiello, *Civilization* 37).

Examining the complications of nineteenth century Argentine national politics is useful in understanding why the Lucía Miranda story proved so attractive to mid-century intellectuals. Along with other Spanish-American nations, Argentina broke away from Spain in 1810. Yet conflicts in Argentina between two political groups provoked civil unrest and schism for many decades to come. The *federalistas* (Federalists) advocated a federal style of republic, with a group of semi-autonomous states. Opposed to the federalistas were the *unitarios* (Unitarists), who fought for a centralized rule, with Buenos Aires as the seat of political and economic power. The civil wars that erupted over the next twenty years created a power vacuum that was filled by *caudillos*, or provincial military rulers. One such *caudillo* was Juan Manuel de Rosas, a *federalista* who became Governor of the province of Buenos Aires, and the country's de facto ruler from 1829 to 1852. Upon his fall from power, the *unitarios* gained control and Buenos Aires seceded from the Confederation of Argentine Provinces.

During the next decade, Argentine moderates were faced with the task of constructing a new kind of Argentine nation: one based on a constitution that would bring order to a divided region and political leadership to a people accustomed to *caudillo* rule. Juan Bautista Alberdi's *Bases* (1852) served as the most direct inspiration for the constitution that resulted, and as a whole stressed unity at the expense of individual rights. Alberdi's concern about private rights revolved around the question of property. In writing about the 1862 reunification of the Argentine nation, Jeremy Adelman comments that among the commonly held goals that would eventually re-unite Buenos Aires and the Confederation were "defense of property and the promotion of economic growth" (8). As a perceived threat to economic growth for white Argentines in the pampas, the indigenous tribes represented an obstacle to the prosperity of the nation, which was being defined as exclusive of its indigenous population.

In early 1850s Argentina, many national politicians and writers dreamed of creating a nation that was white and Europeanized, a feat that would be accomplished in their view by European immigration. In *Bases*, Alberdi also laid down some of the deeply racist beliefs that would determine the future composition of the Argentine population. His slogan "gobernar es poblar" characterized the conviction of Argentine founders (inherited from scientific racism) that "if one were to populate a given region or country with Europeans and their descendants, European modes of 'progress' would inevitably follow" (Andrews 102). In *Facundo* (1845), the colorful and highly fictionalized biography of the great *caudillo* Facundo Quiroga, Domingo Sarmiento defined the parameters of Argentine literature for several generations, both before and after its appearance. With the book's subtitle *Civilización y barbarie* (*Civilization and Barbarity*) Sarmiento popularized this dichotomy as the defining theme of Argentine cultural discourse. For Sarmiento and other Argentine thinkers, civilization referred to white, Europeanized culture, and to the inhabitants of the great cities. Barbarism referred to non-white, indigenous, African-Argentine, and gaucho culture, and to the rural inhabitants of the pampas. Unlike European intellectuals of the era, Argentine intellectuals did not embrace the space of nature as one of truth and divinity. In fact, the traditional dualism of city and country was usually reversed. In the novels *Lucía Miranda*, and in the period following the 1860s, barbarism is shown as occurring outside of the city of Buenos Aires, referring more directly to the inhabitants of the pampas.

There is no doubt that in the nineteenth century, indigenous raids on white settlements resulted in white women being kidnapped. However, there is a disjunction between the historical reality of the women captured and the myth of the *cautiva*; this slippage between the real women and the symbol of the *cautiva* that emerged in nationalist discourse is significant because of the specific character of bodies that would be used to represent the nation. The literary *cautiva* is generally a young, beautiful white married woman who—in the story's mid-century incarnations—is marked for a romantic death by her refusal to have sex with her captors. Like David William Foster's description of Amalia (the title character of José Mármol's novel [1851, 1855]) the *cautiva* is "a stereotyped incarnation ... of all the traditional virtues and charms of pure woman" (5).

The character Amalia was fashioned by Mármol to represent qualities that Mármol saw as belonging to the *unitarios* whom he saw as the rightful leaders for the emerging nation of Argentina: Amalia was educated, Europeanized, urban (a positive trait for nineteenth century Argentina), white, wealthy, kind and, of course, civilized. In the novel, Amalia and her friends stand in stark contrast to the depiction of the *federalistas*, the party led by dictator Juan Manuel de Rosas. Mármol represented the Rosas supporters as uneducated, lacking in Europeanization, rural of mixed race, cruel and barbaric. In "Reading the Warning: The Reader and the Image of the Captive Woman," Bonnie Frederick adds that "angelic beauty and virtue ... help to establish the 'good rape,' that is, the rape that is regarded by society as an act of unprovoked violence against a woman whose own behavior is above reproach" (6). And in writing about *cautiva* narratives in general, Laura Malosetti Costa posits that the bodies of the white victim and her indigenous captor acquire their meaning against the space of the pampa, which is "el marco en el que [la imagen de la cautiva] creció y adquirió su máxima significación" ("the frame within which the [image of the cautiva] grew and gained its greatest significance) (297). Like other *cautiva* narratives, the story of Lucía Miranda was used to represent actual stories of captured women; thereby engendering new fictions at the same time that it helped re-write historical reality.

The white public's fascination with the rape of white women by indigenous men centered not only around the invasion of the white body, but around the nineteenth century fear by white Argentines of racial mixing. The obsession with what was termed miscegenation, and the supposedly fatal consequences that might result, found focus in narratives—like Ascasubi's *Santos Vega* (1872)—about women who were rescued from indigenous camps, and were later killed in raids on forts by their own children. What the obsession with racial mixing does is to hide the usual method in the New World — that is, white men raping native women — and to place a taboo on any suggestion that indigenous people and Europeans might create future Argentine citizens together (Iglesia 35). Frederick calls the stories of captive women "a kind of morality tale, insisting on the necessity of preventing the union of Indian men and Spanish women" (9).

In addition, white Argentine fears of tribal attacks had grown more intense during the late 1850s. David Rock points out that in Buenos Aires province "the Indians had again moved northward such that by 1860 the frontier line in some parts lay closer to Buenos Aires than it had forty years before" (123). In 1860, the pampas represented potentially valuable territory that was perceived as belonging to the nation, lands that were seen as being under attack from indigenous tribes. There was a strong sentiment that the land needed to be reclaimed in the defense of present and future property owners. Rarely did nineteenth century nationalists pause to consider that they were, in fact, the true attackers. As a result of the violence of the colonial system towards the indigenous inhabitants, the only indigenous groups in Argentina that were still reasonably intact by the 1800s were the nomadic people of the western and southern pampas.

As a tale of colonial origins that presented the indigenous tribes as having always been the enemies of peaceful white settlers, the use of the myth of Lucía Miranda paralleled the growth of a nationalist discourse that had brutal effects at the level of national policy. While not as clearly documented as the genocide of the indigenous people of the United States, the killing and forced resettlement of the indigenous people of Argentina was equally cruel. For centuries, the colonial Spaniards, followed by the white Argentines, had been enslaving indigenous tribes and displacing them from their lands. David Rock notes that in Argentina, as in the rest of the Americas,

> the coming of the Spaniards shattered the delicate balance of Indian society and swiftly effected a sharp demographic decline. Spanish confiscations, forced labor, and resettlement caused malnutrition and lowered resistance to European disease among the native population. Forced labor for Indian females and the occasional forced segregation of the sexes led to a sharp fall in the birthrate and an increase in the infant mortality rate [19].

James Scobie reports that the conquistadors "based their principal towns and major economic centers on Indian agricultural communities" of the north-west (30).* The reason for the Spanish settlement in the northern and western part of the country had to do with access to forced indigenous labor: the Spaniards chose those groups with a history of agriculture.

---

*Specifically, Scobie refers to "the Guaraní of Paraguay, Corrientes, and Misiones; the Huarpes of Cuyo; the Comechingones of the Córdoba hills; the Tonocotés of the Río Salado in Santiago del Estero; and the Diaguitas of Tucumán" (30).

The immediate disintegration of community, family, customs, and even language was tragic: Scobie notes that since many of the Spaniards had come to the Río de la Plata after spending twenty years in Perú, they imposed the Quechua language on the groups of the Andean region of Argentina, "further robbing these natives of their linguistic identity" (54). At times entire tribal groups of native people — such as the Huarpes of Cuyo — were sent wholesale to other regions as slave labor. Because of the practices of forced labor resettlement, between the years 1580 and 1680 the native population declined by more than two-thirds in the northern and western parts of what is now Argentina. The nomadic people of the western and southern pampas avoided a similar fate until the 1870's.

The existence of a free indigenous population was considered threatening to white Argentines in the nineteenth century. The native people who remained in Argentina actively resisted the occupation and the continued intrusion by white settlers on the land they had occupied for so long. The whites, however, regarded the Indians of the south — the Araucanians, of which the Ranquels were part — as the invaders. Since the arrival of the Spaniards in Chile, the Araucanians had migrated to southern Argentina from Chile, with the largest movement taking place during the early nineteenth century as the indigenous population of Chile lost ground to the new republic" (Lynch 12). The Argentine government took decisive and violent action in 1879 in order to gain access to the vast reserves of land that remained white Argentina's greatest asset, and to keep control over parts of Patagonia to which Chile had begun to lay claim (Rock 154). As the government wanted more land for expansion — and as there were ready buyers — General Julio A. Roca actually funded his eradication of the indigenous tribes of the south through the sale of property: the same territory which had been occupied by native people for centuries. Rock comments that Roca's military expedition, which accomplished what nineteenth century Argentines called the conquest of the desert,

> subdued, drove out, or exterminated the scattered Teheulche and Araucanian tribes in the region, stopping at last their depredations against the southern *estancias* and opening land access to Patagonia [154].

The destruction of the native people of Argentina was complete. In referring to Brazilian national discourse of the nineteenth century, Peter Beattie notes, "The rape of the innocents by rampaging 'barbarians' has long been a rallying cry for war mobilization" (69).

The desire by the growing nation to contain and put boundaries around lands that were still not under the control of urban Buenos Aires required a narrative that would re-create indigenous territory—seen as limitless, uncontrolled, and racially marked—as a space that belonged to the white nation. Moreover, in the re-imagining of territory as national space, the territory in question in *Lucía Miranda* was particularly significant. *Lucía Miranda* takes place along the Paraná River, a place name that has special significance for the late 1850s, when Paraná was the seat of the Confederation, and when Argentine politicians and intellectuals yearned for a united republic. Lucía herself becomes a site of desire for national union.

The emergence of the white female body in the nineteenth century as a national symbol—what Mary Louise Pratt calls the "uneasy coexistence of nationhood and womanhood"—brought with it certain paradoxes: the female body is both a symbol of national unity and a seductive emblem of trouble (53). In the *Lucía Miranda* novels, Lucía appears as a sexually unstable body that actually creates lust in indigenous men. The white female body—and therefore the construction of national space—is scripted into national discourse by an erotic epic whose end is death and whose goal is the destruction of the obstacles to national prosperity.

The concept of the displacement of violence onto a symbolic female body becomes highly suggestive in a twentieth century context. The body of Evita Perón, for example, functioned culturally as a site of political power both before and after her death. Nation-space became any space around the body of Evita: her body was such a powerful cultural totem that the location of her body became an obsession for Peronists and anti–Peronists alike. In her life, Evita was portrayed as being held captive by her devotion to the *descamisados* to such an extent that she supposedly sacrificed her health to "her" *pueblo*. In death, the captivity of her body by the Argentine military represented for many the plight of the Argentine nation.

The nation-space occupied by her corpse was of supreme significance to that body's usefulness as a political icon: political battles and social legends erupted over the strange manner in which her body was embalmed, where she would be buried, how she was buried (or unburied), the travels of her body throughout the world, and the use to which her body was put as a totem for Juan and Isabel Perón. Evita's eroticized body still leads a charged afterlife in national political and social ideology (the media storm created by Tomás Eloy Martínez's 1996 *Santa Evita* is just one example). The two novels *Lucía Miranda* are therefore part of a continuum in Argentine cultural history.

The tropes of nation and space surrounding the captive white female body in national discourse continue to haunt Argentine culture to this day.

Rosa Guerra's *Lucía Miranda*: The Palimpsest of Land

Este infame proceder de los Timbúes convirtió en ódio la amistad de los españoles, y su pasada alianza, no les quedó otro partido que abandonar el Fuerte Espiritú Santo [...].

Con esta retirada quedó del todo evacuado el Río de la Plata, término fatal de tres espediciones, que deberian desalentar el espíritu de conquista [...].

Es de presumir que si la causa de la humanidad hubiera entrado directamente en el proyecto de estas empresas, hubieran sido menos desgraciadas.*

(This vile act by the Timbúes turned the Spaniard's friendship, and their past alliance, into hatred; there was no other path but to abandon the Fort of Espiritú Santo [...].

(With this retreat, the River Plate was completely evacuated, a fatal end to three expeditions [...].

(It must be presumed that if the cause of humanity had entered directly into the project of the three expeditions, they might have (ended) less disgracefully) [77].

Rosa Guerra, a normal school teacher and journalist who died in 1894, was a friend of Juan María Gutiérrez, and the editor of *La Educación*, in which she passionately defended a woman's right to an education that would place her at the intellectual level of men (Masiello 37). Building on the oft-used argument that educating women would serve the nation, Guerra exhorted the government: "Educate our daughters in view of the fact that they are destined to be mothers of a generation which, under such noble and holy auspices, soon awaits us" (qtd. in Masiello, *Between Civilization* 65). In "Mejorar la condición de mi secso," Nancy Sternbach argues that Guerra used a double-voiced discourse in order to make her feminism palatable to the government, and that she was in fact staking out a subject position for woman-as-citizen. Since Guerra's journalistic writings engaged women's intellectual and political space — and since she was speaking to and for white women — it is ironic that her version of the Lucía Miranda story deals so completely with potential nation-spaces which become dangerous when occupied by a white female body.

In her 1860 version of the Lucía Miranda story, Guerra describes an intimate story of a friendship gone wrong. As the novel begins, Lucía is already established as a presence in the fort. The chief (called Mangora in

*I have retained the spelling and accentuation of the original text.

this version) is presented as the prototypical noble savage. As a frequent visitor to Lucía and Sebastián's home, he listens to Lucía expound on the beauties of Christian married love and the pleasures that supposedly await him if he converts to Christianity and marries a Spanish woman. Mangora's love for Lucía is presented as an example of *méconaissance*: Guerra evidently believes that Lucía does not understand the true nature of the "savage," who thinks of earthly and not of heavenly pleasure.

The key to this odd text can be found in the introduction. Describing what she "saw" as she wrote the novel, Guerra claims that she had a vision of "la hermosa y simpática Lucía, en dulces y sabrosas pláticas con el cacique Mangora, contrastando maravillosamente su vestido a la europea, con el singular traje del salvaje" ("the beautiful and kind Lucía, in sweet and rich conversations with the chief Mangora, her European dress contrasting marvelously with the strange costume of the savage") (15). This reduction of historical and ethnic categories into an exoticizing fashion statement signals the author's obsession with bodies. Every incident in Guerra's *Lucía Miranda* becomes a vehicle for descriptions of the characters' bodies, which are described in detail as they change, often radically, depending upon the circumstances of the narrative.

And it becomes clear that bodies in this text — and, most significantly, how Lucía's body becomes problematic in the space of the New World — determine the inevitably tragic outcome. In the introduction Guerra also claims to have written the novel as a wedding present for a friend, a claim that seems designed to draw attention to the novel's focus on married love. In Guerra's novel, Christian marriage serves as the boundaried space that fixes identities. There is an interesting play between the idea of one's "work" ("*obra*") and one's "duty" ("*deber*"). Lucía has come to see her "work" as that of teaching Mangora about the delights of Christian married love. The culmination of that work is to marry him off to a Spanish lady. However, the novel seems designed to demonstrate that Mangora, as a "barbarian," is incapable of understanding the "sacred" space of Christian marriage. Lucía's work comes into conflict with her duty to her husband, especially since she is seen as being romantically attracted to Mangora. Duty in the novel becomes synonymous with avoiding the union between white women and indigenous men. Marriage and fidelity serve to forestall the possibility of creating Argentine citizens who might contain any traces of those barbaric indigenous bodies.

While marriage serves as a space that references the avoidance of interracial unions for Europeans, nation-space is the land occupied by the indigenous people. This becomes clear in a scene — right before Lucía is kidnapped by Mangora — in which Lucía's body serves as the nexus for a number of associations about land use, property, undiscovered wealth, scientific travelers, and even Christian religious ecstasy. During this scene, the fragmented indigenous landscape becomes a painterly, Europeanized horizon, while Lucía's body moves from being represented as imperfect and three-dimensional to being portrayed as a perfect image in a painting. At the same time her body loses some of the sexuality it is said to inspire in the men around her. As the representative of the nation, Lucía stands for the perceived vulnerability of white Argentines against the indigenous people. The way in which her body is transformed within nation-space demonstrates the beginning of the transition in the representation of the emblematic citizen.

Lucía Miranda begins in much the same way that Jane Austen began her satire on the gothic novel, *Northanger Abbey* (written in 1817): a listing of all the traits that the heroine does not possess:

> Era la Miranda, no una de esas heroínas pertenecientes a todos los poetas y novelistas [...]. No tenía quince años, ni labios de coral, ni dientes de perlas, no ojos color de cielo, ni cabellos de ángel, ni sus divinos ojos estaban siempre contemplando el firmamento, ni menos se alimentaba de suspiros y lágrimas.
>
> (La Miranda wasn't one of these run-of-the mill heroines found in the work of every poet and novelist [...]. She wasn't 15 years old, nor did she have coral lips, nor pearl-like lips, nor eyes the color of the sky, nor angel-like hair, nor were her divine eyes always contemplating the firmament, nor did she nourish herself through whispers and tears) [19].

Lucía represents the absence of qualities we might expect to find in a typical European heroine — that is, of physical qualities. However, instead of (à la Jane Austin) continuing on by informing us of any defects in Lucía, Guerra counterpoises the statement with one about the literary value of her novel. While Guerra insists that she is not one of those run-of-the-mill novelists with a startlingly beautiful and insipid blonde heroine (as Argentinean readers might find in any of a dozen literary journals at the time), Guerra is careful to place the novel in a European context, informing us that "Lucía Miranda era más bien una de las mujeres de Balzac, en todo el brillo y fuerza de la edad, en toda la plentitud de la hermosura, en toda la elegancia de las formas" ("Lucía Miranda was more like a woman from Balzac, in the brilliance and force of youth, in the plenitude of her beauty, in the elegance of her form") (19). Lucía as a character, however, does not seem to hold any of the mysteries that a Balzacian character might have. Nearly as flat a character as Amalia, Guerra's Lucía Miranda speaks in sermonizing language about the beauties of Christian love and never acts in a way that is contrary to what we are told about her. What Lucía Miranda and a woman in a Balzac novel might have in common, however, is that their desires lead them to a tragic end. In the case of Lucía Miranda, her body and the ways she uses it make her a culpable figure in Guerra's re-telling, which points up the erotic components of the tale. In writing about the myth in general, Malosetti notes that

> aquello que define a esta primera cautiva, el desencadenante de la tragedia, es su cuerpo de mujer blanca, que provoca en el indio una pasión irrefrenable. La imagen de la cautiva es, desde sus primeras formulaciones, una imagen erótica.
> (that which defines this first captive, the unfolding of the tragedy, is her white woman's body, which provokes an unstoppable passion in the Indian. The image of the *cautiva* is, from its first formulations, an erotic image) [298].

What sets Lucía apart from her fictional sisters is the fact that Guerra believes — and obviously intends — her novel to exist as a kind of historical document. As well as beginning the novel by giving us the exact location of the fort of Espíritu Santo, down to the latitudinal markers, she refers to the unreliability of indigenous history (an aside which is comical when considering the spurious truth of the Lucía Miranda story) mentioning that "los indios no tenían crónicas, y aventurarnos a supociones, sería exponernos a pasar por poco verídico" ("the Indians didn't have chronicles, and to venture suppositions would be to expose ourselves to being called hardly truthful") (18). Notice how Guerra has suddenly included the reader in this charge; the history of Lucía Miranda is one that includes the reader, who might also be responsible for the lack of truth in the production of this national tale.

Guerra's documentation of Lucía Miranda includes information about her body that connects her to biblical history. Lucía is a character whose body — its ethnic characteristics and its earthy eroticism — produces the reactions from the *cacique*. "Era el verdadero tipo español, hermosa como la primera mujer que Dios diera por compañera al hombre, esbelta como el más bello árbol del paraíso, seductora como nuestra amorosa madre Eva" ("She was the true Spanish type, as beautiful as the first woman that God gave to man as companion, svelte as the most beautiful tree of Paradise, seductive as our amorous mother Eve") (19). Lucía now connects to a pre-history in which she possesses the same qualities as Eve, the primal figure of Judeo-Christian femininity who betrays mankind. Like Eve, Lucía is the seductive woman who destroys paradise on earth.

In her descriptions of Lucía's body, Guerra presents Lucía as a collection of body parts, in a page-long description in which each part is given a paragraph. We go from her figure, in general, to her arms, foot, and face. As in the description of Amalia in Mármol's novel of the same name, Lucía is often described in terms of artistic models, but with different results from the sanitized rendering of Amalia.

> Su estatura era lo que se llama regular, y sus formas tan propor-cionadas, que sus brazos habrían podido servir de modelo al más hábil esculto. Su pie diminuto como generalmente lo tienen las andaluzas, y su talle tan flexible y delicado, que bien podia hacer su cintura de una liga, como dice Eugenio Sue.
>
> (Her stature was what is called regular, and her figure so pro-portionate, that her arms could have served as a model for the most able sculptor. She had a tiny foot, as Andalusian women generally have, and her waist was so flexible and delicate, that she could make her belt from a garter, as Eugène Sue says) [20].

However, the character Amalia's eroticism is described in the two dimen-sional language of painting, with the effect that the character is unable to act on desire, framed as she is by a static historical past. In terms of artis-tic referents, Lucía's body parts are described in the three-dimensional terms of sculpture. Far from being a static image, the description of these sculptural body parts—even those referring to the stone used—denotes movement. For example, the turn of phrase "al más hábil esculto" pro-duces the image of a sculptor handling a sculpted arm—Lucía's arm. In addition, her hair is described as being "black as ebony," while

> su garganta de alabastro, ondulosa, y sus lindísimos hombros perdían casi su redondez, deslizándose en sus contorneados brazos perfecta-mente armonizados con su regularmente abultado seno, donde azu-laban las transparentes venas [...].
>
> (her alabaster throat, which was undulous, and her incredibly beautiful shoulders which were almost losing their roundness, led to well shaped arms which were perfectly harmonized with her regularly formed bust, where transparent veins ran blue [...]) [20].

Lucía, unlike Amalia, is a woman who can touch and be touched; but she is still an object referring to a historical figure. We can "read" her as Guerra's fictional representation of a static historical past, but this is a past where bodies cause trouble.

The reference to her Andalusian background is significant; remem-ber that she is a "typical Spanish beauty," whose attraction must be explained by Guerra in order for us to understand her powers of seduc-tion. A nineteenth century reading of the passage is called for here: Lucía's

Andalusian origin implies that she might be part Moorish. For this reason, Guerra is uneasy with calling her beautiful. However, the body described by Guerra does seem so astonishingly lovely that it is surprising that Guerra continues to assure us of this fact for two pages. "No era linda ni blanquísima en la extensión de la palabra, ni tenía color de rosa, pero simpática e interesante: una mujer que no se podía mirar sin amar" ("She wasn't beautiful or pure-white in the full sense of the word, nor was she rose-colored, but she was sweet and interesting: a woman at whom one could not look without loving") (21). At the end of the description come the assurances that her entire body — her appearance and the way in which she moved and spoke — all contributed to her appeal. "Su andar, su hablar, el menor de sus movimientos [...] atraían todos los corazones, tanto españoles como indios" ("Her walk, her speech, her slightest movements [...] attracted every heart, the Spanish as much as the Indian") (21).

It is the fact that Lucía has placed her body in the public domain that makes her a figure of wrong, a fact that is constantly stressed by the author. After the first description of how Lucía has taught Mangora about the delights of married love, Guerra writes: "Fue imposible a Mangora seguir contemplando tantos encantos y seducciones, sin quedar locamente enamorado de Lucía" ("It was impossible for Mangora to keep contemplating so many charms and seductions without falling madly in love with Lucía") (22). In fact Guerra does seem to endorse an erasure of the white feminine body from the colonial enterprise because of this troubling problem. Calling Lucía "la Elena de los españoles," ("the Spaniards' Helen") Guerra continues: "Si hubieran de hacerme otras conquistas, se había de prohibir a los expedicionarios por una real orden, llevaran a los paises conquistados mujeres hermosas" ("If they were to embark on other conquests, there should be a royal order prohibiting the expeditions from bringing beautiful women to conquered countries") (47). In Guerra's view, white women, particularly beautiful ones, interfere with the aims of the conquest. This is an interesting point of rhetoric, because it uncovers the genocidal motives of the colonial enterprise. Previously, Guerra has talked about the friendship and cooperation between the two communities, but now the problem becomes clear. The reference to Helen of Troy introduces the idea of two warring communities. The bodies of women are particularly troublesome because they muddy the waters of the conquest and show the truly violent nature of the Spanish presence in the colonies.

Returning to the erasure of the body, it becomes clear that Guerra's problem with beautiful women on American soil has to do with the fear of what would be called racial intermixing. In the morality of nineteenth century Argentine narrative, Lucía Miranda's sin was not her attempt to

Christianize the Timbúes, but her belief that Mangora should marry a Spanish woman like herself. The proposed marriage is referred to as the act that would "completar su obra" ("finish her work") of teaching Mangora about European ways and religion. That marriage would bring into question the power relations between the conquered and the conquerors, as well as invoking the invasion of what was a sacred space for the conquerors—the space inhabited by the white female body. In reading Sarmiento through Cooper, Doris Sommer mentions Cora's "racial slippage," signified by her dark hair and her critique of pure whites. This was the reason, Sommer suggests, that Cooper kills Cora off, in a "cathartic sacrifice of social impurities, that became necessary if the nation was to be established in the clearest possible terms" (57).

Similar misgivings about racial mixing characterize Guerra's *Lucía Miranda* as well. Lucía herself is marked in the novel by the potential of her relationship with Mangora. While Sebastián is off on the expedition in the jungle, Mangora presses his love on Lucía.

> En ese momento el cacique era tan feliz, su actitud tan humilde, su acento tan tierno y apasionado, que era preciso que Lucía estuviera tan enamorada de su marido, y que Sebastián fuera tan tiernamente enamorado de Lucía, para que la virtuosa esposa no faltara a sus juramentos.
>
> (At that moment the *cacique* was so happy, his attitude so humble, his tone so tender and passionate, that it was lucky that Lucía was so in love with her husband, and that Sebastián was so tenderly in love with Lucía, so that the virtuous wife did not break her vows) [42].

With this passage, Guerra seems to suggest that Lucía might easily fall in love with Mangora and break her vows by having her agree to his plan to make her queen of his subjects. Lucía's belief that all Christian subjects are equal—no matter what their race—makes her a doomed character for her nineteenth century readers. The paradisaical possibilities of the Paraná region into which she brought her body (a body already condemned by gender) are seen as being destroyed through her attempt to bring white and indigenous bodies together.

The taboo of incest appears here under various guises. Lucía Miranda treats Mangora as a brother. Her fraternal affection for him is mentioned several times. After Mangora's death, his brother Siripo inherits the same passion for Lucía's body. Any discourse of family politics that might interrupt the narrative by suggesting that the Timbúes, too, had families is erased by the appearance of this taboo, which presents the two leaders as bad brothers, to one another and to Lucía. This can be extended to represent all the Timbúes: as brothers to one another the Timbúes are seen as traitorous, violent, and full of incestuous longing. The discourse that made them brothers to the Spaniards is ruptured by Lucía Miranda, a character who means to arrange the marriage of a Timbúe man to a Spanish woman. The potential legitimate partnership, which suggests that Spaniards and (baptized) indigenous people are equal, proves to be too disturbing to be contained by Guerra's narrative.

The double inversion of the historical facts of sexual relations between the Spanish and the Timbúes in Guerra's narrative (a wedding between a willing Timbúe man and Spanish woman versus the rape and forced concubinage of indigenous women by Spanish men) demonstrates the difference between the manner in which white and indigenous female bodies are represented. Lucía sees it as her duty to avoid having attentions forced upon her by the native men. Her fear — and the idea that this would be a fate worse than death — is clearly shown. At the same time, Sebastián is asked to choose a woman from among the beautiful young Timbúes. There is no suggestion that the young Timbúe women might have feelings about being given to Sebastián; their bodies are subsumed under the sign of the barbaric. For Guerra, white female bodies inhabit a space that serves as a nexus for fear whereas indigenous female bodies are represented as those sexually willing and passive barbarians who can be given freely to the Spaniards. Iglesia refers to this displacement as a means by which the sexual slavery of indigenous women during the conquest is re-written to demonstrate that "el asentamiento del español con la india es forzoso" ("the relations of the Spaniard with the Indian woman is forced") (*Cautivas* 53).

The sense given by the narrative that the Spaniards are willing to defend "their" women while the Timbúes are not, mimics the ways in which indigenous and white use of the land is portrayed by Guerra. The indigenous houses are described as "chozas esparcidas sin orden en los valles, [que] ocupan una inmensidad de terreno" ("sparse huts without order in the valleys [that] occupy an immensity of land) (33). The land itself is described as "precious," and the native people are shown to use it in a profligate way, occupying an unboundaried territory.

One of the most representative and significant passages concerning the relationship between bodies and spaces in the novel takes place after Sebastián has departed on his expedition farther up the Paraná, and after Mangora has declared his love to Lucía, has been rejected, and has sworn to take revenge. In this scene, the Paraná area is constructed as nation-space, and ideas about land use and the wealth of the region are put forth by Guerra.

Beginning the chapter entitled "La Paraná" the passage occupies four or five pages, starting with a description of the flora of the region, and ending with a description of Lucía kneeling as she prays to the sky, an image that appeared later as emblematic of the *cautiva*, such as in one of the many paintings of *cautivas* executed by Juan Manuel Blanes in the nineteenth century. During the passage, the focalization of the land is fragmented. The position of focalization changes several times, re-constructing the viewer of the imagined scene. At the moment that the description moves from the land to Lucía herself, the position of focalization changes to that of Mangora; another instance in which the erotic is displaced onto the painterly. In this example, it is noteworthy that the erotic viewer ends not as the reader but as the "barbarian/Other," suggesting that unlike the assumed viewer of the erotic in *Amalia,* the erotic viewer of *Lucia Miranda* was being constructed in a position outside citizenship.

The lengthy descriptions of the land describe the area as Paradise on earth.

> La márgen derecha del Paraná donde estaba levantada la fortaleza, era un verdadero Eden. Fuentes naturales brotan de la tierra y refrescan los bosques, cristalinos arroyos serpean por los montes de limoneros y naranjos y dan savia a sus raíces; brazos de ríos en caprichosas ramificaciones se dilatan por los valles; pájaros de vistosas plumajes, y preciosas avesitas de melancólicos cantos son los habitantes de los bosques
>
> (The right bank of the Paraná where the fort stood, was a true Eden. Natural fountains gush from the earth and refresh the trees, crystal brooks snake through the clusters of lime and orange trees, and nourish their roots; the capricious branches of rivers wander through the valleys; birds of striking plumage and precious little birds that sing melancholy tunes are the inhabitants of the woods) [33].

In spite of having declared the area to be Paradise, the description also contains phases that introduce the sinister: nature is not only refreshing and fertile, but also capricious and melancholy.

Guerra follows this introduction of the sinister, with a note about the wealth of the region, which seems straight out of a travel narrative. "El Paraná es el más rico jardín del mundo, sus fértiles y productivas islas se puede decir con verdad, forman un archipélago en este soberbio y caudaloso mar de agua dulce" ("The Paraná is the richest garden in the world, its fertile and productive islands it can be said with truth, form an archipelago in this proud and abundant sea of sweet water") (32). This comment — made in the present tense — introduces an idea that will be repeated many times in the text, that the Paraná is a rich area just waiting to be tapped by the Spaniards.

The first change of focalization comes with the introduction of a new observer to the scene: a scientific observer who will be able to make sense out of this wealthy but (what Europeans would consider to be) uncharted terrain:

> El hábil botánico, que tiene la paciencia de estudiar el origen de las plantas, y conocer las razas por sus pétalos, debe estudiar allí una ciencia oculta habilmente por la mano de la Providencia en los secretos de la naturaleza
> (The able botanist, who has the patience to study the origin of plants, and know the species by their petals, should study there a science that has been ably hidden by the hand of Providence in the secrets of nature) [32].

In this sudden change of tone, the scientific emerges. According to this formulation, the region hides its secrets, which can be decoded through scientific method by an expert. This passage, following the description of the wealth of the region, suggests that the area is one that God has "hidden," and that is waiting for the scientist. Guerra suggests a belief about land use that was common to colonial discourse: that the first-world scientist — and not the native inhabitant — has the patience to decode what seems mysterious and sinister, both appropriating it and making it understandable. The fact that the Timbúes certainly had a complex mastery of the plant life and terrain is never suggested.

Guerra's shift in focalization introduces the notion that natural space itself encourages that which is capricious and disordered, and that only the conquering scientific gaze can make sense — and what was for Guerra, the proper use — of the region's wealth. Historically, of course, colonial use of land in South America would often include the total destruction of indigenous species of plants and animals. Guerra's ideas about the disorder of natural space hide the true chaos and destruction caused by the arrival of Spaniards to the region.

The next paragraph suggests another shift in focalization, this one in which the land itself resists being viewed and understood. "El terreno naturalmente quebrado y caprichoso hace que la vista se dilate y pierda en sus engalanadas colinas [...]" ("The terrain, naturally broken and capricious, makes the view wander and lose itself in its bannered hills [...]") (32). The fragmentation of sight continues with the description of the Timbúe settlement that follows, but places the fragmentation within the context of indigenous rule. The houses are described as "chozas esparcidas sin orden en los valles, y sobre las preciosas colinas, [que] ocupan una inmensidad de terreno, pues que el cacique era señor de un crecido número de vasallos" ("huts spaced without order in the valleys, and over the precious hills, [that] occupy an immensity of terrain, as the chief was the lord of a growing number of vassals") (33). Because of the way the sentence is structured, as a phrase indicating logical sequence ("pues que"), both the mention that the Timbúe settlements take up an immense territory and the supposed disorder of their arrangement are connected by the narrative to Mangora's rule over his "vassals." The "natural" order of things, Guerra seems to believe, may lead to a capriciousness and disordered state which is reflected in what she perceives as the poor use of the land by the Timbúes. The notion that Mangora rules over "vassals" is an implied way for Guerra to tell a nineteenth century audience that a modern, European style of civilization is needed in what Guerra obviously considers to be a backwards, feudal place.

Guerra then places another fictional observer in a spot in which to compare the two settlements:

> Colocada una persona en un lugar céntrico desde donde se pudiera observar los habitantes de la costa, y los de las selvas, sería curioso ver, la diferencia y contraste que ofrecieran las habitaciones y modo de vivir del hombre civilizado de las ciudades, con la del inculto salvaje, habitante de los bosques.
>
> (If a person were situated in a central place from where s/he could observe the inhabitants of the coast and those of the jungles, it would be curious to see the difference and contrast offered by the habitations and way of living of the civilized man of the city, with that of the uncultured savage, inhabitant of the forests) [33].

Here the dichotomy civilization/barbarism is framed in a way that describes the geographic distribution of Argentina: with the coastal region inhabited by *criollo* or European settlers and the interior occupied by the indigenous people. Guerra does not describe those "differences and contrasts" that she suggests in the narrative: the fort itself is never described by Guerra in the novel. One effect of this absence is that the fort exists as a given, as the stable place among the fragmentation of the space of Timbúe society. In describing the myth of Lucía Miranda, Cristina Iglesia writes: "Lugar propio y cerrado, escenario de la primera parte de la acción, la fortaleza en la que Lucía reside funciona como espacio 'real,' 'verdadero' en el nivel mítico [...]" ("A self-contained and closed place, scene of the first part of the action, the fort in which Lucía resides functions as a 'real,' 'true' space on the mythic level [...]") (48). Another effect of the absence of description of the contrasts between the two settlements is that it suggests that only the anonymous observer (who exists in Guerra's narrative in the subjunctive, the mood of possibilities) can adequately describe and contain those differences.

While up until now the narration has suggested a nineteenth century viewer, Guerra brings back the focalization of the colonial Spaniards, in order to return to the sixteenth century and to set the scene for Mangora's reappearance, noting that "los indios con sus vistosas plumajes, habían dejado de ser ya un objeto de curiosidad para los españoles, desde que, hacia dos años vivían casi en contacto con ellos" ("the Indians with their showy plumage had stopped being an object of curiosity for the Spaniards since for almost two years they had lived in contact with them") (33). The last time that "showy plumage" was mentioned, it was in the context of the bird life: the Timbúes are constructed as part of the natural landscape, no more significant to the production of meaning in this world for Guerra than the plant and animal life.

Following these rapid shifts in focalization, we are brought back to Lucía herself. For several pages, Lucía's state of mind seems to reflect the landscape around her; and suddenly, instead of a fragmented landscape, what she sees offers clarity. "Detrás de los valles, colinas y montes, se veía un horizonte de oro, diamantes y rubíes; un horizonte! como no es posible a la más hábil pluma ni pincel, describir jamás" ("Behind the valleys, hills, and mountains a horizon of gold, diamonds and rubies could be seen; a horizon! Like the most able pen or brush could never describe") (34). The landscape, far from being an object of study, is again attributed to the glory of God.

The moment of ecstasy that Lucía undergoes when staring at the godly horizon has another effect on how her body is described as well. Following a passage that describes her beauty in her moment of agony, Lucía undergoes a process of whitening, "ese tinte sonrosado [...] lo había sostituído el blanco pálido de la perla" ("that sun kissed color [...] had been substituted by the pale white of a pearl") (36). This process of whitening concurs with the slow movement in the story towards Lucía's death. Before her death she becomes more white, more European, and the fragmented, moving parts of her body coalesce into a still, flat image.

> En su dolor, Lucía estaba celestial. ¿Era una de las húries del serallo de Mahoma? No, era una de las vírgenes de Rafael. Sus labios no se movían, no articulaba una palabra; pero sus incomparables ojos elevados al cielo, su actitud humilde y suplicante y las ajitadas emociones de su seno, decían más que las más fervientes oraciones; oraba en secreto.
>
>   (In her pain, Lucía was celestial. Was she was one of the houries of Mohammed's harem? No, she was one of Raphael's virgins. Her lips did not move, she did not say one word; but her incomparable eyes elevated to the sky, her humble attitude and the supplicant and

agitated emotions of her heart, said more than the most fervent prayers; she prayed in secret) [36].

The passage focuses on Lucía's possible resemblance to one of the Mohammedan nymphs of paradise, a possibility rejected in favor of an ultimately Christian, pure, and European image: a virgin in a Raphael painting. Mimicking the process by which the fragmented landscape becomes the painterly horizon, Lucía's body moves from being imperfect and three-dimensional to having the static perfection of a flat pure-white icon. Instead of existing in body parts, she is a recognizable whole. The sudden perfection of Lucía's body becomes significant after the raid on the fort, when Mangora is carrying the unconscious Lucía amidst the terrible storm that is raging: "su seno y espaldas quedan en toda su desnudez, no es una mujer, es una figura de alabastro" ("her breast and shoulders are there in all their nakedness. She is not a woman, she is a figure of alabaster") (56). In the previous descriptions of Lucía, alabaster is a material that reflects movement and life; the sculptural images are always paired with tactile descriptions of Lucía's body. Once Lucía's body is transformed into that of Raphael's virgin, alabaster becomes a material of stillness and death. The historic sacrifice of Lucía Miranda has already turned her into a statue of herself, an unbreachable fortress of purity.

As in the (imagined) death of Sarmiento's mother in *Recuerdos de provincia*, the death of Lucía has the effect of reconfirming order, according to Bronfen's theory that "cultural norms are reconfirmed or secured, whether because the sacrifice of the virtuous, innocent woman serves a social critique and transformation or because a sacrifice of the dangerous woman reestablishes an order that was momentarily suspended due to her presence" (181). Through death, Lucía Miranda is revealed as both a virtuous woman and a dangerous one. While gazing down at Lucía's still body, and certain that she is dead, Mangora appeals to the Christian God: "¡Dios de Lucía! [...]. Yo no había nacido para el crimen, y solo el amor, el amor por una mujer tan hermosa y perfecta, me ha hecho cometer tan horrible perfidia" ("God of Lucía! [...]. I was not born to commit crime, and only love, love for such a beautiful and perfect woman, has made me commit such a horrible sin") (57).

Mangora is ultimately deemed innocent of his crime by Guerra, for she describes him as "Mangora, cuyas virtudes y caballerescas acciones, habían sido oscurecidas por una pasión desgraciada [...] siendo él mismo una de las sangrientas víctimas" ("Mangora, whose virtues and noble actions, had been obscured by a shameful passion [...] was also one of the bloodied victims") (65). It seems like an error on the writer's part to speak of a perfect woman as the cause of the destruction of the fort, since there seems to be no true perfection for Guerra when it comes to women or land. For Guerra, the paradise on earth that is the Paraná requires the scientific observer to categorize, the soldier to restore order, and the writer to erase alterity—by the woman whose body attracts all the trouble and by the Timbúe whose passion for her body creates so much shame.

The separation of the Europeans from the so-called savages becomes especially apparent in the days before Sebastián and Lucía are killed. Mangora has died and his cruel brother Siripo has fallen in love with Lucía and has made the same demands on her virtue as Mangora. Although under house arrest, Sebastián and Lucía are able to send letters to one another. The letters are the means by which Lucía can assure Sebastián that she would rather die than "complacer en lo más mínimo las impuras pasiones del cacique" ("satisfy in the most minimal way the impure passions of the *cacique*") (70). Lucía is also able to assure Sebastián of her guilt in having "la desgracia de inspirar amor a estos salvajes" ("the disgrace of inspiring love from those savages") (71). While informing her that he is the culpable one, Sebastián indirectly lays the blame on her again, because he claims responsibility for having brought her to "tierra de salvajes" ("the land of the savages") (71). The problem, again, is presented as the presence of the white female body in the land.

The final pages of the novel depict the martyrdom of Lucía and Sebastián as a martyrdom of conjugal love. Sebastián and Lucía's perfect love means that at the end of the novel—when they have been able to meet in secret and are discovered by the *cacique*—"Todas las fuerzas de los bárbaros no pudieron desunir aquellos dos cuerpos tan estrechamente unidos, como lo estaban sus amantes corazones" ("All the force of the barbarians could not tear apart those two bodies so intimately united, as were their loving hearts") (76). Before being burned, they are united even more closely by one-hundred arrows that "atravesaron aquellos dos cuerpos, que aun después de muertos no fuera posible separarlos" ("crossed those two bodies, that even after death were not possible to separate") (76). The last lines of the novel leave no doubt about the connections between race, duty, and married love. "Fueron unos mártires. ¿Quién puede dudarlo? Mártires de su deber, y del amor conyugal" ("They were martyrs. Who can doubt it? Martyrs to their duty, and to conjugal love") (76). Their duty—it should be noted—as Sebastián and Lucía assure one another repeatedly, is to keep her from being violated by the Timbúes. In the colonial ideology behind *Lucía Miranda*, the white female body, vulnerable to attack on moral and physical grounds, a bearer of citizens that is prone to the disgrace of producing half–European/half-indigenous children, must be protected to the death.

Eduarda Mansilla's *Lucía Miranda*: Enclosing Narratives

Although Rosa Guerra rushed her manuscript to press upon hearing that Mansilla had written a novel by the same name, it is hard to imagine two more different versions of the same tale. While Guerra's version begins almost a year after Lucía has arrived at the fort, Eduarda Mansilla begins at a point before the birth of Lucía, focusing much of her attention on the tragic love story between Lucía's adoptive father, Don Nuño de Lara, and a wealthy and beautiful Neapolitan widow, Nina Barberini, who chooses the nunnery after her beauty is destroyed by smallpox. The fact that a third of the novel moves between the environs of the Neapolitan court and Lucía's childhood home in Andalucía means that the contrast between the New World and the Old is marked.

In addition, Mansilla's version is considerably more complex than that of Guerra: upon reaching the New World, the first encounter with the Timbúes is described, along with several supposed descriptions of Timbúe rituals and ceremonies. The *cacique*, Carripilún, is the father of both Marangoré (as he is called in Mansilla's version) and Siripo. The original agreement between the Spaniards and the Timbúes is made with Carripilún. The death of Carripilún exposes the jealousy between Marangoré and his younger brother Siripo, who—discovering Marangoré's passion for Lucía—constantly tempts his brother with descriptions of Lucía's body. Siripo has fallen in love with Lucía himself in creating the narrative of Lucía's body for his brother. Lucía herself is a more conflicted and somewhat richer character. She emerges from Mansilla's story not only as an educated and outspoken woman, but as a spiritual leader for the Spaniards and the Timbúes. In addition, she functions as a trickster figure, outwitting the Timbúe soothsayer who intends to kill her because of her exposure of the Timbúe demons as fraudulent spirits.*

Most startling when read against Guerra's novel is the difference in how marriage figures in Mansilla's story. In Mansilla's *Lucía Miranda*, Marangoré appears first as the heir to the Timbúe leadership. He is married to the daughter of a leader from a neighboring tribe in a ceremony that (through their invitation to witness these sacred rites) ritually cements the alliance between the Spaniards and the Timbúes as well. Marangoré's

---

*In the 1860s, as throughout the nineteenth century, white Argentine knowledge of Indigenous customs and rituals was limited. Mansilla's representation of the "sacred rites" of the Timbúes was probably drawn from a number of sources that homogenized the experience of remarkably heterogeneous cultures.

love for Lucía is therefore doubly taboo. Moreover, Mansilla proposes a mixed-race marriage as a possibility: the second pair of young lovers of the novel is the young Timbúe girl Anté—who has converted to Christianity—and her fiancé, the young Spaniard Alejo. Alejo and Anté are the witnesses to Sebastián and Lucía's death. The novel ends with Anté and Alejo fleeing into the pampa, which "les brinda su inmensidad" ("offers them its immensity") (160), serving as a shadow land between cultures of all kinds.

Indigenous territory as nation-space is a vague and contradictory concept in Mansilla's novel. Lucía has a privileged relationship to the land—one that is seen as allowing her insights into Timbúe culture—and towards which her feminine spirituality allows her an undefined power in the natural order. At times Lucía is compared to an object of nature, and she is seen as receiving real, sensual pleasure from her environment. However, while Lucía's body relates to nature, the Timbúes are represented by Mansilla as *being* objects of nature. In addition, the qualities of wildness and unrestrained desire that Mansilla ascribes to the indigenous people are related to this deterministic connection between their bodies and land. Physical space in Mansilla's narrative is divided first between Europe and the New World. Within the New World, physical space is divided between the river area (where the Spanish settlement lies and where the Timbúes live) and the pampas, where the men go to hunt. Lucía is not represented within the nation-space of the pampas, which is figured first as a space where bonds between men are formed, and later as a potential nation-space that can resolve potential conflicts in the representation of nation and citizenship.

The fact that Eduarda Mansilla places half of the novel in Europe is not surprising considering her history.* Belonging to an illustrious family of Federalists, Eduarda Mansilla lived a great part of life in Paris, in diplomatic circles. Mansilla's version, much more than Guerra's, stresses the class origins of her characters. Lucía Miranda comes from noble parentage: her father is Don Alfonso de Miranda, "joven hidalgo, pobre y valiente [...]" ("young nobleman, poor and valiant [...]") (6). While dying on the battlefield, Don Alfonso entrusts his friend Nuño de Lara with guardianship of his only child Lucía. Lucía was born as the result of Alfonso's illegitimate union with a lower-class beauty "de origen morisco, hija de padres artesanos, que, desde al primer momento se hizo dueña de su corazón, nuevo hasta entonces al fuego de las pasiones" ("of Moorish origin, child of artisan parents, and who, from the first moment they met became mistress of his heart, which

---

*A more detailed history of Eduarda Mansilla de García can be found in Chapter Two.

until then had been new to the fire of passion") (6). Lucía Miranda is already marked by illegitimacy and a "mixed" parentage. While a baptized Christian herself, Lucía is of Moorish descent. In Mansilla's version, then, and according to nineteenth century morals, Lucía already bears some dishonor from her parents. The fact that Lucía's mother set Don Alfonso "aflame" with passion continues the motif of female culpability that runs through the *cautiva* stories (and nineteenth century narrative in general). In Mansilla's eyes, Lucía's mother (whose name is also Lucía) gets an easy pardon for her "crimes" by dying immediately following childbirth. "Por último, y como prueba del perdón que el cielo ofrecía a la delincuente, Lucía murió a los diecinueve años después de dar a luz una niña, tan bella como su desgraciada madre" ("Finally, and as proof of the pardon that heaven gave to the offender, Lucía died at nineteen, after giving birth to a daughter who was as beautiful as her disgraced mother") (6).

Instead of being raised by a loving mother and a happy family, this illegitimate Lucía is raised by a poor couple into whose care her unhappy father has given her before going off to die on the battle fields of Italy. Her godfather is Nuño de Lara (who figures so prominently in the story of Lucía's death) and he leaves Lucía again in the care of this couple, while he goes to live in Milan. There, he carries on with the beautiful Nina Barberini. A great deal of the novel is taken up by don Nuño de Lara's love affair with Nina, who is described as

> una de esas criaturas a quienes la fortuna parece complacerse en tratar como a una verdadera hija mimada. A los veinticinco años poseía una de las más bellas fortunas de Nápoles, un nombre ilustre y la más hermosa figura de mujer que en aquella tierra clásica de la belleza podía verse.
>
> (one of those creatures that fortune appears to get pleasure in treating as a truly spoiled daughter. At twenty-five years old she possessed one of the most beautiful fortunes in all Naples, an illustrious name and the most beautiful figure of woman that could be seen in that classic place of beauty) [10].

Nina sees Nuño de Lara at a ball and contacts him, inviting him to her home. Put off by her reputation as a coquette, Nuño de Lara asks a friend:

> ¿Qué puede quererme tan orgullosa dama? Tú sabes bien cuán enemigo soy de [...] esas seductoras criaturas, que en nombre del amor y de la constancia, destrozan sin reparo el corazón del hombre [...].
>
> (What should such a proud lady want from me? You well know what an enemy I am of [...] those seductive creatures who in the name of love and constancy destroy the heart of a man [...]) [12].

Nuño de Lara turns out to be mistaken about Nina, who is neither proud nor destructive. Once they have declared their love to one another, she tells him the story of her birth: she is the child of a poor, half-mad girl from a fishing village and the dissolute son of local nobility. Nina's mother died a year after her birth, the dissolute heir perished a little later, and Nina's paternal grandmother adopted Nina, made her heir to a huge fortune, and raised her in luxury in Rome. Nuño is touched by the story, which he sees as proof of Nina's humility, and she, in turn, is enchanted that Nuño's young charge Lucía is another orphan with a similarly tragic history.

Before Nuño and Nina can get married, however, Nina is stricken with smallpox, which leaves her horribly disfigured. Refusing to see Nuño before she locks herself away in a convent, she instructs him in writing to look at the statue in the garden, a statue of Diana for which Nina served as the model. "Mira ese frío mármol, contempla la inmóvil rigidez de esa figura sin vida; he ahí tan sólo lo que resta en el mundo de la que fue antes tan bella, tan amada" ("Look at that cold marble, contemplate the immobile rigidity of that lifeless figure; that is all that remains in the world of what was once so beautiful, so loved") (36). In Mansilla's *Lucía Miranda*, the old world seems to have its analogous recipe for a tragic union: the mixing of classes and illegitimate birth. The seductive beauty produced by these unions— seen as doubly illegitimate — always leads to tragedy. The death of Nina informs the reader that Lucía's future is similarly burdened.

The separation between new world and old in the novel always seems to carry with it a historical lesson for new world adventurers. Besides the oral histories that imply that tragic endings come with illegitimate and inter-class unions, written history also carries instructive lessons for the future explorers. Lucía's passion for reading — she is educated far above most women at the time, due to the interest of the local priest, Fray Pablo— is significant. While education at first separates her from Mariana, her adoptive mother, it unites the family when Lucía begins to read aloud. "Hogar" becomes a place where educated women instruct the family, which was precisely the model of republican motherhood for many nineteenth century Argentine feminists.

Lucía's choice of reading matter, however, becomes another clue to her fate in the Americas. What Lucía reads to the family is "El Cid." The story becomes the means by which we understand that the lessons drawn from history depend upon the skill of the reader. From "El Cid," Lucía declares, "Cuán cierto es que la felicidad nos espera siempre cariñosa, para calmar nuestros males" ("How certain is it that happiness awaits us dearly, to calm our ills") (47). Lucía's declaration becomes a source of bitterness to don Nuño, who reminds her that she has not yet finished the tale, and says, "no tardarás mucho en ver de nuevo aparecer a la desgracia, como compañera inseparable del hombre" ("you won't have to wait long to see disgrace appear yet again, as the inseparable companion of man") (47). The language used here recalls the Biblical description of womankind. One of the reasons that Lucía cannot understand her future is a gendered one: in the terms of nineteenth century beliefs, she, like Eve, is of the gender that is man's inseparable companion. "Disgraced" ("desgraciada") is a term used often throughout Mansilla's novel to refer to women in love, but even more significantly, to women who insert themselves into the act of making history.

The reference to El Cid seems to resonate with the new world as well. Masiello notes that while "the epic past serves as a model for the Spanish conquest of America [...] it also foreshadows the epic hubris that Lucía reveals in her engagement with the Indians" (42). I would argue that the epic also serves Mansilla's somewhat conflicted views on civilization and barbarism. For in Spanish history, El Cid represents "un tipo de hombre nuevo: el que viva en la frontera" ("a type of new man: one that lived on the border") (Ubieto et al., 155). This "new man" of the *Reconquista* dealt equally well with Christians and Muslims and acted according to his own convenience: "reservado y cauto por necesidad, podía ofrecer el más alto ejemplo de desprendimiento junto al acto de máxima crueldad" ("reserved and cautious by necessity, he could offer the highest example of selflessness next to an act of maximum cruelty") (Ubieto et al., 155). The warrior who lived in a world between "infidels" and Christians, who lived by frontier justice, sounds, in fact, like the *caudillos* of nineteenth century Argentina. One of Rosas's political strengths, in fact, was his ability to make alliances with indigenous tribes. The gauchos of the pampas were also seen as figures that lived in this shadow land between cultures. Lucía's connection to El Cid as a figure of happiness might demonstrate her *méconnaissance* of the project awaiting the Spaniards in the New World. And, in keeping with Mansilla's exhortations concerning women's education in *El médico de San Luis*, Lucía demonstrates what Mansilla might see as the danger of the overeducated woman: her education makes her aspire to more than her gender and social status would normally allow.

The discourse of the female body in Eduarda Mansilla's *Lucía Miranda* blends the common nineteenth century figuration of women as ethereal nature with another representation that reflects a more earthy relationship to land. In this way, Mansilla de García reflects the paradoxes in cultural depictions of women and nature in the nineteenth century.

> Sentíanse aquellas rústicas criaturas, especialmente atraídas por la
> belleza de Lucía, encontrando singular agrado en tocar sus finos cabel-
> los, que comparaban ellas, con las negras y relucientes plumas del
> tordo; ensaizando de continuo la blancura de su tez llamándola ros-
> tro de luna, cuello de leche [...]).
>
>   (Those rustic creatures felt especially attracted by Lucía's beauty,
> finding singular pleasure in touching her fine hair, which they com-
> pared to the black and shining feathers of the thrush; constantly
> touching the whiteness of her skin, referring to her face of moon,
> neck of milk [...]) [123].

Lucía's body is compared by the Timbúes to nature itself, and the feminine force of nature, the moon. The moonlike purity of Lucía, which presents her body as ethereal and white in comparison to the Timbúe women's,
is contrasted by Mansilla with the sensual pleasure Lucía receives from the
New World.

When she bathes in the river daily, the Timbúe men spy on her, a fact
of which she is unaware. Siripo tells Marangoré:

> no es más bella la esbelta garza que refresca y lava sus plumas en las
> claras aguas del arroyo, que la hermosa Lucía, cuando sueltos los lar-
> gos cabellos, baña su desnudo cuerpo en la pura corriente del río, que
> amoroso refleja su imagen.
>
>   (the svelte heron that refreshes and washes its feathers in the clear
> waters of a stream is no more beautiful than the lovely Lucía, when,
> her long hair let loose, she bathes her naked body in the pure current
> of the river, that lovingly reflects her image) [146].

Here the evident pleasure that Lucía takes from her environment is commented upon. Not only is she compared to an object of nature, but nature
in the form of the river is reflecting the image of her body "amorously."
In comparison to the other Spaniards, Lucía's relationship to her environment is a privileged one; she receives more sensual pleasure from
interacting with the environment of the New World than do her compatriots.

> Lucía más que nadie, goza con el espectáculo encantador de aquella
> naturaleza, en su más lujosa manifestación, aspirando con delicia las
> perfumadas y blandísimas auras, que traen [...] la amenidad y fra-
> gancia que de sí exhalan las arboledas y florestas del Nuevo Mundo,
> como en los más floridos y risueños meses de la coqueta Andalucía.
>
>   (More than anyone, Lucía enjoyed the enchanting spectacle of
> nature, in its most luxurious manifestation, breathing in with delight
> the perfumed and soft breezes, that bring [...] the amenity and fra-
> grance emitted by the forests and flowering plants of the New World,

as during the most florid and pleasing months in coquettish Andalucía) [109].

"More than anyone," of course, means more than any other Spaniard: Lucía has already begun to occupy that shadow land between cultures. She is able to negotiate both cultures—serving as interpreter between the Timbúes and the Spaniards—because of this physical connection to the land. The land itself, in typical nineteenth century language, is alternately compared to a coquettish earthy woman and considered a realm of feminine spirituality.

While Lucía's relationship to the land is sometimes described as sensual, her intimacy with the land is not as primordial as that of the indigenous people. For while Lucía's body relates to nature, the Timbúes are represented by Mansilla as *being* objects of nature. In addition, the qualities of wildness and unrestrained desire that Mansilla ascribes to the indigenous people are related to this deterministic connection between their bodies and land. In describing the first encounter between the expedition and the Timúes, the indigenous people are pictured as actually emerging from the earth: "con los cuerpos casi desnudos, con las cabezas cubiertas de plumas y en la más completa inmovilidad, semejaban estatuas de barro" ("with semi-nude bodies, heads covered with feathers, and almost immobile — they looked like statues made of mud") (113). The indigenous people appear first as bodies and — even more significantly — as statues. However, these are not civilized statues of marble or alabaster. Mansilla has described New World statues, made from the earth itself. The racist discourse of nineteenth century views towards the indigenous population includes the notion that, unchanging and made of the basest of materials, the bodies of the natives represent ground zero of nature.

Mansilla makes a much more deterministic connection between bodies and land in her novel than does Rosa Guerra. For Mansilla, land seems to determine character, much as it did for many nineteenth century Argentine thinkers:

> El hijo del desierto, nacido al aire libre de las pampas, cuyos ojos abiertos a la calurosa luz del sol, abrazan desde el primer día la inmensidad de la Pampa y la esplendente bóveda del cielo, imágenes de libertad y amor; el, sin mas ley que su deseo, sin más guía que el altivo pensamiento, siente delante de Lucía, subyugada su rebelde naturaleza.
>
> (The son of the desert, who was born in the free air of the pampas, whose eyes opened to the hot light of the sun — embracing from the first day the immensity of the Pampa and the splendid arch of the sky, images of liberty and love, without any other law than desire, without another guide than his own high thoughts—felt his rebellious nature subjugated in front of Lucía) [149].

Here Lucía is able to wield a certain spiritual power over Marangoré's "wild" spirit. As in Mansilla's *El médico de San Luis*, Lucía's connection to spirituality is shown as lifting her above the physical realm, allowing her to rule over the natural world. This fits Bram Dijkstra's description of the relationship between women and nature in mid-nineteenth century Europe. Referring to the figure of woman in Coventry Patmore's "The Angel in the House," Dijkstra remarks: "The earth was her servant, nature an abject slave in her capacity to transcend the call of the flesh" (83).

In his chapter "The Cult of the Household Nun," in *Idols of Perversity*, Dijkstra refers to the discourse of feminine spirituality in nineteenth century Europe, in which — in fiction, art, and even domestic manuals — women became "the safe keeper of [man's] soul" (11). Dijkstra refers to the popularity of the works of French historian Jules Michelet who, in his 1859 *La Femme*, referred to the duty of woman as one of supporting and keeping God for her husband. "She [...] who in the wretched days, when the heavens are dark, and everything is disenchanted, will bring God back to him, making him find and feel Him on her bosom" (qtd. in Dijkstra 12). Michelet also referred to the changelessness of woman, who "follows the noble and serene epic that nature chants in her harmonious cycles, repeating herself with a touching grace of constancy and fidelity" (qtd. in Dijkstra 12). The circulation of Michelet's ideas can be seen in Mansilla's work, for many of her women characters represent some aspect of the "household nun" who is so spiritual that she's almost missing a body.

Mansilla's Lucía, even with (what was for the nineteenth century) a checkered past, is a woman with an inner battle of which she is not aware. Self-willed, outspoken, well-educated, she assumes a self-sacrificing spirituality after her marriage. Upon marrying Sebastián, she becomes the figure of spiritual purity that Michelet extolled. Without any evidence of sexual desire (unlike Guerra's Lucía, who feels desire for Mangora) Mansilla's Lucía has a body so graceful it can barely support her and skin so white that the Timbúe women compare it to the heavens. However, her very corporeality is what will kill her because, as in Guerra's version, it is Lucía's body that inflames the *cacique*.

Lucía's body contains so many contrasts that, like the white female body in Guerra's novel, and like most women in nineteenth century fiction for that matter, the body becomes a conjunction of beautiful parts that, in its overdetermination, is shown to create desire from the men who view it. In a scene where Marangoré is watching her pray at Fray Pablo's tomb, Mansilla's language even suggests a secret self-knowledge on Lucía's part, by which she participates actively in this seduction by her body of the *cacique*.

Con creciente avidez, descubre uno a uno, los tesoros que encierra en casto conjunto el cuerpo de la bella española; parécele por momentos, que la joven la mira cariñosa, que lee en sus ojos el tormento cruel que ella sola le causa [...].

(With growing avarice, he discovers one by one, the treasures that the body of the beautiful Spaniard encloses; it appears to him at times, that the young woman looks at him fondly, that he reads in her eyes the cruel torment that she alone causes him [...]) [149].

While we are not told whether Lucía herself is really aware of the torment she is creating, Mansilla suggests that this seduction can be read in her body by the men that view her.

Just as Guerra provides a kind of rationale for Lucía's death because of her impolitic plan to push forward a marriage between Mangora and a Spanish woman, Mansilla provides a rationale for Lucía's death with her assumption of spiritual power. By this, I mean that under the terms of what appears to be Mansilla's own philosophy of women as the spiritual guides in the private sphere, Lucía's assumption of leadership in this area is portrayed as another example of her hubris. Whereas—in the terms of nineteenth century values—the perfect household nun should support her man spiritually, Lucía serves as spiritual leader for all the Timbúes and the Spaniards following the death of her mentor, Fray Pablo, who has accompanied the expedition. Lucía even thinks of the Spaniards as her "tribe": "Gracias a tan bellas disposiciones, el ascendiente de Lucía sobre su pequeña tribu, como ella graciosamente llamaba a las pocas familias españolas que en su compañia habían venido, era cada día mayor" ("Thanks to such beautiful qualities, the ascendancy of Lucía over her little tribe, as she humorously called the few Spanish families, that had come with her, was greater each day") (116). As the spiritual leader/interpreter, Lucía becomes an active matchmaker, creating a marriage between the young Spaniard Alejo and the indigenous girl Anté and negotiating the cultural laws of the Timbúes so that both cultures will be satisfied. Whereas in Guerra's novel, the match that Lucía was arranging was between a Spanish woman and the *cacique* himself, Mansilla presents two attractive and innocent young lovers who will become the star-crossed people who have to flee into the pampas.

In his wish to get rid of Lucía, Gachemané, the spiritual leader of the Timbúes, declares that Lucía is an evil spirit. This scene is one of the most intriguing of the novel. The paradoxes of the scene are many, not the least of which is that Lucía is nearly killed by Gachemané for her conscious spiritual leadership, only to die later for the erotic power that seems to emanate from her body. While Lucía repeats the *cautiva* motif where women are portrayed as the emblem of trouble, she actually does function as an evil spirit in the story, bringing about trouble for the Timbúes and the colonists.

Sebastián has gone on an expedition with most of the able-bodied Spanish men and many Timbúe men as well. In their absence Gachemané has told the *cacique* chief (Marangoré's father) that Lucía is an evil spirit, and she calls his bluff by asking to enter the sacred space of the Timbúes and see for herself the demons who call for her death:

> Pido [...] me permitas ir, yo y los míos, al lugar sagrado, en donde evocarás mañana al rayar el alba los espíritus malos: ellos pronunciarán nuestra sentencia, ellos decidirán si somos aún dignos de conocer los misterios de vuestras sagradas creencias.
>   (I ask [...] that you permit me to go, me and mine, to the sacred place, where tomorrow at the first rays of dawn you will evoke the demons: they will pronounce our sentence, they will decide if we are worthy of knowing the mysteries of your sacred beliefs) [132].

In the absence of her husband, she is no longer a passive creature. Asking to be initiated into a spot which is sacred to the Timbúes, willing to risk her own death on the knowledge that she can outwit the soothsayer, Lucía Miranda shares many traits of the classical hero, who often contains elements of the trickster. When the evil spirit does appear, it asks for her death and the death of the other Spaniards: "Que Lucía y los suyos merecían morir despedazados en número de veinte mil pedazos" ("That Lucía and her [people] deserved to die cut up into twenty-thousand pieces") (134). Lucía asks Carripilún that she be allowed to sacrifice her life for theirs. "Déjame penetrar en la chozuela, quizá mis ruegos logren ablandar al feroz monstruo" ("Let me penetrate the hut, perhaps my pleas will succeed in pacifying the fierce monster") (136). Lucía's adoption of masculine norms for feminine ends is made clear. Moreover, she adopts the mode of the masculine colonizer in showing disrespect for the beliefs of the Timbúe. In her role as spiritual leader of the Spaniards, she will penetrate this sacred space, in order to soften the monster that represents what Lucía considers to be the Timbúe superstition.

Instead of pacifying the monster, however, Lucía exposes one of Gachemané's old wives Upay as the demon. As the result of Lucía's exposure of Upay, many other members of Gachemané's family are beaten to death by the angry crowd of Timbúes. There is no commentary by Mansilla that suggests that the death of Upay is as tragic as the death of Lucía might be. Gachemané is executed that day, in a reversal of fortunes that will be mimicked later by Lucía's own death. The power Lucía assumes in this scene — and the intelligence and wit she exhibits — are uncharacteristic of her character in other parts of the novel. For the reader, the scene demonstrates ways in which Mansilla overflows the boundaries of the formulaic conventions she laid down for herself.

What opens the gates of these boundaries is the figure of the open frontier itself. Mansilla's writing about the pampas exhibits a number of contradictions, until the pampa itself begins to stand for an overdetermined nation-space. Just as Sarmiento read the pampas from the work of the London Geographic Society and the scientific travelers who had traversed Argentina, Eduarda Mansilla might have read the pampa through Sarmiento. And in gaining information about the pampa, she must have depended on second-hand information: she had been born and raised in Buenos Aires, but she very soon became a resident of Europe. Her vision of the pampas is very close to that of Sarmiento, who wrote about the indefinite quality of the land: "Allí la inmensidad por todas partes: inmensa la llanura, inmensos los bosques, inmensos los ríos, el horizonte siempre incierto, siempre confundiéndose con la tierra [...]" ("There, immensity everywhere: immense prairie, the immense forest, immense rivers, the always uncertain horizon, always becoming confused with the land [...]") (32). Sarmiento's views about the open prairie were not original, of course. Writers in both the Americas had taken up the same themes. But Sarmiento stressed the determinism of the land and people to an extraordinary degree. His ending message is that the pampas is a space that defines the Argentine nation, and must be cleared of those bodies that are not national.

Recalling the way in which the pampas emerges in *El médico de San Luis* as a means of a masculine interruption of the overfeminized domestic family, in *Lucía Miranda* the pampas become a space where bonds between men are forged, and suggests — at first — a possible model for an Argentine nation that would contain both indigenous peoples and Spaniards. Marangoré and Sebastián learn to respect and like one another in their forays into the wilderness.

Cobraba Marangoré mayor simpatía a Sebastián; el franco continente del español, su mucha fuerza corporal, la admirable destreza en todas las armas y su carácter abierto y caballerezco, eran cualidades propias para cautivar el ánimo del salvaje. También Hurtado y don Nuño tuvieron ocasión entonces de admirar la caballerosa cortesía de Marangoré, si tal frase conviene a un héroe de las Pampas; y la maestría y agilidad del indio en todos los ejercicios varoniles.

(Marangoré gained great sympathy for Sebastián; the frank countenance of the Spaniard, his great bodily strength, the admirable ability in the use of all weapons, and his open and noble character, were

> qualities that captivated the savage's spirit. Also Hurtado and don
> Nuño had occasion to admire Marangoré's noble courtesy — if such a
> phrase fits a hero of the Pampas — and the mastery and agility of the
> Indian in all manly activities) [126].

The pampas gives men a chance to show off those activities that are considered by the author to be truly masculine. Those activities, in turn, allow each man to demonstrate his character, and the nobility of character that seems to characterize the ideal man in Mansilla's novel.

The stories that men tell one another in the pampas also create a privileged space of male bonding. While Marangoré goes hunting with Sebastián and the other Spaniards, the stories they tell form part of his liking of the Spaniards: "Pasábase Marangoré horas y horas escuchando al viejo Nuño y a Sebastián recordar sus hechos de armas, inflamándose extraordinariamente el intrépido joven con el vivo relato de las guerras europeas" ("Marangoré spent hours and hours listening to old Nuño and Sebastián remember their feats of arms, the intrepid youth becoming inflamed by the vivid story of European wars") (139). This construction of the pampas as a place of male friendship will be seen again in Lucio V. Mansilla's *Una excursión a los indios ranqueles*. In *Excursión*, men of all rank become equals around the campfire. Eduarda Mansilla, however, uses the pampas as a place of indefinite openness, where men prove their masculinity through word and deed. The use of the word "inflamed" in reference to Marangoré's interest in the Spaniard's stories is interesting since, not only does it often refer to sexual passion, but it is used by Mansilla to refer to Marangoré's passion for Lucía. The space of the pampas creates male intimacy and even suggests love between men.

A dichotomy between tame Indians and barbaric Indians pervades Mansilla's novel and complicates the bonds of male friendship. An expedition to destroy the supposedly barbaric Charrúa people is the reason for the absence of the men during the attempt by Gachemané to kill Lucía. The tame Indian motif also penetrates the theme of bad brothers that I discussed in terms of Guerra's novel. The notion of good Indians means that the young Timbúe woman Anté can be whitened through her exposure to Lucía Miranda's rhetoric and, most importantly, through her conversion to Christianity. The partnership between Anté and Alejo seems to be acceptable in the narrative as long as it is controlled in every aspect by Lucía. With the feminization of the history of conflict, Lucía pacifies and obscures what was in reality the brutal history of sexual relations between the Spaniards and the native inhabitants of the New World. Whereas Guerra presented Lucía and Mangora as a brother/sister pair, the pairing in Mansilla's version is not as intimate or prolonged. Here, the fraternal pairing is between men: between Sebastián and Marangoré. The betrayal of family ties also concerns the promise made by Marangoré's father to the Spaniards, and Marangoré's betrayal of his wife: Marangoré is not only represented as a bad brother but as a bad son and husband, too.

The ability to classify the indigenous people as good and bad assumes that "good Indians" know their place. Siripo and Marangoré at first represent the two sides to this particular dilemma; it turns out to be a false dichotomy in the story because according to Mansilla's novel all Indians turn out to be bad. Lucía's righteous anger when Siripo proposes that the men exchange women is not made out of a sense of duty but from the racist horror that an indigenous man would dare to address "mujer cristiana, esposa de un noble español" ("a Christian woman, wife of a noble Spaniard") (158). As much as the violation of the rights of possession, the contrast between the nobility of the Spaniard Sebastián and the supposed lowliness of the native Siripo is stressed. Nobility in this case comes to stand for the privilege enjoyed by white men. According to Mansilla's novel, the male friendship that occurs on the pampas is only good if the whites remain in control.

As in *El médico de San Luis*, the pampas is invoked at the end as a manner of resolving the battle between civilization and barbarism. This romance, of course, suggests a possible future for the Argentine nation: could the children of Anté and Alejo be the future citizens of Argentina? As the young lovers escape into the pampas, the burning bodies of Lucía and Sebastián ignite the entire forest: "El bosque se convirtió en cenizas; hoy no quedan de él ni vestigios" ("the forest is turned into ashes; today there does not remain even a trace of it") (160). The burning of Sebastián and Lucía is witnessed by Ante and Alejo. The novel ends with the beginning of their story.

> A la luz viva del bosque que se enciende, vése un hombre que lleva en brazos una mujer desmayada. ¿A dónde irán? ¿Dónde hallarán un abrigo para su amor? ¡La pampa entera les brinda su inmensidad!
> (In the brilliant light of the burning forest, a man is seen carrying an unconscious woman in his arms. Where are they going? Where will they find shelter for their love? The entire pampa offers them its immensity!) [160].

The erasure of the bodies of Lucía and Sebastián is told against the immensity of the pampas, where the doomed lovers will flee. In Mansilla's romanticizing view, the pampas is the only place that will accept an interracial union; in part, Mansilla suggests, because it is a place that knows "no other law than desire." The pampas has been constructed by Mansilla completely in terms of its use for and its relationship to the white Argentine nation.

Already Alejo is shown shouldering the "burden" of the union into which he entered. The resolution of the idea of interracial romance between a white Argentine and a Native Argentine would not be resolved until 1879, when the idea that an Argentine citizen could be indigenous was effectively denied.

The pampas begins to represent so many contradictory elements in this novel that it too becomes an overdetermined space: representing potential property and the absence of property, the white female body and the "barbaric" savage, freedom from the constraints of civilization, love between men and women and love between men. Mansilla has constructed a space that can contain every contradiction possible, and it is the only way she is able to resolve the novel's open-ended romance between Anté and Alejo.

The two novels entitled *Lucía Miranda* by Eduarda Mansilla and Rosa Guerra, which appeared in 1860, share many of the same preoccupations with the female body, but differ greatly in how nation-space is constructed, and how ideas about interracial unions are presented. Lucía stands for both the symbolic national body (the idea of the nation and its people) and as a partial representation of the emblematic citizen. In terms of the virtues of an idealized citizen in nineteenth century Argentina, Lucía has the purity, Christian ideals, privileged relationship to nation-space, and some of the qualities of the republican mother. However, Lucía's body is portrayed by the authors as an emblem of trouble: her sexual body is seen to inspire lust from the "barbarians." As such her body is seen to provoke the indigenous rage that destroys the civilized space created by the white settlers.

Dijkstra mentions 1860 as the date around which "the theme of woman as nun found its true apotheosis" in Europe (11). As a writer who straddled both sides of the Atlantic for inspiration, Mansilla's *Lucía Miranda* reflects the exaltation of feminine spirituality in marriage, at the same time representing feminine hubris. In Guerra's novel Christian marriage is an enclosed sphere in which "duty" and "obligation" reign. This duty comes from both the man and woman; the woman's duty is primarily to retain her virtue against attacks by "infidels."

How both novelists dealt with the potential of sexual relations between white women and indigenous men is significant, particularly when examining the novels against the history of sexual relations of the conquest. The possibility of intermarriage in these novels is always brief, destroyed not by the colonists' refusal, but by the barbaric violence of the Timbúes. The displacement of the history of violence against indigenous women can be seen in Mansilla's novel in her doomed pair of young lovers, a

Timbúe girl and a Spanish young man. Their escape into the pampas at the end of the novel represents Lucía who, in Guerra's representation, feels desire for Mangora that she might have acted upon if it weren't for the protection of her marriage to Sebastián. The danger that Lucía might consumate her erotic desire for Mangora creates tension in the narrative that can only be resolved by Mangora and Lucía's deaths: the erasure of the bodies that create desire. For Guerra, both Lucía and Mangora possess bodies that bring erotic desire, and therefore, trouble, whereas in Mansilla's *Lucía Miranda*, culpability rests on Lucía and what is presented as the devil-like temptation of Marangoré's wicked brother Siripo.

In Guerra's novel, the space occupied by the Timbúes is seen clearly as potential nation-space, one that Guerra portrays as able to be used fruitfully by white Argentines and one that in Guerra's view (and a view typical of colonialist discourse) is being squandered by the Timbúes. Mansilla's space is both vague and contradictory, becoming overdetermined by the number of qualities that it possesses and bestows upon its inhabitants. As an indeterminate resolution of the co-existence of the Spaniards and the indigenous people of Argentina, the novel introduces the pampas as an extra-legal space that brings love and trouble in equal quantities.

FOUR

Men Around the Campfire, Women in the Stars: Lucio V. Mansilla's *Una excursión a los indios ranqueles* and Eduarda Mansilla's "El ramito de romero"

> *Women, then, are the same under every constellation [...]*
> *on the shores of the majestic River Plate and in the open plains of*
> *the Argentine pampas.*
> *They think that sighing is speaking.*
>
> — Lucio V. Mansilla

The confusion of literature, travel, and personality in Argentine politics of the nineteenth century often seemed to involve Lucio V. Mansilla (1831–1913). A member of a wealthy commercial and military family, Mansilla was already a literary and political figure when he published *Una excursión a los indios ranqueles* (*An Expedition to the Ranquel Indians*) in 1870. Before undertaking his expedition, he had a long history as a traveler. His travels had begun when his father sent him on a commercial trip to India at the age of seventeen. The reason for the trip was ostensibly to cut short a budding romance but it was also to keep young Mansilla out of trouble with the law. As a young intellectual, Mansilla had been collecting books that were banned by his uncle, dictator Juan Manuel de Rosas. According to Mansilla his father called him into his office one day and told him, "Mi amigo, cuando uno es sobrino de don Juan Manuel de

Rosas, no lee *El Contrato Social*, si se ha de quedar en este país" ("My friend, when you are the nephew of don Juan Manuel de Rosas, you don't read *The Social Contract* if you want to stay in this country") ("Por qué" 57).

After traveling for three years through India, Egypt, Constantinople, Italy, France, and Great Britain, Mansilla returned to Buenos Aires, writing a travel narrative called *De Adén a Suez*, which was published in 1855. In 1856, Mansilla was forced to take another voyage—for reasons that might be called literary—after he publicly insulted author José Mármol for the unflattering references in Mármol's novel *Amalia* to Mansilla's mother, Agustina Rozas (Rosas) de Mansilla. Banished from Buenos Aires for three years, Mansilla traveled to Paraná, capital of the Confederation, and then to Santa Fé, where he worked as a journalist. After returning to Buenos Aires, he embarked upon a dual career of military officer and journalist.

In 1870, at nearly forty, he moved in the high society of Buenos Aires, frequented posh gentlemen's clubs, and had had a long, if uneven, military career, rising to the rank of colonel in the "Guerra de la Triple Alianza" or War of the Triple Alliance (1865–1870) in which the combined forces of Argentina, Uruguay and Brazil fought against Paraguay. However, despite his family and class origins, Mansilla was not as successful as he desired. His support of Sarmiento's presidency did not lead to the Ministry of War position he coveted. Instead, Mansilla was given what he considered to be the rather humiliating position of *Jefe de la frontera* ("Chief of the frontier") at a little known outpost near where, for white Argentines of the period, the lands known as Indian Territory began (Iglesia 189). And it was Sarmiento who would give Mansilla his dishonorable discharge from the army, following the investigation into the execution of a soldier under Mansilla's command.

The circumstances of the writing of *Una excursión a los indios ranqueles* are both well documented and vague. Having previously signed a pact with the Ranquels, Mansilla took an expedition of ten men into Ranquel territory for eighteen days in order to clarify the fact that the pact would not be legally binding until ratified by Congress. Mansilla's claims, however, are in question. Carlos Alonso has demonstrated that the reasons given by Mansilla for the journey were completely spurious, and has suggested that Mansilla took leave in order to avoid the unpleasantness surrounding the investigation into the execution (44).

Critical literature is in agreement, however, that Mansilla's excursion into indigenous people's territory, and his subsequent writing about it for *porteño* audiences in the pages of the newspaper *La Tribuna*, represents a rarity: "one of very few works of either North or South American letters which present a vivid and sustained firsthand account of noncombative coexistence between American Indian and white civilization, on Indian land, during any nation's period of consolidation" (McCaffrey, xi). For a nineteenth century Argentine observer, Mansilla's attempt to comprehend the culture of the Ranquels is highly unusual. Like other texts from nineteenth century Argentina, Mansilla's document is something of a mixed-bag: a travel narrative, a diplomatic record, an anthropological treatise, and a military report, told in an epistolary style which also contains elements of the fantastic, detective fiction, and testimonial literature. However, Mansilla's reporting on the indigenous people he encounters is condescending, patriarchal, and ultimately as genocidal in its attitudes as those of his more obviously racist peers: he sees his penetration of Ranquel lands, and the white Argentine conquest of indigenous territory, as a situation in which whites are saving the land from being squandered by the local tribes.

The testimonial aspect of Lucio V. Mansilla's text would become the trademark of the group of Argentine writers known as the "Generation of 1880." Often referred to as the "gentlemen writers," these were mostly members of Argentine high society, and were often journalists or politicians with access to places of privilege. Mansilla often uses his elite, international education to great literary effect in the narrative, producing an undercurrent of musings upon the dichotomy of civilization and barbarism. Mansilla's erudition is highly evident as he weaves quotes from Shakespeare, Byron, and de Staël into the text along with references to Argentine writers such as Sarmiento and Echeverría. The inclusion of the refined European authors seems programmed to produce a culture shock among Mansilla's nineteenth century Argentine public, as European civilization at its highest degree is used to refer to what the nineteenth century public might think of as a primitive and barbaric people. The inclusion of these texts becomes another way in which Mansilla attempts to demonstrate what he evidently perceives to be the cultural superiority of white Argentines.

Lucio's younger sister, Eduarda Mansilla de García, had already begun a serious writing career by the time Mansilla wrote *Excursión. El médico de San Luis* and *Lucía Miranda* had appeared in the early 1860s, while *Pablo ou la vie dans les pampas*, was translated by Lucio V. Mansilla in 1870 and published in serial form in the newspaper *La Tribuna*, which Lucio edited. In the early 1880s Mansilla de García became a regular columnist for *El Nacional*, sending articles on European and North American customs and fashion to *porteño* readers. In her fiction, she had begun to experiment with spiritualism and to place her stories in French settings by the late 1860s. The story "El ramito de romero" was written in 1868, and appeared in *Creaciones* (1883), a volume of short stories with themes that referred to Mansilla's fascination with spiritualism and the fantastic.

"El ramito de romero" involves the spiritual vision experienced by a young French doctor after he kisses a female corpse he finds in the empty surgical amphitheater at his Parisian medical school. Despite the fact that she lived away from Argentina, Mansilla de García read Argentinean newspapers and literature and remained fascinated by subjects that obsessed Argentinean writers. It is also important to remember that Mansilla de García had been enmeshed in Argentinean political life when she was quite young, serving as French interpreter for her uncle at the age of 11. Although it takes place in Paris, what is most significant about "El ramito de romero" is that the story revolves around the same issues of national space and the body that mark *Una excursión a los indios ranqueles*: how knowledge about the nation is produced, how bodies occupy the space of knowledge, and how a sense of "the national" is tied to gendered, class-identified bodies.

In fact, in *Una excursión a los indios ranqueles* questions of knowledge, body and nation-space can be read as part of an ongoing dialogue between Sarmiento and Mansilla. Carlos Alonso notes that

> Mansilla reproduces Sarmiento's essential argument regarding the determination of the gaucho's moral and social constitution by the geographic milieu, only that Mansilla finds the final product to be undeserving of the opprobrium with which Sarmiento had judged him [45].

Corina Mathieu-Higginbotham, among others, has discussed the text as "la respuesta a *Facundo*, la obra que sirve de puente entre ésta y el *Martín Fierro*" ("the response to *Facundo*, the work that serves as a bridge between this and *Martín Fierro*") (82). *Excursión* is an odd bridge of those two narratives, which can be seen as opposing sides of an argument that dealt with the pampas. In the quasi-fictional *Facundo*, the pampas stands for the disorder and chaos that Sarmiento perceives as emanating from the land, and which he wishes to resolve by the taking of the pampas for white settlers. For Sarmiento, the solution lay in the taming of the pampas, a final solution that included the genocide of the indigenous population and the violent disruption of other rural families, including those of the gauchos. In the first part of the narrative poem *Martín Fierro* (1872), José Hernández speaks for the gaucho, in a narrative written in rural dialect. Hernández's poem tells the tale of a man made renegade by the very government that hoped to tame him. Mansilla's text questions every category made concrete by Sarmiento and refers to the same problems that will be attacked by Hernández, but never attempts to resolve the issue. The gaucho is defended at the same time that Mansilla seems to want to express what he perceives to be the ultimately unstable nature of the lower classes.

Many critics remark on the surprising sensitivity Mansilla exhibits in his observations on Ranquel culture. In discussing the ways in which knowledge is produced for a *porteño* readership, Foster mentions the difficulties an elite nineteenth century writer like Mansilla must have faced in writing about the Ranquels, about whom so little was known: "almost in the tradition of the medieval bestiary, *Excursión* is obliged to tame the strange and the forbidding by assimilating it to the language of its exposition and to the quadrants of knowledge of its audience" ("Knowledge" 23). In referring to the comparison between indigenous people and exotic beasts, Foster notes the deeply racist attitudes that most nineteenth century observers of European origin had towards indigenous peoples.

There is no doubt that Mansilla often expresses guilt and doubt over white treatment of indigenous people. However, while Mansilla's text may exhibit some sensitivity in comparison to those of other nineteenth century writers, Mansilla is ultimately dismissive of Ranquel culture, except as it serves to highlight his mockery of *porteño* political and social life. Despite Mansilla's attempt to comprehend the Ranquels and their customs, the text insists upon the difference between cultures of men, and often reverts to a utopianism about the nation that seems to propose for the future only an alliance of privileged white story-tellers like Mansilla himself.* While Mansilla presents Ranquel culture as one in which story-telling is highly significant, there is no sense that the indigenous narratives also produce valuable and highly complex knowledge about their own social formation, which of course, they do.

It is notable that, in a text in which cultural distinctions between men are under discussion, women provide a sameness that often transcends race, ethnicity, culture, and place. In the text, women provide a zero degree of culture that unites them as members of a group but which means that they often lack the distinctions that mark men as citizens. The sameness

---

The epistolary style of Mansilla's text has political and cultural references to this process. The intended recipient of Mansilla's letters would have been significant to Mansilla's readers: Chilean writer Santiago Arcos was the author of La cuestión de los indios: las fronteras y los indios *(1860), a treatise that called for military action against the indigenous people. David William Foster has referred to the implied dialogue with Santiago Arcos as confirming the image that Excursión is "primarily a dialogue between two members of an educated elite" ("Knowledge" 22).*

that Mansilla sees all women as exhibiting "under every constellation" (338) divorces them from any notion of national. In fact, women are "othered" to an extraordinary degree in the text, appearing as the cause of all the trouble related in the stories that men tell around the space of the campfire. Far from being representatives of civilization, women as a group — like the supposedly barbaric indigenous and African-Argentine men — are viewed by Mansilla as part of the chaos that produces social disorder.

In *Excursión*, Mansilla creates a series of spaces in which knowledge about the nation is produced. These nation-spaces are the pampa itself as *tierra adentro* (interior land), the male domain of the circle around the military campfire, and finally the interior lives of the men themselves. These enclosing spaces are represented as producing knowledge about the nation through narrative. The campfire in particular provides a pseudo-utopian nation-space where men of all classes tell the stories that define "lo nacional." These stories are also a window into the inner lives of the emerging national figure, the loyal gaucho, and will be re-told by Mansilla to the nation vis-à-vis the newspaper *La Tribuna*.* Indigenous men, African-Argentine men, and most women are excluded from these knowledge-producing nation-spaces.

In his travels through the pampas, Mansilla, in his role as "causeur," meditates on a number of subjects, from civilization and barbarism to the nature of women. His musings, while disparate, generally lead to a common end: his fascination with the territory known as *tierra adentro* (interior land). Mansilla describes

> el deseo de ver con mis propios ojos ese mundo que llaman Tierra Adentro, para estudiar sus usos y costumbres, sus necesidades, sus ideas, su religión, su lengua, e inspeccionar yo mismo el terreno por donde alguna vez quizá tendrán que marchar las fuerzas que están bajo mis órdenes [5].
>
> (a desire to see with my own eyes that world they call *tierra adentro*, so as to study its customs and ways, its needs, its religion and language, and to inspect for myself the terrain where the forces under my orders would perhaps one day have to march [*An Expedition* 6]).

As David William Foster has indicated in "Knowledge and Mansilla's *Una excursión a los indios ranqueles*," Mansilla's text is obsessed with the production and transmission of knowledge, not only about the Ranquels but also about this *tierra adentro* or inside space of the nation. The line between

---

The newspaper, as Benedict Anderson has reminded us in Imagined Communities, *is a place where the nation was defined in the nineteenth century.*

the known and the unknown for Mansilla and his readers can be marked physically on the map drawn by white cartographers. This is also the same space that will eventually become part of the known nation at a future date when it is conquered by the Argentine army. Moving past the frontier line, Foster notes, creates a sense of patriotic pride for Mansilla "in the face of the opportunity to assimilate the indigenous people of the barbaric unknown into the known world of Christian civilization" ("Knowledge" 24). Mansilla enters this space — which is considered "unknown" to Mansilla and his readers — with the conquest of the indigenous people in mind.

Mansilla's need to know the land actually has to do with his position as a soldier. Whether or not he admits it to himself, he certainly knows that the government's plan is a wholesale takeover of indigenous lands. Mansilla himself seems to have no quarrel with the idea of an invasion of cattle-raising settlers, or with the idea that he would someday be invading the people he was traveling to meet:

> No hay un arroyo, no hay un manantial, no hay una laguna, no hay un monte, no hay un médano donde no haya estado personalmente para determinar yo mismo su posición aproximada y hacerme baquiano, comprendiendo que el primer deber de un soldado es conocer palmo a palmo el terreno donde algún día ha de tener necesidad de operar [6].
>
> (No stream, spring, lagoon, hill, or dune did I leave unobserved as I personally went about determining approximate positions and getting the lay of the land, it being my understanding that a soldier's first duty is to know the whole span of land in which he one day must needs operate [*An Expedition* 5]).

Mansilla's negotiations with the Ranquels had to do with land use — the defining difference between the civilized and barbaric man for him. Mansilla's view — that indigenous people were not using the land and that therefore the land did not belong to them — was one held by colonialists in general. Mansilla examines the pampas through the eyes of the expanding nation: he sees the land in terms of its use for white Argentines.

> Muchos miles de leguas cuadradas se han conquistado.
>
> ¡Qué hermosos campos para cría de ganados son los que se hallan encerrados entre el Río Cuarto y el Río Quinto!
>
> La cebadilla, el porotillo, el trébol, la gramilla, crecen frescos y frondosos entre el pasto fuerte; grandes cañadas como la del Gato, arroyos caudalosos y de largo curso como Santa Catalina y Sampacho, lagunas inagotables y profundas como Chemeco, Tarapendá y Santo Tomé constituyen una fuente de riqueza de inestimable valor [6].

> (Many thousands of square leagues have been conquered. How
> lovely the land lying between the Cuarto and Quinto rivers for rais-
> ing cattle! Indian barley, common beans, clover, and grasses all grow
> lush and fresh among the pasture lands; great hollows such as the
> Gato Gorge; long, plentiful streams such as the Santa Catalina and
> the Sampacho; deep and inexhaustible lagoons such as Chemecó,
> Tarapendá and Santo Tomé provide an incalculably bountiful source
> of wealth [An Expedition 5]).

Mansilla's voyage into the unknown interior will re-create the pampas as
a place for white settlers to produce wealth for the nation.

Many of the nineteenth century writers who described Latin American wilderness did so in the guise of scientific travelers, who were record-
ing the difference between European and American natural history.
The reasons for their voyages often concerned the eventual use of the land
they were observing for European gain. The question of the perceived
squandering of the land by indigenous people was part of the violent discourse of national expansion. In a comment that could refer to most
situations of nineteenth century expansion on indigenous land, Howard
Morphy refers to the question of landscape in nineteenth century Australia,
indicating that "Europeans moved into what (to them) was a previously
unutilized environment, their objective being to release its potential"
(206).

While the scientific travelers were supposedly collecting information
about the land, most of that information resulted in an obfuscation of history, an erasing of the memory of the indigenous people who had inhabited the land for centuries. Howard Morphy refers to changes in land use
when he states: "The European [colonial] landscape has been created
through a process which involved a change in land use and a break with
the previous history of the land, amounting almost to a denial that the
land had a previous history" (206). In Argentine history, this denial would
foretell the genocide of indigenous people during General Roca's invasion
of the "desert" when

> Indian resistance had been wiped out and close to nine million hec-
> táreas of 'liberated' land passed into the hands of the less than four
> hundred individuals who had financed Roca's blitzkrieg-like expedi-
> tion [...] [Foster, "Knowledge" 19].

While Mansilla's voyage — presaging the obliteration of the same people with
whom he was signing a treaty — produced a record of Ranquel culture,
it also concerned the question of the (white) nation's relationship to
the space of the pampas. Like other scientific travelers, Mansilla was

gauging the land in terms of its eventual occupation by white Argentine settlers.

Mansilla's work as a scientific traveler cannot blur the fact that story telling forms the heart of this text and reflects Mansilla's dreams for the nation. In *Una excursión a los indios ranqueles*, nation-space is found in the intimate groupings of men. Most significantly, the war in Paraguay, and the resultant camaraderie which Mansilla claims to have found in the military, is called upon in the text to create a hero's epic which excludes women from the process of nation-building and therefore from the nation-spaces occupied by heroic men. For Mansilla, national utopia is the military campfire, around which class distinctions are supposedly lost in an orgy of story telling. Mansilla's overriding authority in the text — as a first-person narrator who refers to himself as an observer able to negotiate the civilized and frontier worlds— makes him the organizer of these stories. For Mansilla, the lands occupied by indigenous people represent the absence of civilization; that is the absence of Christian settlers. In the text, campfire produces a kind of civilization for Mansilla in the midst of this perceived absence; the circle around the campfire is represented as a utopian civilization of men in which rank is unimportant but in which gender and race are not.

The notion of the inside space of indigenous territory is significant when examining how Mansilla creates a sense of nation through the use of the campfire. The creation of the sense of nation through spatial means addresses the three knowledge-producing spaces I have identified in the text: 1) *tierra adentro*, which is inside both physically (far from the coast) and conceptually (as lands that white Argentines see as interior [hidden] in relationship to their settled nation); 2) the military campfire, a space which is also both physical (a circle of men) and conceptual (as a space which is repeated every night in a different place yet retains the same qualities), and 3) the conceptual space of storytelling by Mansilla and his men.

In fact, Mansilla's narrative is thematically organized by the intimate gatherings of men. Mansilla's comments on human nature often arise from moments in the text where men gather in close conversation: from the clubs of Buenos Aires to the officers' clubs of the forts, from the gaucho campfires to the Ranquel tents. Yet more than any space where men gather, the campfire has a special place in Mansilla's imagining of the nation: "El fogón argentino no es como el fogón de otras naciones. Es un fogón especial" ("An Argentine campfire is not like the campfire of other nations. It is a special campfire") (62). The special quality to which Mansilla refers has to do with how gatherings around the fire (in his mind) tend to dissipate social rank and ethnic differences:

El fogón es la delicia del pobre soldado [...]. Alrededor de sus resp-
landores desaparecen las jerarquías militares. Jefes superiores y
oficiales subalternos conversan fraternalmente y ríen a sus anchas [21]
   (The campfire is every poor soldier's delight [...]. Military rank
disappears in its glow. Superiors and subordinates converse frater-
nally, laugh heartily) [*An Expedition* 20].

What makes these campfire gatherings so emblematic of the text itself
is that at the campfire Mansilla becomes both a witness to and a producer
of gaucho stories. Often reminding his readers that the story would have
been forgotten if it were not for him, Mansilla appears to be trying to
reproduce the *fogón* through the pages of *La Tribuna*, just as the epistolary, conversational style of the narrative seems aimed at reproducing the
atmosphere of the literary salon. Control of the nation, however, is still
reserved for those storytellers with access to the national print medium —
men like Mansilla himself.

That Mansilla should penetrate the pampas only to re-create a men's
club is not surprising; In *Literatura y realidad politica* David Viñas has provided a well-known analysis of the clubman phenomenon in Mansilla's *oeu-
vre* (1964). What is most fascinating to my discussion of bodies and spaces
is how the question of space becomes ultimately fluid in regard to men who
produce narrative, and, in turn, how the question of nation becomes inseparable from the idea of a narrative space physically occupied by men. David
William Foster has noted:

> As a first-person narrator self-charged with recounting his own
> exploits [...] the Mansilla of *Excursión* cannot help but project the
> validity of his own scrutiny of the phenomena of the Tierra Adentro,
> at least as a zero degree of narrative practice [25].

Mansilla carries the assurance of "knowing" with him wherever he goes. What
becomes evident in Mansilla' text is that knowing has a spatial component
that has to do with the access to a national audience through the newspaper.

In *Imagined Communities*, Benedict Anderson discusses the printing
of the newspaper as a "figure for the secular, historically clocked imagined
community" that, Anderson claims, is partly created in its pages (35). In
the chapter titled "Creole Pioneers," Anderson discusses the newspapers
of South America as created by and for "a specific assemblage of fellow-
readers, to whom [...] ships, brides, bishops and prices belonged" (62).
In mid-nineteenth century Argentina, it was still true that the writers creating the newspapers (as editors) belonged for the most part to an elite
group of public men. This is significant in demonstrating how the control
over the print medium related to control over nation-spaces.

As an elite man, Mansilla had great freedom in moving between and making judgments upon different kinds of public and private spaces. His gender, family connections, and class status gave him freedom to move around Argentina, as well as giving him access to the press. The number of arenas occupied by Mansilla was astounding: few readers (which included the Ranquel *cacique*, who was a regular reader of *La Tribuna*) would have been included in all of them. Mansilla could move between the salon, the genteel men's club, the brothel, the campfire, and the Ranquel tent. With unimpeded access to any part of the nation, Lucio V. Mansilla had specialized and privileged knowledge that he could impart to his audience.

It is impossible to read *Una excursión a los indios ranqueles* with gender in mind, without seeing that in the ultimately fluid social categories among men that Mansilla constructs in his text — where musings on the definitions of "civilized" lead him to reflect that such distinctions are often arbitrary and random — women represent a figure of sameness. Yet the stable nature of women is hardly a positive trait in Mansilla's view. It is somewhat disappointing to find — in this writer who supported his sister's writing career — that his attitude towards women could be summed up as "Can't live with 'em, can't live without 'em." Mansilla can hardly pass a chapter without remarking on the untrustworthy nature of women. Violence between men is blamed on women: "There are heroes because there are women," he announces in the beginning of the book (17). And later, he claims that "Un hombre debe tener palabra con las mujeres, aunque ellas suelen ser tan perfidias y tan malas; las cosas han de tener algún fin" ("A man must keep his word with women even though women are so often perfidious and bad. Things must have some purpose to them") (351). There are multiple references of the same order, demonstrating that women become "Other" in Mansilla's text to an excessive degree.

But precisely one of the difficulties in engaging with this complex text is the evasive, peripatetic quality of Mansilla's writing. Known to espouse beliefs which he did not hold, Mansilla often makes comments that seem designed to undercut his own access to places of privilege; comments that make him, as it were, just one of the boys. In a phrase that pits the language of the body against the written word, for example, Mansilla holds up the gaucho as an example of loyalty, abnegation, and honesty. In order to deal with the gauchos, Mansilla muses, "Hay que sentir y callar. Por eso una mirada, un abrazo, un ademán con la mano, dicen más que todo cuanto la pluma más hábilmente manejada pueda describir" (20) ("You have to feel and keep quiet. Because a look, a hug, a hand gesture, say more than anything the most skillful pen could describe" [21]. One of the ways

in which men connect in their storytelling has to do with women. The supposed undependability and manipulative power of women colors almost
every anecdote told around the campfire. Women's bodies, however, are
excluded from the campfire; if women do appear, they are conspicuously
silent. Silence seems to be a characteristic of women which is scorned by
Mansilla:

> Está visto que las mujeres son iguales en todas las constelaciones [...];
> lo mismo a orillas del majestuoso Río de la Plata, que en las dilatadas
> llanuras de la Pampa Argentina.
>   Suspirar, creen que es hablar.
>   Confieso que es un lenguaje demasiado místico para un ser tan
> prosaico como yo. [338]
>   (Women, then, are the same under every constellation [...] on
> the shores of the majestic River Plate and in the open plains of the
> Argentine pampas.
>   (They think that sighing is speaking.
>   (I must confess that it is too mystical a language for as prosaic a
> sort as I) [An Expedition 332].

Mansilla is not prosaic; his writing, history, and celebrity make that statement untrue. Yet in this remark, geography is tied to women in a way that
is consciously ironic: the romantic grandeur of land is contrasted with the
supposed sameness of women. The citation also suggests that the occupation of physical space by women has no effect on the space itself; women
are not seen by Mansilla as essential to changes in land use or occupation.

The appearance of *cautivas* in the text deviates from their appearance
in earlier literary texts. Here, the captive white women are no longer the
tragic victims of other tales. An entire range of captive experience is represented by Mansilla, but he almost never directly refers to the captives'
speech. As opposed to the Lucía Miranda story and other captive tales, the
women held prisoner by the Ranquels do not represent the nation or the
idealized citizen. Neither is there any urgent sentiment in Mansilla's text
that the nation has a responsibility to rescue the female captives. Instead
a captive man — an old school chum of Mansilla's— is ransomed. For the
female captives' mistreatment, Mansilla often seems to hold women (other
captives or native Argentine women) responsible.

The indigenous women that appear do so mostly as background sup-
ports for their husbands. Mansilla includes a discussion of the sexual freedom enjoyed by single Ranquel women that is obligatory to nineteenth
century texts on indigenous cultures. While pretending to believe that this
mode of behavior is an improvement on white Argentine sexual mores,
Mansilla simply uses these descriptions as a means of pointing out what

he believes to be the unstable and contradictory nature of sexual and gender relations among the Ranquels.

Yet the mediating factor between the Ranquels and the *criollos* in Mansilla's text is the figure of women. The first indigenous people that Mansilla meets on his journey are women, who offer food to him and his soldiers. In particular, one woman becomes highly significant to the text and to Mansilla's negotiations: Carmen, whom Mansilla describes as "lovely and astute." Mansilla is vague about his relationship with her, which he describes as "intimate," but he is clear that the Ranquel *cacique* has chosen Carmen because "tiene mucha confianza en la acción de la mujer sobre el hombre" (8) ("he places great trust in the effect of a woman on a man"; [*An Expedition* 7]). Mansilla even suggests that Carmen might have served as a second Malinche, in an odd reversal of power relations.

> Carmen fue despachada [...] por el Talleyrand del desierto, y durante algún tiempo se ingenió con bastante habilidad y maña. Pero no con tanta que yo no apercibiese, a pesar de mi natural candor, de lo complicado de sus misión, que a haber dado con otro Hernán Cortés habría podido llegar a ser peligrosa y fatal para mí, desacreditando gravemente mi gobierno fronterizo. [8]
>
> (So it was that Carmen was dispatched [...] by the Talleyrand of the desert and for some time exercised her charge with considerable craft and skill. Not so well, however, that I should fail, despite my natural guilelessness, to sense the complexity of her mission, so that had I been contending with another Hernán Cortés, it might have been perilous, indeed fatal to me, gravely discrediting my frontier government [*An Expedition* 7]).

In a reversal of power relations, Mansilla becomes Moctezuma, with the cacique cast in the role of the conqueror, Cortés. By referring to Mariano Rosas (the Ranquel chief took Rosas's surname after being held captive on Rosa's ranch as an adolescent) both the Spanish conqueror and — in ironic terms — as a "Talleyrand" while referring to himself as the Aztec king and to his "candor," Mansilla's language underplays the power relations at work behind the treaty, i.e. that Mansilla really was there to help conquer the Ranquels. And with hints about his relationship with Carmen, Mansilla then uses the episode to engage in some self-congratulation that serves to heighten his reputation as a ladies' man and diplomat:

> Pasaré por alto una infinidad de detalles, que te probarían hasta la evidencia todas las seducciones a que está expuesta la diplomacia de un jefe de fronteras, teniendo que habérselas con secretarios como mi

comadre; y te diré solamente que esta vez se le quemaron los libros
de su experiencia a Mariano, siendo Carmen misma la que me inició
en los secretos de su misión.

El hecho es que nos hicimos muy amigos, y que a sus buenos
informes del compadre debo yo en parte el crédito de que llegué pre-
cedido cuando hice mi entrada triunfal el Leubucó [8]

(I will spare you the endless details, though they would give evidence of the blandishments to which the diplomacy of a frontier captain is susceptible, especially where secretaries of the caliber of my
comadre Carmen are involved. I will only say that this time Mariano's
book of human experience went up in smoke, it being Carmen herself who initiated me in the secrets of his mission.

(In short, we became close friends, and I owe the creditable reputation that preceded my triumphant entry into Leubucó to her good
offices) [*An Expedition* 7].

The language of Mansilla's description of the "diplomacy" is erotic (more
so in Spanish than in McCaffrey's translation): the "seductions" to which
he is "exposed," and the way in which Carmen "initiates" him into secrets
suggest an eroticism which Mansilla as frontier chief comes out of as the
victor. In so doing, Mansilla — in a multiplication of personae that will not
surprise readers familiar with his prose — becomes both Moctezuma and
Cortés, vanquished emperor and cagey conqueror. The question of whether
a sexual relationship existed at all is not as significant as the fact that Mansilla's— and by extension, the Argentine government's— relationship with
the Ranquels is described in sexual terms.

This is an erotic history with no domestic romance or even domestic
tragedy to suggest a model for the formation of the Argentine people. Carmen's relationship with Mansilla is described as it relates to the construction
of Mansilla's personae, and as it heightens his celebrity. The self-proclaimed
savior of "his" frontier government, by his self-perceived ability in the text
to see through a woman's seductions, becomes emperor (Moctezuma) by his
own seduction of the same woman. Sylvia Molloy's characterization of Mansilla in "The Unquiet Self" as an adolescent rings true here when the erotic
language that includes seduction and exposure leads to an initiation. This is
where Mansilla's characterization of his supposed candor begins to have its
effect. In Mansilla's language, his mission to the Ranquels is characterized
by these diplomatic secrets. Diplomacy is not only sex, but also sex in the
brothel, with the Ranquel woman as prostitute.

This episode recalls Mansilla's statement (cited by Molloy) that
"Todos perseguimos la sombra de algo, que no alcanzaremos jamás: pasar
por lo que no somos" ("We all pursue the shadow of something, which
we will never reach: to pass for what we are not) (qtd. in "Imagen de

Mansilla" 746). Through Carmen, Mansilla can become Moctezuma, and the power, privilege, and marginalization of Moctezuma can shadow his prose. The episode also seems to relate to Cristina Iglesia's discussion of the text as one in which a military expedition becomes a pleasure jaunt. She relates this in part to Mansilla's need to keep the image of himself as an exotic figure, who "se exhibe como un ciudadano de la frontera: Mansilla está instalado en este espacio, parece conocer sus códigos y disfrutar de su estadia" ("behaves like a citizen of the frontier: Mansilla is installed in this space, he appears to know its codes and enjoy his stay") (189). Part of his successful working of the "codes" of the border region, however, is based on his past as a man of leisure. Mansilla's knowledge of the "codes" of sexuality and pleasure allow him to succeed in his diplomatic mission, semi-official though it may be. Clearly he casts the mission as one in which the safety of the border region is at risk. Relating this back to the text as a reply to Sarmiento, Iglesia writes that by converting his expedition into one of pleasure, Mansilla is also poking fun at the serious Sarmiento.

> La humillación que Sarmiento, ahora Presidente de la república, le ha infligido, al enviarlo a un lejano y oscuro puesto de frontera en lugar de ofrecerle el Ministerio de guerra que Mansilla esperaba, se convierte de una estadía placentera.
> (The humiliation that Sarmiento, now President of the Republic, has inflicted on him, on sending him to a far-off and obscure frontier post instead of offering the Ministry of War that Mansilla wanted, has become a pleasure trip) [189].

What is most intriguing about Carmen, however, is that she is one of the only women in the text who is mentioned by name, and who seems to carry any kind of individual personality. All the other women are *chinas* (a term indicating a lower-class, rural, or indigenous woman) and *cautivas*.

One of the reasons that critics may be correct in calling *Una excursión a los indios ranqueles* a bridge between *Facundo* and *Martín Fierro* is that *Excursión* signals the end of literary romanticism in Argentina where the territory of the nation is concerned. Whereas romantic writers projected the pampas as a space of isolation (Echeverría), a generator of backwardness (Sarmiento) or an extra-legal space of confusion (Guerra), Mansilla views the pampas in his tripartite role as Europeanized traveler, military man, and diplomat: he looks at the land in terms of its use-value for the nation. His desire to see "tierra adentro" comes from a need to study and analyze. Even the terminology that Mansilla uses to refer to the pampas—the interior—indicates that in *Excursión* the pampas is conceived of as part of the nation: the possibilities for constructing "civilization" on the pampas are now made real.

The elite world of salon life was one in which Lucio V. Mansilla's sister Eduarda was very comfortable. In the newspaper *El Nacional*, in 1879, Sarmiento took pains to praise the work of Eduarda Mansilla, whose contributions to the newspaper's society pages he describes as giving intimate knowledge about Argentine women. In describing Mansilla, who wrote articles on fashion and manners for *El Nacional*, Sarmiento calls her "mujer muy mujer y lo que es más, habituada a los refinamientos del 'High life' europeo en cuyo medio ha brillado muchos años en París y en Estados Unidos" ("a very womanly woman and what's more, accustomed to the refinements of the European 'High life' in whose midst she has shined for many years in Paris and in the United States") (47). This "womanly" quality of her writing, Sarmiento claims, means that the delicacy with which she wrote enabled her to reveal knowledge about the inner workings of women. In reference to this supposedly gender-specific knowledge, Sarmiento marvels that "por no tener la 'mot' del enigma, lo hemos estado viendo toda la vida, sin comprenderlo" ("because we didn't have the clue to the riddle, we have been seeing it all our lives without knowing it") (48).

The knowledge gained reveals more about what constituted "Argentine women" in nineteenth century thought than about the women themselves. "¿Quién habría, por ejemplo, descubierto que las mujeres se visten para examinarse y criticarse mutuamente, si alguna grande autoridad [...] no revelase el secreto" ("Who else would have known that women dress up to examine and criticize one another, if some great authority [...] had not revealed the secret") (47). Sarmiento describes women as creatures obsessed with fashion: "lo que despierta las facultades descriptivas, la imaginación, el juicio, la penetración femenil, el sentimiento de las armonías es el traje" ("what wakes the descriptive faculties, the imagination, judgment, feminine penetration, the sentiment of artistic harmony, is dress") (48). Whereas fashion was considered a rightful subject for Argentine men, like Alberdi, to express political subjects, its discussion by women was mocked.

There is also a class bias to the knowledge gained, which Sarmiento foregrounds without noting the slippage between "women" and "upperclass women" in his text. The upper-class women who attend balls and fêtes in Eduarda Mansilla's columns become both the representatives and producers of knowledge about Argentine women in Sarmiento's essay. Sarmiento's characterization of Mansilla also insists upon her class status when discussing her place in the corpus of Argentine writers. For

Sarmiento, Eduarda Mansilla can produce knowledge about women due to an unspoken agreement between men. Beginning the essay by describing Eduarda Mansilla as the perfect example of a lettered, Argentine woman writer, Sarmiento ends by claiming that

> una escritora, y más si pertenece a la alta sociedad, no está sujeta a la crítica que podemos soportar nosotros, pues que una autora [...] nunca deja de ser una mujer, una dama que escribe bajo la égida de la cultura, de la caballerosidad y del respeto de los hombres.
>
> (a woman writer, and more if she belongs to high society, is not subject to the critique that we can endure, since a lady author [...] never stops being a woman, a lady who writes under the aegis of the culture, the gallantry, and the respect of men) [49].

In this formulation, women writers—particularly if they are "ladies," are isolated from the general body of Argentine writers. Sarmiento refers to women writers as those who walk "solas en las calles, así escriben en libros y diarios. 'Ne touche pas à la reine!'" ("alone on the streets, as they write in books and diaries. 'Don't touch the queen!'") (49).

In general, the language of Sarmiento's essay creates a picture of Eduarda Mansilla and other women writers as beings who can awaken refinement and a sense of spirituality in men. For Sarmiento, the secrets revealed by Eduarda Mansilla awaken "La Luz [...] en nuestro espíritu" ("The Light [...] in our spirit") (48) while her "mano delicada y artística nas haga sentir de nuevo, lo que escapó a nuestros groseros sentidos" ("delicate and artistic hand makes us feel again, what escaped our gross sentiments") (49). This perceived ability of women to awaken the refined in men is common to nineteenth century writing. In Sarmiento's prose, the spiritual dimension of this awakening is seen to be a positive force for the nation: the content of women's prose exempts them from criticism among other national male authors.

The ability of women to awaken a sense of spirituality and refinement in men is one of the themes of the short story "El ramito de romero." The story is told by a young medical student from Normandy, who is studying in Paris. In the story, the narrator, Raimundo, first discusses his lovely young cousin Luisa who believes that his new, overly scientific way of thinking will lead him to lose his soul. Before he leaves, she gives him a small sprig of rosemary, which he carries in his vest pocket. Upon going to the medical school to meet a professor he finds himself obsessed with the rosemary, staring at it, examining it, and smelling it; the rosemary reminds him again of his cousin. At that moment he spies a cadaver lying on a table. Astounded by the perfect beauty of the dead woman, the narrator touches and caresses her arm. After touching the cadaver, Raimundo loses consciousness and imagines that the dead woman embraces him and that she invites him to the land "donde se elabora la naturaleza inorgánica" ("where inorganic nature is prepared") (37). As they begin to float into this nether region, she requests that he leave his soul, which, she tells him, resides in the rosemary sprig in his pocket. The doctor refuses, because the dead woman informs him that the rosemary flowers "te dejan una luz que puede cegarte o darte mayor lucidez" ("will shine a light on you that can blind you or give you greater clarity") (37). The dead woman then takes him to a place of archetypal forms. As well as witnessing perfect colors, music, tastes, and smells, the narrator sees perfect souls: "fruto de dos seres verdaderamente amantes" ("the fruit of two beings who are truly in love") (39). The narrator also sees the representation of the entire march of human progress "sin indicado sin pasado ni presente, diferencias puramente humanas" ("without indicating either past nor present, purely human differences") (40). Finally he joins in a dance with fictional characters: from Goethe, Walter Scott, and George Sand.

Understanding the importance of love, the soul, and the imaginary world, the doctor returns to consciousness, finding himself in the home of his aunt and cousin in Normandy. His spiritual excursion with the corpse is explained as the result of "un ataque cerebral" ("a cerebral attack") (44). The cadaver, he discovers, was that of "una pobre actriz del Vaudeville, cuya historia es terrible y grotesca a la vez [...]" ("a poor actress from the Vaudeville, whose story is at once terrible and grotesque [...]") (44). In his aunt and cousin, Raimundo finds that women can be "seres sobrehumanos" ("superhuman beings") (44) in their devotion in the sickroom. The story ends with the narrator's marriage to his cousin. While sitting beside her at the wedding banquet, the narrator sees that she carries the sprig of rosemary, and the story ends with "Los labios pronuncian la palabra ¡amor! y el corazón responde: ¡Inmortalidad!" ("The lips pronounce the word love! and the heart responds: Immortality!") 46).

As a means of reading questions of nation-space in *Una excursión a los indios ranqueles*, I will use the regional emphasis in "El ramito de romero" to discuss the split between city and province in Argentina, and as a means of understanding the sense of nation. Many of the same concerns involving the make-up of Argentine nation-space that appear in *El médico de San Luis* appear in "El ramito de romero" in a different form. In particular, the dichotomy of city and province, the questions about the kinds of citified knowledge that are suitable for provincial use, and a discussion of the position of women in family life are employed within "El ramito de romero." The emphasis on Normandy in the story is equally split between the Normandy that represents traditional country life and the Normandy that has to do with a sense of regional identity.

As a way to re-read *Una excursión a los indios ranqueles*, the shorter story is fascinating precisely because it can be read as a response or imitation of the gentlemen-scholar style. Told in the form of a direct address to another friend from medical school, the conceit — like that of Lucio V. Mansilla's prose — is that the story has been written to a particular friend, for his eyes alone:

> tú no reirás de mis inconsecuencias; así al escribir esta narración para ti solo, como si hablara conmigo mismo; voluntariamente he dejado en la primera parte, ciertas frases, ciertas ideas bien contrarias a tu modo de pensar.
>
> (you won't laugh at my digression; that is, on writing down this story for you alone, as if I were talking to myself; I have willingly left in the first part, certain phrases, certain ideas contrary to your way of thinking) [44].

As well as imitating the testimonial style favored by Lucio in his autobiographical work, Eduarda's story uses literary and scientific allusions. Most significantly, as in Lucio V. Mansilla's text, the use and acquisition of different kinds of knowledge are addressed and resolved through the ways in which the bodies occupy space and represent nation-space.

Two kinds of knowledge are considered to be opposed in the text, both of which are associated with particular spaces: spiritual/emotional knowledge, which is associated with women, family, and traditional provincial life, and scientific knowledge, which is associated with single men, lack of emotional ties, and modern city life. Both of these kinds of knowledge are represented in the story as forming a "balanced" nation-space. As the story begins, the narrator's obsession with materialism — and rejection of a spiritual and emotional life — leads to a devaluation of women and family. An argument with his lovely young cousin Luisa occupies the first part of the story; then Raimundo reveals to his friend Carlos that he has argued with Luisa because of his (Raimundo's) lack of respect for women: "Ya conoces tú mi opinión sobre la mujer o sea el elemento femenino en la creación; contribuir el desarrollo vital y nada más; lo contrario no es sino sentimentalismo enfermizo que pasará" ("You already know my opinion about women or whatever you want to call the feminine element of creation; to contribute to the development of [new] life and nothing more; anything else is just weak sentimentalism that will pass") (33).

The narrator's devotion to materialism is mirrored by his description of his cousin's body in the beginning of the story. When he discusses Luisa,

Raimundo describes her first as a body. His description implicitly requests that his friend (the imagined reader of the story) become the creator of that body:

> imagina un cuerpo diminuto, con movimientos inquietos, que recuer-
> dan los de la ardilla; pon sobre un cuello blanco, muy blanco y que
> creo suavísimo, una cabecita coronada de rizos rubios; evoca una
> fisonomía, en la cual campean alternativamente la dulzura y la mali-
> cia, agrega una manecita preciosa, que siempre despierta en mi el
> antojo de chuparla como alfeñique [...]
>
> (imagine a diminutive body, with nervous movements, like those
> of a squirrel; put on top of that a white neck, very white and which
> I believe to be very soft, and a little head crowned with blonde curls,
> evoke a physiognomy, in which alternately move sweetness and mal-
> ice, add an adorable little hand, that always awakes in me the desire
> to suck it like sweet almond paste [...]) [32].

The description evokes a sensuality in the desire to touch Luisa's body: Raimundo believes but does not know that her neck is soft; he desires to but cannot suck her hand. The intimate description, therefore, demon-strates that Raimundo lacks knowledge — erotic knowledge — that he would like to possess.

The space of knowledge occupied by single men in Mansilla's story does not give them erotic possession of the bodies of bourgeois women but does give them the power to deconstruct the corpses of marginalized women. While Raimundo cannot touch his cousin, he is able to touch dead women at the medical school, during autopsies. Raimundo takes apart women's bodies with a sense of desire and a certain reverence for the beauty of form: he believes more in the body than in the spirit. While his friend refers to the body as "mortal covering," Raimundo refers to the bodies he dissects as "the triumph of organized matter" (33). The act of possession that allows Raimundo and other men to take apart the naked bodies of women has to do with the marginal, public spaces that these dead women inhabited while living: the brothel and the theater. The pos-session of bourgeois women is obviously reserved for the private space of the home.

The notion of spaces reserved for men and marginalized women brings me back to Lucio V. Mansilla's *Una excursión a los indios ranqueles*, a text that I have described as producing nation-spaces through the inti-mate groupings of men. Eduarda Mansilla's story, like Lucio's text, is projected as a dialogue between two elite men of leisure, although Eduarda's dialogue is consciously a fictional one. In *Excursión*, however, the conversational style of the narrative and the creation of male spaces of storytelling are designed to reproduce in writing those elite public spaces inhabited by men of leisure. The gentlemen-scholars of the Generation of 1880 were the same men who moved from the club and literary salon to the brothel and backstage at the theater. For Lucio V. Mansilla, these male spaces are those that are most productive in the construction of the nation. In Eduarda Mansilla's story, those marginal public spaces produce sterility and a rejection of the traditional values of family and home that (in her view) were the domain of bourgeois women. For Eduarda Mansilla, a lack of respect for bourgeois women must be followed by a rejection of family.

While he cannot touch his cousin, Raimundo can and does caress the body of the dead actress that he finds in the examining room. What may have made this scene potentially more titillating to the nineteenth century reader is the fact that the class status of the cadaver is not given until the end of the story. In his description of the cadaver, the narrator focuses on her perfections. The body of the dead actress attracts him first through her beauty, which he associates with works of art. Her arm is compared to that of "la Venus de Milo," while her hair has "juegos de luz, que hubieran encantado a Rembrandt" ("plays of light, that would have enchanted Rembrandt") (36). As in Rosa Guerra's characterization of Lucía Miranda, the reference to statuary indicates that —for nineteenth century readers— the dead woman has an erotic body, meant to be touched. And using the language both of art and of science, Raimundo "dissects" her in his description by referring to her body as a conjunction of parts:

> El brazo que atrajo mi atención desde el principio era sin duda alguna la parte más perfecta de ese conjunto de perfecciones. La ondulación de la línea del cuello, después de perderse suavemente, según las reglas de la estatuaria, para marcar el arranque del brazo, iba poco a poco elevándose en la curva más deliciosa y ondeada.
>
> (The arm that attracted my attention from the first was without a doubt the most perfect part of that perfect whole. The undulation of the line of the neck, after disappearing smoothly according to the rules of statuary, to mark the break of the arm, went up little by little into the most delicious and wavy hollow) [36].

The female body in this description is— as Raimundo claims— a "ser sobrehumano" ("superhuman being") who produces in him an irresistible erotic desire. The body itself—a dead body whose soul has departed —is confused with spirituality.

> Aquel brazo sin vida me produjo un enternicimiento irresistible. ¡Cuán hermoso, cuán terso era, cuán provocante! El deseo es la

voluntad. Rápida como la electricidad, mi acción se produjo a la par
que mi deseo: mis labios se posaron amorosos sobre aquel brazo
divino y perdí la conciencia de mi existencia normal.

(That arm without life produced in me an irresistible feeling of
tenderness. ¡How beautiful it was, how resplendent, how provocative!
Desire is will. As rapid as electricity, I acted along with my desire: I
pressed my lips amorously on that divine arm and I lost consciousness of my normal existence) [37].

Acting upon this desire is what provokes the "ataque cerebral" that sends
him back to Normandy. It should also be noted that the desire to kiss the
corpse's arm recalls Raimundo's more erotic desire — which he does not
act upon — to suck upon the fingers of his cousin's hands. The corpse
becomes a substitution for the body of Luisa. The confusion of the material body — particularly this marginalized body — with the spiritual domain
associated with bourgeois women produces sickness in Raimundo.
Raimundo's rejection of what appears in the story as feminine bourgeois
norms is characterized as an illness. It is during this illness that Raimundo
is shown as regaining his soul, and during his recovery that the values of
women, home, place and family — so prized by the narrative — are regained
as well.

In his excursion into the spiritual realms, Raimundo does not see the
dead woman as a unified body: she appears instead as two "brazos
amorosos" ("loving arms") (37) around his neck and a voice that speaks
into his ear. Although she has regained some semblance of life, her body is
again fragmented. There is a suggestion that once Raimundo has acted upon
his desire there might be a playing out of that erotic will. The dead woman
seems to tempt him at one point by asking him to leave his soul behind.
"Tu alma me importuna [...] y como sé que no tienes especial interés en
conservarla, vamos a dejarla aquí" ("Your soul bothers me [...] and as I
know that you don't have any special interest in keeping it, let's leave it
here"; 37). It is clear that the dead woman is tempting him away from Luisa,
for she asks him to give up the sprig of rosemary, to which his soul is linked.
The narrator refuses and it is at this point that he loses physical contact
with the dead actress. In refusing to give up possession of the rosemary that
represents both his cousin's body and his own soul, Raimundo has already
made a choice about the kind of knowledge he will accept. The physical
separation from the fragmented body of the cadaver mimics his movement
away from a completely materialistic mode of thought.

The voyage into the land of spirituality is one in which Raimundo
discovers the essential nature of the world in which he lives, and in which
he rediscovers his soul. The disembodied voice of the dead woman tells

him that he has come to the land of "el arquetipo de la form en su más pura manifestación" ("the archetype of form in its purest manifestation") (36). Archetypes include all manner of physical sensations: colors, sounds, the essence of all plants and flowers—which are found to relate not to the body but to the soul. Raimundo asks himself whether "lo dulce, lo amargo, lo agradable, como gusto, como olores, como tacto, no significan sino lo que despierta en nosotros esta o aquella sensación." ("the sweet, the bitter, the agreeable, like tastes, smell, touch only mean anything in that they awaken in us this or that sensation") (38). Raimundo finds the spiritual element in his admiration of material form.

Most significant to my argument about bodies in the text is that when Raimundo sees "perfect beings," he finds they are without bodies: "cabezas sin cuerpo con bella fisonomía y dos alas en el nacimiento del cuello" ("bodiless heads with a beautiful physiognomy and two wings at the base of the neck") (39). And yet the *most* perfect beings are those with four wings who are

> el fruto de dos seres verdaderamente amantes, que al acercarse desprendieron de su esencia la chispa inmortal que poseían latente en su organismo: esas almas privilegiadas fruto del amor, son escasas, su encarnación no es duradera; y nunca tardan en ascender a las regiones superiores.
>
> (the fruit of two beings who are truly in love, who in the moment of union give off from their essential beings the immortal spark that they had latent in their organism: these privileged souls, fruit of that love, are rare, their incarnation is brief, and they never delay in ascending to the higher regions) [39].

Perfect married love—the story suggests—produces perfect souls. This perfect love has a bodiless dimension that is far from the erotic desire provoked by the corpse of the dead actress.

Yet bodies of women in the "real world" of the story remain as symbols of bourgeois family life. Raimundo awakens to find his aunt standing in front of his bed. She is a solid housewife dressed in the national costume of Normandy: "mi tía Juana, con su cofia piramidal, su delantal blanco y su manojo de llaves" ("my Aunt Juana, with her pyramidal headdress, her white apron and her bunch of keys') (43). His aunt's presence as this traditionally dressed figure is seen to be key to his recovery. " ¡Cuántas veces mis ojos debilitados siguieron distraídos y curiosos sus movimientos!" ("How often my weak eyes—curious and distracted—followed her movements!") (43). His cousin Luisa, however, who is also sitting by his bed when he awakes, is described in almost saintly terms, "con las manos juntas y los ojos elevados hacia el cielo" ("with her hands pressed together and her eyes raised to heaven") (43). Women's bodies now signify respectability and are connected to both spirituality and traditional family life.

Women, for Raimundo, show almost superhuman qualities in the manner by which they can cure sickness. It is through his care by his aunt and his cousin that he regains his respect for womankind. The work of women in the sickroom is described as "su santo ministerio" ("their saintly ministry") (45). Gazing upon his cousin's body (which he contrasts to that of his aunt) he declares:

> Y si mi tía, con cincuenta años y proporciones exhuberantes, parece sustraerse a las leyes de gravitación y sus dependientes, ¿qué diré de la chiquitina, con sus formas graciosas, casi infantiles y su semblante de rosas? Aquello era un paraíso terreste y celeste a la vez, Carlos, que reunía el verdadero arquetipo de la felicidad humana.
>
> And if my aunt, 50 years old and of exuberant proportions appears to defy the laws of gravity and its dependents, what can I say about the little girl, with her graceful, almost childish form, and her rose-like face? That was a paradise on earth and heaven at the same time, Carlos, which brought together the true archetype of human happiness) [45].

Luisa's body is now described in ethereal terms as the spiritual space that the narrator visited during his vision. The future for that ethereal body, of course, can be seen in the robust and earthly proportions of the aunt. For Mansilla de García, the spiritual glory of the daughter leads to the solid stability of the mother and, by continuation, of the national family.

The themes of province and city that appear so prominently in *El médico de San Luis* also appear in "El ramito de romero" in relation to the questions of knowledge and family. Country and city are seen to be intimately linked to the kinds of knowledge that best suit citizens of the nation. Provincials in Mansilla de García earlier novel are seen to bloom in their native land as long as they are given an education suited to their situation. The mixture of (English) scientific attitudes mixed with (Argentine) emotional understanding creates what the narrative presents as the ideal national family. In "El ramito de romero" Raimundo's concerns for his scientific studies have led him to ignore not only his family but his "country" (Normandy) in favor of life in Paris. His conversion to a love of family and place is represented at the end by his meditations on the Norman-ness of the ancient abbey where he is married.

In "El ramito de romero" the regional markers of life in Normandy are also used to represent the dichotomy of science and spirituality. In contrast to the modernity of his Parisian medical school, the narrator refers to the antiquity of Normandy and its people. He refers to the male guests at his wedding as "esos robustos descendientes de los compañeros de Guillermo el Conquistador" ("those robust descendants of the companions of William the Conqueror") (46) suggesting a continuity that differs from the fragmented quality of his life in Paris. The abbey where he is married is referred to as "la antigua Abadía, que encierra tantas reliquias de pasados tiempos" ("the ancient abbey, that encloses so many relics of past time") (46). The indefinite quality of past time is related to the infinite quality of love; Old Normandy is where the narrator finds love.

Looking at "El ramito de romero" in relation to Argentina of the late nineteenth century, one can see that the same domestic ethos is at work, including the notion — present in *El médico de San Luis*— that the home is a place that women create as "a curative unit that can rehabilitate [those] infirm" men who "represent the illness of the state" (Masiello, 79). In "El ramito de romero" nation-space is represented most clearly in the sickroom, a place ruled by white, bourgeois women. Not only can white bourgeois women cure, but the absence of the spiritual knowledge associated with the bodies of these women actually produces illness. The young medical student who attempts to control scientific knowledge becomes ill in this loss of the feminine. Far from saying that bourgeois women merely reproduce the family — or are Republican mothers who will raise future citizens for the nation — Mansilla de García is claiming a place for such women in which the private becomes the public interior: she presents these women as the soul of the nation. And far from seeing domestic spirituality as the trap for women that it is, Mansilla de García constructs a regressive nation-family in which the home becomes a place of strength in which men regain their souls. The emblematic citizen for Mansilla de García is clearly the young medical student, with his spiritual connection to *lo nacional* found in home and woman.

In *Una excursión a los indios ranqueles*, the emblematic citizen has a split personality: Mansilla sometimes privileges the gaucho, who becomes a down-to-earth, loyal figure fighting for the good of the nation in the text. Women may be useful to the nation but are never considered in the guise of citizens or as spiritual advisers. Mansilla's projection of himself as the winner in the battle for Carmen's loyalty means that, for Mansilla, Carmen serves to indicate the superiority of white male narrators like Mansilla. Mansilla represents himself as the ultimate emblematic citizen who can traverse all possible spaces of the nation (from *porteño* salon to pampean campfire) with success. The storytelling around the campfire, which

Mansilla constructs as a utopian space where men of all classes converge on an equal footing, mimics the narrative-producing spaces of the elite world of salon life in Buenos Aires. As Mansilla is "reading" the pampas as a potentially useful space for the nation, he creates these circles of elite male civilization around the campfire.

FIVE

The Injured Body:
Martín Fierro and the Public
Hygiene Movement

José Hernández's *Martín Fierro* (*La Ida* 1872, *La Vuelta* 1879) was an instant popular success when it first appeared in Buenos Aires.* A long narrative poem in two parts—the second which appeared seven years after the first—*Martín Fierro* was written by Hernández (1834–1886) with the self-proclaimed wish of defending the gauchos, the rural inhabitants of the pampas, from injustice. The poem contains many of the ideas regarding national policies in the interior that Hernández had developed in a long career as a journalist, during which he wrote passionate articles on frontier politics, land distribution, immigration policies, and the condition of the gaucho.

In *Martín Fierro* the male, rural, semi-barbaric gaucho is represented as the emblematic citizen of Argentina, marking the final transition in the relationship between the body, citizenship, and nation-space in nineteenth century Argentina. As a symbol of Argentine national identity, the figure

The first edition of Martín Fierro—published in November 1872—ran out after two months (Sáinz de Medrano 17). Ricardo Rojas notes that from 1872 to 1875, eight editions appeared in Buenos Aires, and a ninth in Rosario (92). Hernández himself claims in the introduction to La Vuelta that in the six years since the publication of La Ida 48,000 copies had been sold. He also reports that the first printing of La Vuelta comprised 20,000 copies. Angel Rama comments that "El primer índice de la importancia de la obra no fue de carácter estético sino primariamente sociológico: la demanda del lector" ("The first indication of the importance of the work was not of an esthetic nature but primarily of a sociological nature: the public demand [102].

of the gaucho has been enduring, and *Martín Fierro* is considered the hall-mark of Argentine national literary culture even today. However, this highly masculinized emblematic citizen Fierro was as removed from real gauchos as the highly feminized emblematic citizen Amalia was removed from real women. Moreover, the gaucho who emerges as the emblem of national identity in *Martín Fierro* is not the unlettered countryman of other *gauchesca* works. The gaucho Fierro is a *payador* (a ballad singer and folk poet), a master of folk culture: his adventures mark him as an epic hero. As such, he stands for the master-narrators of Argentina: the elite male writers who are producing national prose. Furthermore, as the second part of the poem (*La Vuelta*) emphasizes resignation and obedience over the first part's advocation of rebellion, *Martín Fierro* also presents a gaucho who can function within the new civilized pampas of the late nineteenth century.*

In *Martín Fierro*, the white-occupied pampas emerges as the predominant nation-space of the narrative. Fierro crosses white-occupied territory to the frontier with indigenous lands, returning to white-occupied lands in Part II in order to preach a message that suggested the incorporation of the gaucho into the nation. The pampas and the relationship of the rural gaucho to the land-owning elites who formed the rural oligarchy was a subject of continuing national debate during this period. The desire of the elites to gain firm control over the economic possibilities of these vast lands resulted in the brutal control and displacement of the gaucho, and eventually the destruction of the gaucho way of life. Although the poem registers this erasure, the gaucho is seen as the only true master of the space of the pampas: the gaucho dominates nation-space in this text.

Another space that refers to the literary struggle for national identity in this text occurs in two scenes in which Martín engages in duels with El Negro and El Moreno, two African-Argentine men: one is an actual knife fight, the other a *payada*, a duel of balladeers. The space in question is the physical and conceptual space of the *payada*: the physical space, like a circle around the campfire, appears wherever two dueling gauchos meet. The conceptual space of the duel has to do with the fraternity of gauchos themselves. In both instances, Martín defeats the African-Argentines after engaging in a discourse surrounding racial difference. Martín's brutal racism is a challenge to the African-Argentines, who, however, lose the battle. His victory over the two African-Argentine men with whom he duels (and the

---

*Many critics have observed that the rebellious tone of the first part, written when Hernández was a journalist, changes in the second part, published during Hernández's successful campaign for a seat in the national senate.

death of one of them) has the effect of erasing the African-Argentine from the space of the duel, and from the possibility of belonging as a gaucho.

African-Argentine bodies are not the only bodies that are displaced in the poem. Lower-class women, indigenous men, and immigrants are represented—through their displaced bodies—as not belonging on the pampas. Through the figure of Martín Fierro, the gaucho body becomes a body of exclusion, and part of a discourse of subordination over marginalized bodies that are coded similarly. While protesting and registering the destruction of the gaucho body, the poem effectively fragments other bodies—female, immigrant, African-Argentine, and indigenous—excluding them from citizenship by submitting them to a process of feminization that makes them powerless. Once a marker of cultural power, femininity now marks the absence of power. The prototypical gaucho, Fierro, becomes both a destroyer of marginalized bodies and a witness to their destruction. This marks an apparent paradox, because the gaucho was most often a *mestizo*, a person of mixed ancestry. Slatta has noted that, in practice, the gaucho could be a man of any race: gauchos were defined by the profession they exercised, not by their skin color. However, the representation in literature of the gauchos' racial status changes during the late nineteenth century. In *Amalia*, the gaucho of the Rosas era was associated with barbarism, and with supposed racial inferiority. The gaucho of *Martín Fierro* is called *blanco*—"white"—signaling a shift in the racial figuration of the gaucho body in literature.*

The destruction of marginalized bodies in *Martín Fierro* recalls the discourse of public hygiene (public health) texts of the late nineteenth century. The push for improved public hygiene began in the 1870s, in part because of several outbreaks of cholera and yellow fever in the late 1860s and early 1870s, the most tragic being the yellow fever epidemic of 1871, which killed more than seven-thousand people in Buenos Aires. In medical texts on the subject, the calls for improved public hygiene grow more and more fervent in the early 1870s. In *Sex and Danger in Buenos Aires: Prostitution, Family, and Nation in Argentina*, Donna Guy claims that because of the participation of public health (Guy translates *higiene* as "public health" to make clear that it parallels this field of medicine) physicians such as Guillermo Rawson, Eliseo Cantón, and Edwardo Wilde in national politics, "politics became inseparable from issues of public health" (78).

The perception of the race of the gaucho depended upon the political use to which he was being put: the unitarios cast the gaucho (considered an ally of Rosas) as a mestizo, and therefore in the eyes of white Argentines, a "barbarian."

This web of public hygiene, racial transgression, and folk culture owes its complexity to the tortured political and national history of the time. *Martín Fierro* recalls the tensions involving territory and control over the gaucho body that abounded in Argentina in the 1870s, a country that had barely recovered from a grueling war (the War of the Triple Alliance, 1865–1870) and had only recently re-united (in 1862) after many years as a split nation. After 1862, Argentina had begun to attract foreign capital, and train lines began to span the pampas surrounding Buenos Aires. As the opportunities for profit grew, property owners in Buenos Aires province, in particular, began to complain about the lack of a constant labor supply and about the free gauchos who ignored private property ownership and wandered the pampas, killing cattle in order to survive. In 1865, the *Código Rural* (Rural Code) that was instituted by the national government imposed draconian measures on the rural population. Laws of vagrancy meant that unemployed gauchos were forcibly recruited into military service or resettled as laborers for large ranchers. The measure guaranteed that workers were virtual slaves to the ranchers, who could also fire the workers at will.

While the articles regarding vagrancy were repealed in 1870, it was 1880 before forced recruitment was ended. The war with Paraguay was an obvious reason for the measure. But following the end of that war, the proscripted gauchos were also used to fight the indigenous population on the pampas. Even before the war with Paraguay began, Sarmiento wrote to Mitre (future president of Argentina, but at the time, governor and military chief of Buenos Aires) and advised him to use the gaucho body. In a September 1861 letter, Sarmiento encouraged Mitre, in cruel terms, to break down that body into blood:

> No trate de economizar sangre de gauchos [...]. Este es un abono que es preciso hacer útil al país. La sangre es lo único que tienen de seres humanos.
>
> (Don't try to economize on the blood of the gauchos [...]. This is a contribution we must make for the good of the country. Their blood is the only thing that makes them human beings) [qtd. in Sáinz de Medrano 31].

The feeling that the gaucho was only useful to the nation as a military tool is repeated in Hernández's poem. In *La Vuelta*, the son of Martín's friend Cruz tells him that

> El gaucho no es argentino sino pa hacerlo matar
> (The gaucho is not Argentine except when they want to make him kill) [V.3869].

The poem begins as Martín Fierro narrates the bitter story of his troubles. As the result of government policies intended to rid the pampas of unemployed gauchos, Fierro is forced into military service, and taken from his home to an army post on the frontier with indigenous lands. After experiencing intolerable punishments and back-breaking labor, he deserts his post and returns home, discovering that his wife and children are gone. As the result of this loss he becomes a gaucho *matrero* (killer-gaucho), and murders two men: El Negro ("the Black Man") and the gaucho *guapo* (handsome gaucho). Surrounded by soldiers sent to capture him, Fierro is saved when one of them, Cruz, decides to desert as well. Cruz tells his own story of betrayal and loss. They decide to go live, as did other deserters and marginalized Argentines, in one of the indigenous settlements, or *tolderías*.

La Vuelta begins by recounting the miseries Fierro and Cruz experience while living among the indigenous people. Cruz dies in an epidemic; Fierro saves a *cautiva* from a brutal indigenous man, and after killing him, returns to civilization. He then encounters two of his sons—referred to simply as el Hijo Mayor ("the Oldest Son") and el Hijo Segundo ("the Second Son")—as well as the son of Cruz, who is called Picardía. Martín's oldest son tells the story of the inhuman conditions in the penitentiary. The second son has joined up with Viscacho, a curious old thief who has been appointed by a corrupt judge as the second son's master. Picardía recalls his abandonment and suffering. Following the stories of his sons and Picardía comes the famous *payada* (duel of balladeers) between El Moreno ("The Dark-Skinned Man") and Martín Fierro. After Fierro's victory over El Moreno, Fierro, his sons, and Picardía decide to separate, each going in a different direction. The poem ends with Fierro advising the younger men to obey authority and stay out of trouble: a stark contrast from the earlier advocation of rebellion.*

The figure of Martín Fierro was recognized as being related to citizenship as early as the 1870s. In an 1879 letter to Hernández, thanking him for having sent an autographed copy of *La Vuelta*, Mitre describes *Martín*

---

*La Ida *is divided into thirteen cantos and has 2,316 verses.* La Vuelta *contains 33 cantos and 4,894 verses. In* Historia de la literatura hispanoamericana, *Oviedo paraphrases Martínez Estrada, noting that the strophe is of Hernández's invention: "una sextina que por su esquema básico de rimas (abbccb) parece provenir de la décima tradicional" ("a sestina that through its basic rhyme scheme (abbccb) appears to come from the traditional décima") (63). (A décima is a Spanish stanza consisting of 10 verses of eight syllables. In Hernández's strophe, the first two verses present a theme or question; the next two develop or complement it, and the last two condense the thought and answer it, producing a remark or proverb [Oviedo 63]).*

Fierro as "una obra and un tipo que ha conquistado su título de ciudadanía en la literatura y en la sociabilidad argentina" ("a work and a type [of man] who has conquered the title of citizenship in Argentine literature and society") (13). The popularity of the poem was commented upon by Pablo Subieta in 1881, in a series of articles about *Martín Fierro* that appeared in the newspaper *Las Provincias*. Subieta refers to the poem as "la leyenda más popular que aprende de memoria el niño, que la canta el payador, que la murmura el carrero y la lee con deleite la cándida doncella" ("the most popular legend that the child learns from memory, that the troubadour sings, that the cart-driver murmurs, and that the innocent girl reads with delight) (44). Subieta's characterization of the readers of *Martín Fierro*, seems to be related to his feelings about the use of the poem as a teaching tool for Argentine citizenship. Subieta describes *Martín Fierro* and its eponymous hero, as a summation of all the beliefs and institutions that comprise the nation:

> Martín Fierro no es un hombre, es una clase, una raza, casi pueblo; es una época de nuestra vida, es la encarnación de nuestras costumbres, instituciones, creencias, vicios y virtudes; es el gaucho luchando contra las capas superiores de la sociedad que lo oprimen; es la protesta contra la injusticia, es el reto satírico contra los que pretendemos legislar y gobernar, sin conocer las necesidades del pueblo; es el cuadro vivo, palpitante, natural, estereotípico de la vida de la campaña, desde los suburbios de una gran Capital, hasta las tolderías del salvaje.
>
> (Martín Fierro is not a man: he is a class, a race, almost a people; he is an era of our life, he is the incarnation of our customs, institutions, beliefs, vices and virtues; he is the gaucho battling the upper echelons of a society that oppresses him; he is the protest against injustice; he is the satiric retort to those of us who pretend to legislate and govern without knowing the needs of the people; he is the living picture — palpitating, natural, stereotypical — of country life, from the suburbs of a great Capital, to the encampments of the savage) [36].

Subieta's statement makes it clear that he views the work as a protest against the status quo of arbitrary justice in rural Argentina. Even in a statement in which Subieta is calling the character Martín a warrior against oppression, the critic defines "country life" as a phenomenon in which various registers of space could be found, from the national, "the suburbs of a great Capital" to what nineteenth century Argentines would consider extra-national, "the encampments of the savage" (36).

The two parts of the poem *Martín Fierro* represent a linear movement: from the (national) pampas across the frontier into indigenous territory in Part I, (or *La Ida*) and from indigenous territory back into the pampas in Part 2 (or *La Vuelta*). Even the names of the poem (*The Departure* and *The Return*) demonstrate that the poem stands in relationship to the frontier, a space from which Fierro must return. When examining the pampas as a space that was in the process of becoming nation-space and the *tolderías* as an extra-national space, it is significant that the return of Fierro from the *tolderías* follows his murder of an indigenous man. Fierro returns to "the nation" after the destruction of the indigenous body.

In discussing the poem, Subieta relates the notion of a wounded and corrupted body several times. In fact, Subieta compares the Argentine nation to a sick and wounded body that Hernández has exposed through the poem:

> En el fondo de ese poema sencillo [...] se encuentra la verdad; [...] al través de las diafanas y elegantes vestiduras de nuestro toilette social, se descubre la llaga cancerosa que corroe las entrañas del organismo.
>
> (At the bottom of this simple [...] poem one finds the [...] truth; through the diaphanous and elegant clothing of our social toilette, one discovers the cancerous wound that eats away at the entrails of the organism) [40].

The use of metaphors of sick and wounded bodies mirrors the discourse of public hygiene. In public hygiene texts, the city and nation appear linked; sometimes appearing as bodies, with the city a defective organ or limb. In his *Conferencias sobre higiene pública*, in 1876, Dr. Guillermo Rawson, professor of public and private hygiene in the Facultad de Ciencias Médicas, refers to the narrow streets of Buenos Aires as "pulmones demasiados pequeños que necesariamente amenazan afixiar a la sociedad bonarense" ("too small lungs which threaten to asphyxiate Buenos Aires society") (2).

In the discourse of nineteenth century public hygiene, space is organized vis-à-vis its control by experts. During the yellow fever epidemic of 1871, this control penetrated what had previously been "private" spaces: the houses of those who had contracted the disease. It is no coincidence that the plans to fight yellow fever — with the use of quarantining and disposal of bodies— recalls the system used to combat the plague in seventeenth century France (Foucault, *Surveiller et punir* 198–199). Medical and hygiene writers of Buenos Aires at times referred to the yellow fever epidemic as a *plaga* (plague). However, in Buenos Aires, only the neighborhoods seen to be responsible for the initial outbreak of yellow fever — neighborhoods of Italian immigrants and African-Argentines— were subjected to these measures.

The measures for public hygiene became a means of controlling marginal populations in the city through the vigilant eye of the new inspectors of hygiene. Luis M. Drago, member of the Facultad de Medicina, notes that as part of the municipality's plans, each inspector of hygiene

> Vigilará para que todas las ordenanzas municipales vigentes, y las que posteriormente se dicten sobre barridos de calles, remoción de basuras, mercados, y sobre Hijiene en general tengan el mas exacto cumplimiento; debiendo ser objeto de su constante observación, las casas de inquilinato, y bodegones notorios por la aglomeración de personas, y otras circunstancias contrarias a la salud pública.
>
> (Will watch so that all the municipal orders in place — and those that will later be made about the sweeping of streets, removal of trash, the markets, and on Hygiene in general — will be complied with correctly: what must be the object of his constant observation are the boarding houses, the cheap bars that are notorious for crowding, and other circumstances contrary to the public health) [185].

The inspector of public hygiene, therefore, would become a means of controlling prostitution and the immigrants who crowded cheap bars.

The organization of public space is a necessary element to the discourse on public hygiene. In an article titled "Hijiene pública"* in the 1870 edition of the *Revista Médica quirúrgica*, Dr. Pedro Mattos, a member of the Facultad de Ciencias Médicas, presents public hygiene as a totalizing regimen that regulates public spaces, which remain under the watchful gaze of the discourse:

> Desde el aire que nos rodea, hasta los artículos que se espenden para el consumo de la población; desde los lugares en que se benefician ó espenden la sustancias que sirven para la alimentación, hasta aquellos en que vamos a descansar para siempre; desde los sitios en que se elaboran los objetos de nuestro uso, hasta aquellos en que van los obreros á recobrar la salud perdida en los primeros, todo, todo está sujeto á la hijiene.
>
> (From the air that surrounds us, to the articles that are made for the consumption of the population; from the places in which the substances that feed the people are prepared or made, to those places where we go for our eternal rest; from the sites in which the objects of our daily use are made, to the sites where workers go to recover the health lost in the former, every [place] is subject to hygiene.)

The reference to the "place in which food stuffs are prepared" alludes to the battles within the press over the *saladeros*, the salted beef plants that

I have retained the original spellings in all documents from the nineteenth century.

operated within the city limits. The language used to describe the plants, refers to them as a "foco de corrupción" ("site of corruption"). These terms—and the descriptions of the bloody filth produced by the plants—recall the language used by Esteban Echeverría in "El matadero," a short story in which figures of barbarism kill and violate a young *unitario* who has wandered into their midst. Echeverría's story, which was written in 1839, was only published in 1871 (as it happened, during the yellow fever epidemic) in the journal *Revista del Río de la Plata*. Echeverría's story describes bodily fragmentation and destruction: the decapitation of a child and the torture—and suggested sexual violation—of the young follower of the Unitarist party who wanders into the slaughterhouse. The African-Argentine and other mixed-race figures in the story represent the Rosas government. The comparison between the butchers of the story and the butcher Rosas is clear.

The echoes of "El matadero" are a useful reminder that the categories of civilization and barbarism might still be in play, and still be used to reference certain marginalized bodies over those of the white elite. And, indeed, at times the language used to discuss public hygiene means that hygiene begins to work as a synonym for civilization while lack of hygiene functions in place of barbarism. Pedro Mattos refers to public hygiene in moral and national terms:

> Tan importante es para nosotros la hijiene, que la consideramos con relación al órden material de la sociedad, lo que la libertad al órden moral; y la carencia de cualquiera de ellas, deja los pueblos al capricho de un déspota que cada día, cada hora está dispuesto á conculcar sus derechos ó cegar una cabeza; como á atacar la salud y la vida de innumerables individuos, y diezmar las poblaciones.
>
> (Hygiene is so important to us that we consider it in relation to the material order of society, as liberty is to the moral order; and the lack of either of these leaves the people at the caprice of a despot who each day, each hour, might assert his rights, or take off a head; or attack the health and life of innumerable individuals, and decimate the population) [*Médico* 347].

The description of a despot who might "take off a head" from an Argentine citizen sounds very much like a description of any Argentine *caudillo*, or like Juan Manuel de Rosas himself. It echoes the language used by José Mármol when writing about Rosas in his 1851 *Amalia*—in scenes where Rosas appears shaking hands with blood-splattered killers. In public hygiene texts the *lack* of hygiene is related to certain kinds of people: exactly those same marginalized groups who are the butchers of Echeverría's tale.

In hygiene texts of the late nineteenth century women also appear as figures of trouble. Taking a cue from nineteenth century French texts, writers such as Luis Maglioni called for the abolition of wet nurses and for greater state intervention in child welfare. Referring to the fact that the future health of tomorrow's citizens would be shaped by their care as children, Maglioni observes, as if shocked that things are managed so badly, "Todo este gran cuidado, para lo que es y para lo que ha de ser una gran base de salud pública, está encomendado a las madres de familia" ("All this great care, for what is and for what must be a great foundation of public health, is left to the mothers of families") (253). Mothers are further criminalized in Maglioni's text:

> Como, de éstas, no todas se conducen bien; como muchas tratan mal a sus tiernos hijos; como algunas son hasta criminales con ellos; es justo y necesario que la sociedad intervenga y reglamente este asunto [...].
>
> (As, among these women, all do not behave well, as many treat their tender children badly; as some of these women are even criminal with their children; it is just and necessary that society intervenes and regulates this matter [...]) [253].

In addition, Maglioni repeats European warnings on the "descuido de la lactancia maternal" ("neglect of maternal lactation") and refers to an opinion shared by many nineteenth century authorities that "la vanidad, el lujo, la ostentación [...] hacen que muchas madres se convenzan de que ellas no son las que deben criar a sus hijos [...]" ("vanity, love of luxury, ostentation [...] make many mothers convinced that they are not the ones who should raise their children [...]") (254). The discourse of public hygiene — in which hygiene can be said to stand for civilization — implies that women are potentially dangerous and careless caretakers of the nation.

The 1871 Código Civil, instituted after 1871, treated women in the same fashion. Donna Guy refers to the ways in which women's civil liberties were diminished by the new code: "Considered minors, they were completely under the control of husbands or fathers and technically could not manage their own money or property; nor could they work without patriarchal permission" [Sex 44]. As the nation moved towards its eventual reorganization in 1880, the bodies of women were subjected to even greater control by the state.

Guy also discusses the 1875 decision by municipal authorities to legalize and regulate prostitution. Noting that the law provided no protection for women from pimps or disease, Guy observes that the law "promised men of all classes the ability to distinguish public women from the general female population" (*Sex* 53). Guy provides multiple examples of the ways in which efforts by public health physicians (*higienistas*) to regulate the health of prostitutes were governed by the physicians' categorization of venereal disease as a immoral condition spread by prostitutes of a lower class, and having little to do with the men who frequented them. "Higienistas had their own conceptions of illness and deviant behavior, both of which were developed to instill class and gender-directed norms through legalized female prostitution" (*Sex* 89). In discussing the regulation of prostitution, Guy remarks:

> Prostitution became a metaphor for upper- and middle-class fears about the lower class and the future of the Argentine nation. If it were possible to alter and control the sexual mores of poor women, then these women could clarify gender relations between classes, reshape the lower-class family to fit more bourgeois models, and define women's work as reproduction and nurturing rather than production [*Sex* 44].

The discourse of public hygiene, in the nineteenth century, was therefore involved in controlling and categorizing the bodies of women with a view towards the future health of the nation.

Immigrants and foreigners fare badly in discourse surrounding public hygiene as well. In several texts from 1871, yellow fever (*la fiebre amarilla* in Spanish) is referred to alternately as a woman ("esta viajera" ["this woman traveler"]) and a foreigner, ("el mas terrible huésped extranjero que ha visitado nuestras costas" ["the most terrible foreign visitor ever to visit our shores"]); ("Estado Sanitario" 81). In an editorial from *El Nacional* in 1871, reprinted in the *Revista Médico-quirúrgica*, the editor notes: "Tres cuartas partes de las víctimas del flájelo son de *nacionalidad italiana*" ("Three-quarters of the victims of the disease are of *Italian nationality*") (101, emphasis in the original). The editorial ascribes this to the lack of hygiene among "the kind of" ("la generalidad de") Italians who live in Buenos Aires, whom the writer describes as "gente muy ignorante, estúpida y supersticiosa" ("very ignorant, stupid, and superstitious people") (100). Like venereal disease, yellow fever takes on the characteristics of a female gender, the working class, and a non-*criollo* ethnicity. These are, therefore, discourses that worked to subordinate certain groups of people who are coded similarly.

The immigration policy put in effect following 1852 had more than an increase in European population as its objective. Germani remarks:

> The primary and explicit objective of the immigration was not only to populate the desert, finding inhabitants for an immense territory which to a large extent remained uninhabited or only contained a low density but, and above all, to modify substantially the composi-

tion of the population; and the basic objective highlighted the other
aspects of the plan: education and the expansion and modernization
of the economy [qtd. in Lewis 12].

Immigration policies, as Marvin Lewis has observed, were designed to erase
the African-Argentine and indigenous populations from the pampas. However, the immigration policies fashioned by Alberdi brought working-class
immigrants who were not the civilized inhabitants dreamed about by
Sarmiento. The new immigrants were not simply willing to sacrifice themselves to slow starvation on the pampas. Instead they congregated in the
cities, bringing about new dangers, in the eyes of Argentine national thinkers,
and new kinds of barbarism, to be combated by scientific control.

The occupation of certain spaces by "dangerous" bodies, therefore,
identified certain spaces as needing regulation and transformation. In the
discourse that emerged from *Martín Fierro*, the gaucho becomes a citizen
who experiences the openness of the pampas by declaring that those open
spaces belong to one kind of citizen alone. The same bodies that made
spaces dangerous in the city of the public hygiene texts were excluded from
citizenship on the pampas in *Martín Fierro*.

The exception was the figure of the gaucho himself. It cannot be forgotten that the emblematic citizen of Hernández's poem was not privileged in the political discourse of the era. Donna Guy is correct in pointing
out the similarities between the gaucho and the prostitute, observing that
"urban women accused of licentious or suspicious behavior were treated
like gauchos (cowboys), who were arrested for being unemployed" (39)
and that "[l]ike the gaucho the prostitute was both admired and feared
for her freedom and independence [...]" (40).

In referring to the usage of the *gauchesca* genre, Josefina Ludmer has
made clear the connection between the body of the gaucho and the genre's
formation. Ludmer has shown the effect and use of laws (instituted in 1865)
that subjected the gaucho to proscription and forced labor (16). The laws of
subjection represent the first element of a chain of uses that define the *gauchesca* for Ludmer. The second element is war: the wars which "abren la prác-
tica del uso militar del gaucho y su desmarginalización" ("open the practice
of the military use of the gaucho and of his dismarginalization") (17). For
Ludmer, the conjunction of laws and wars articulates and gives meaning to
the genre as a whole, and she sets out a chain of use that leads to a deter-
mined end, with the integration of the gaucho into Argentine law:

> a) utilización del "delincuente" gaucho por el ejército patriota;
> b) utilización de su registro oral (su voz) por la cultura letrada: género
> gauchesco. Y en adelante:

c) utilización del género para integrar a los gauchos a la ley "civilizada" (liberal y estatal).
(a. use of the "delinquent" gaucho by the national army;
b. use of his oral register [his voice] by literary culture: gauchesque genre. And as a result:
c. use of the genre to integrate the gauchos into "civilized" law [liberal and state]) [17–18].

Ludmer then states that this chain she has set out describes "el pasaje entre la 'delincuente' y la 'civilización' y sitúa el género como uno de los productores de ese pasaje" ("the passage between 'delinquency' and 'civilization' and situates the genre as one of the producers of this passage") (18).

The gaucho body is the focus of this process, or passage. The use of the body is both discursive and actual: "El gaucho puede 'cantar' o 'hablar' para todos, en verso, porque lucha en los ejércitos de la patria: su derecho a la voz se asienta en las armas" ("The gaucho can sing or talk for everyone, in verse, because he fights in the armies of the Fatherland: his right to the [national] voice is based in weapons of battle") (18). The gaucho is given the right to speak because of his sacrifice (of the body) for the Fatherland.

The body of the gaucho is therefore related intimately to the recodification and use of the pampas as nation-space — because it is linked to the loneliness and expanse of the desert as a place to flee, as an illegal space where the gaucho body is not subject to the emerging national law. In this illegal space the gaucho roams, creating the narrative that unites the outlaws. In *Martín Fierro*, the gaucho flees from the nation (in *La Ida*) and then returns to recount his story to the nation (in *La Vuelta*). In so doing, he also spreads his body across the pampas figuratively (through his travels), bringing the pampas "back" to the nation through the linking medium of his voice.

As an example of the non-gaucho body, the immigrant body is put in a position of inferiority. And the constant use in the poem of the word "gringo" establishes a native/other dichotomy that is clear and unambiguous. *Martín Fierro* complains about the stupidity of the "gringos" and about the "frontera gringada" ("gringo frontier") (I. 891). The use of the word "gringo" in this case (at this time used most often to refer to Italian immigrants) establishes the place of the pampas as one in which *extranjeros* (foreigners) are not welcome. Complaining about the *gringos*, Martín intones,

> Cuanto llueve se acoquinan
> como el perro que oye truenos.
> ¡Qué diablos!, sólo son güenos
> pa vivir entre maricas.

> (When it rains they are terrified
> like the dog who hears thunder.
> What devils! They are only good
> for living among pansies.) [I. 913–917].

In general, the gringos are shown not to understand the environment of the pampas; their reaction is one of fear. Josefina Ludmer has demonstrated how Italian or Spanish figures in gaucho narratives are feminized. Referring to a play with words in which *Inglaterra* (England) becomes *Hinca-la-perra* (which might be translated as "Screw the bitch"), and *napolitano* (Neapolitan) becomes *papo-litano* (*papo* refers to a woman's pubic area), Ludmer observes that:

> para definir al gaucho como hombre argentino hay que cambiar el sexo, el género, del extranjero. Los gringos enganchados son mujeres y llevan esa inscripción en los nombres de sus patrias, que son partes diferenciales del sexo femenino. La patria del gaucho pertenece, ella sola, al género masculino.
>
> (in order to define the gaucho as an Argentine man one has to change the sex, the gender, of the foreign man. The gringos forcibly placed in military service are women and wear this inscription in the names of their countries, which are the different parts of the feminine sex. The Fatherland of the gaucho belongs, alone, to the masculine gender) [49].

The citizenship/body of the immigrant man is excluded from masculinity, and therefore from participation in the Argentine nation.

The destruction of the body of the African-Argentine man is related directly to the racial categories invoked first by Martín himself. Each time Fierro provokes a fight with an African-Argentine man (a knife fight with El Negro and the *payada* [duel of balladeers] with El Moreno), the two men are seen to be his near-equal in skill. The question of race is always central to the opposition between the two men. The knife fight in which Martín kills El Negro is provoked by Martín's use of racial slurs, in a *coplita fregona* (humorous couplet) that he recites to the black woman whom he sees waiting outside the dance:

> A los blancos hizo Dios,
> a los mulatos San Pedro,
> a los negros hizo el diablo
> para tizón del infierno
> (God made the Whites,
> San Pedro made the Mulattos,
> The Devil made the Blacks,
> to have chalk [coal] in Hell) [I. 1166–1170].

Because El Negro is angered by this insult, a fight ensues. Martín then proceeds to carve up the body of the African-Argentine with his knife. In the *payada*, El Moreno invokes his own blackness immediately, and, when challenged by Fierro to sing a "canto of heaven," refers to racial distinctions that allude to the *coplita fregona* that Martín Fierro himself recited in his early encounter with the African-Argentine woman:

> Pinta el blanco negro al diablo,
> y el negro blanco lo pinta.
> Blanca la cara o retinta,
> no habla en contra ni en favor:
> de los hombres el Criador
> no hizo dos clases distintas
> (The white man paints the devil black,
> and the black man paints him white.
> God does not speak against or in favor
> of men whether their face is white or colored:
> the Creator did not make two distinct classes [of men]) [V. 4067–4072].

At the end of the *payada*, El Moreno reveals that he has challenged Fierro as a means of avenging the death of his eldest brother, El Negro. The two brothers have each lost in their duels with Fierro: moreover, El Negro and El Moreno are portrayed as unable to defend the honor of their "race." In this way, the duels have the purpose of excluding African-Argentines from nation-space.

Throughout *Martín Fierro* women are disappearing figures. Critics have often remarked on the depiction of women as part of the property of Fierro, when he claims that "Tuve en mi pago en un tiempo/hijos, hacienda y mujer" ("I had in my possession at one time/ children, hacienda and woman") (I 289–290). In referring to the "barbarity" of the indigenous people, Martín remarks that "Cuanto el hombre es más salvaje/trata pior a la mujer" ("When a man is most barbaric/he treats a woman the worst") (V. 3001–3002).

> Pa servir a un desgraciao,
> pronto la mujer está;
> cuando en su camino va,
> no hay peligro que la asuste;
> ni hay una a quien no le guste
> una obra de caridá.
>
> No se hallará una mujer
> a la que esto no le cuadre.
> Yo alabo al Eterno Padre,

> no porque las hizo bellas,
> sinó porque a todas ellas
> les dió corazón de madre
>
> (To serve a wretch,
> a woman is ready,
> when she chooses her path
> there is no danger that scares her,
> nor is there a woman who does not like
> a work of charity.
>
> (A woman cannot be found
> who doesn't fit this picture.
> I praise the Eternal Father,
> not because he made them beautiful,
> but because to all of them,
> he gave a mother's heart) [V. 3013–3024].

By the time we meet the *cautiva*, we are prepared for a picture of suffering motherhood. To be a mother in *Martín Fierro*, however, does not signal — as it does in *Recuerdos de provincia*— a powerful force in generating republican sons. The *cautiva* mother is pitiful precisely because she has lost her child, killed by her indigenous master (himself the child's father).

Indigenous women are not included in the figure of women, however. As in Lucio V. Mansilla's *Una excursión a los indios ranqueles*, indigenous women are shown to make white women suffer in captivity. In Canto VII of *La Vuelta*, the actions of one indigenous woman — the mistress of the *cautiva* — indirectly cause the death of the captive woman's baby. The indigenous woman has accused the captive woman of practicing witchcraft, and the indigenous man who owns the captive insists that she confess, and finally, "a su tierna criatura/se la degolló a los pies" ("tore apart her tender baby at her feet") (V.1102–1104). The destruction of the baby — part Christian, part indigenous— is perhaps used as an example of the ultimate act of barbarity. In addition, the cruelty of the indigenous man has to do with the body:

> Esos horrores tremendos
> no los inventa el cristiano.
> Ese bárbaro inhumano
> (sollozando me lo dijo)
> me amarró luego las manos
> con las tripitas de mi hijo.
> (Those tremendous horrors
> are not invented by the Christian.

That inhumane barbarian
[she told me this sobbing]
then tied my hands
with my son's intestines) [V. 1111–1116].

The body of the child is turned inside out; a tremendous horror "not invented by the Christian." Destruction of the body is blamed on the "barbarians" who are not seen to be worthy parents. Unlike the picture of paternal love among the indigenous people that exists in *Una excursión a los indios ranqueles*, the indigenous parents in *Martín Fierro* are portrayed as incapable of taking care of future generations. The indigenous man's destruction of a *mestizo* child signals the perceived refusal of the indigenous people to consider a national future that includes their mixing into *criollo* culture. The violence against the indigenous people, and the uncomfortable specter of *mestizaje*, is then laid at the feet of the indigenous man who would tear apart his own child. Along with the discourse of the *cautiva* tale — which I have described as one of revenge — *Martín Fierro* adds to the national sentiment that the indigenous people were unworthy to be considered citizens of the nation.*

As in other texts I have examined, male friendship and the bonds between men seem to tie the narrative (and the nation) together. In his reading of homoerotic elements of the story, Gustavo Geirola has identified the relationship between Cruz and Fierro as the only domestic love story that occurs in the narrative. Geirola's reading of the story stresses the gaucho's entry into the Law of the Father, noting the protection of narcissism in this inter-gaucho family. Geirola's essay is particularly useful in that it demonstrates that the new national family is not based on the heterosexual domestic unit but eventually on the homosocial alliance made between Fierro, his sons, and Cruz's son. In Canto XXXII can be found Fierro's advice to the younger men to respect the law, work hard, and stay true to your brothers. Fierro refers to the space of the pampas as being transformed by the behavior of the gaucho: "Bien lo pasa hasta entre pampas/ el que respeta a la gente" ("He that respects other people will do well even in the pampas") (V. 4643–4644). The new respectful Fierro, according to Geirola, represents a new order. Geirola refers to Martín's advice as:

The typical Christian, however, might have objected to the woman's tenderness towards her child. In Una excursión a los indios ranqueles, *Lucio V. Mansilla expresses a sentiment that was common as a reaction to women captives' reluctance to leave their children (which was usually a condition of their release): "No me resolví a decirle: Déjelos usted; son el fruto de la violencia! Eran sus hijos!" ("I couldn't bring myself to say: Leave them here. They are the fruit of violence. They were her children!") (360).*

words of wisdom gained by way of brutal historical experience in order to give way to a petit bourgeois masculine order, one that guarantees the union between men who have been feminized by the Law and protected from assuming castration by virtue of macho, racist, and xenophobic illusion [325].

The feminization of the gaucho that places them, according to Geirola, under the control of the law, is combated in this formulation by the rejection of indigenous people, African-Argentines, and women.

The discourses on the body at work in the national narrative *Martín Fierro* and the discourse of public hygiene present many similarities as well as some significant differences. While both discourses effectively fragment and disperse female, non-white, immigrant bodies, there is a notable dissimilarity in the kinds of spaces attributed to these bodies. The public hygiene texts concentrated on the city and its relation to the nation; the normative body of public hygiene was the urban, *criollo* male. In *Martín Fierro*, the open space of the pampas— seen at first to be outside the control of the law — is the focus of national identity. The normative body is a mythical gaucho, part of a masculinist discourse that excludes feminized bodies from citizenship. In both discourses, however, the end effect is a sense of coherence in the relationship to space. In the public hygiene movement, a normative male citizen — a white scientist — regulates the activities of the city/nation by opening up access to all spaces of the nation, making them submit to a regulating function that views all non-normative bodies as potentially diseased or dangerous. In *Martín Fierro*, a very clear demarcation between the pampas as nation-space and as extranational space is made, and the gaucho (in *La Vuelta*, that is) chooses to return to the newly made nation. Those bodies that might occupy this space are then fragmented and destroyed. The body of the African-Argentine, for example, is excluded from the potential nation-space of the *payada*. The difference between national and extra-national space now has to do not with where that space exists, but with who occupies it: the nation-space is where the indigenous people, African-Argentines, immigrants, and public women are *not*. The gaucho body was used as a body of exclusion, and a means of constructing a highly masculinized national identity which wedded an emerging national space (the pampas) to a social formation in which bonds between elite white men (speaking in the voice of the gaucho) were made sacred.

The discussion of the body of the emblematic citizen brings into question the nature of the literary body in nineteenth century texts. While trying to define "the body" for this project, I concluded that the body was as changeable a site of cultural meanings in nineteenth century Argentine cultural discourse as it was in the twentieth century and is in the twenty-first. What is clear, however, is that the body of the emblematic citizen in Argentine literature from the 1850s to the 1880s seems to "transport" gender across time and space for white male writers, who used the representation of class, gender, and regionality as a means of voicing their own beliefs about the national future.

In the context of my argument about the relationship between the emblematic citizen and nation-space, this usage raises the question of how the representation of the body translates into beliefs about citizenship and property. In each of the texts I examine in this book, the emblematic citizen is often constructed as an object of ownership. The texts seem to identify potential citizens and — during the course of the texts — move them to the status of property. Amalia is constructed as one of the many items in her boudoir; Sarmiento's mother is displaced by objects of furniture, the body of Lucía Miranda stands for the idea of national property, and the bodies of the gauchos of *Una excursión a los indios ranqueles* and *Martín Fierro* are manipulated for the needs of large property owners or the national government. It appears that emblematic citizenship as a category imagined in these narratives signifies a kind of dehumanization of the subject. In certain cases, the emblematic citizen is one who can be "owned" by the ruling elite.

The constitution of certain types of spaces as "nation-spaces" suggests the metaphorical importance of property in the construction of Argentine national identity in literature. Ideas about citizenship in literary narratives in the period from 1850 to 1880 revolved as much around the question of space as they did around the question of subjectivity. The necessity that Sarmiento and others saw for populating Argentina with European immigrants involved the vast spaces of the pampas and Patagonia, spaces that Argentine whites saw as "wasted" by indigenous peoples. In the racist views of national thinkers such as Sarmiento and Alberdi, the lands of the pampas would become useful to the nation as a whole when these territories became property and could be controlled and managed by white Argentines.

As lands that were defined to a certain extent by the activities of the gaucho, the pampas represented, to national founders, an excess of freedom. Slatta has remarked on the disapproving comments of British travelers to the pampas and their observation that the gaucho did not need to labor in order to eat: in the mid nineteenth century, meat was not sold on the pampas because anyone with a knife could go out and get dinner (Gauchos 47). For nineteenth century national founders, this was not the basis for a modern nation on the pampas, since modern agriculture and ranching required a plentiful supply of obedient laborers. In their dreams about a pampas inhabited by Europeans, Sarmiento and Alberdi envisioned hard-working, tranquil farmers, peons, and sheepherders. In addition, the introduction of railroads, refrigeration, wire fencing, windmills, and livestock breeding gave the promise, in the eyes of Argentine ranchers and national modernizers, of a changed pampas. In order to produce capital, this new pampas was divided up as private property, and the labor force coerced into working: the vagrancy laws of the 1870s responded to the needs of large *estancieros*.

In the literary narratives I have examined, nation-space is defined by the kinds of citizens who occupy the space, while the bodies of those citizens are in turn fragmented and displaced: objectified within space. The construction of nation-space as property is responsible in part for this dehumanizing movement in the texts. My observation regarding the construction of the emblematic citizen as property raises a number of questions about the connection between concepts of nation-space, frontier, and citizenship. In this book, I have not addressed how the relationship between body and space in the literary narratives of the period from 1850 to 1880 might refer to the constitution and consolidation of class privilege among the oligarchy through the accumulation and use of property. In addition to the technological modernizations that were beginning to be enacted, this particular period saw the formation of the modern nation through territorial and legislative cohesion: in the 1860s national institutions such as the legal system, national customs office, and national treasury were put in place. These institutions were involved in promoting the expansionism that supposedly furthered the interests of the "nation," but which ended by enriching large landowners.

Reading ideas of nation-space in the literary narratives of this period specifically through the idea of property might clarify certain tensions in the texts of this period. The question of property is much more clear when examining nation-space as geographic territory than, for example, when projecting it as a circle around a campfire or as a provincial parlor. But even in these more conceptual representations of literary nation-space, the idea of property haunts the narratives. In *Amalia*, Amalia is able to create her elegant Unitarian boudoir because of income from her Tucumanian properties. In Sarmiento's *Recuerdos de provincia*, the question of who owns the "hogar paterno" becomes a powerful subtext in the battle over old traditions and new. The circle of men around the campfire in *Una excursión a los indios ranqueles* that establishes a white Argentine space on the pampas, is formed by soldiers who represent the nation's desire to take over the lands occupied by the Ranquel people.

The knowledge-producing space-within-a-space of male narrative on the pampas refers to another circle of men in Buenos Aires: the landowning peers of Lucio V. Mansilla, whose interests these gaucho soldiers are serving.

Analyzing these narratives through the idea of property is also a means of further analyzing shifts in the representation of emblematic citizens. In these literary narratives, the body of each citizen-subject functions as an object of property, denying the possibility of agency. The relationship to nation-space means that as well as serving as a site of struggle over identity, the limited circle of nation-space serves as an enclosure, metaphorically fencing in those potential citizens. I have noted the enclosing movement of literary nation-space throughout this book: Amalia's boudoir produces her body as a static historical object, the white-occupied pampas of *Martín Fierro* is the space in which Martín roams, preaching a message of resignation. Enclosure in this case represents both inclusion and entrapment. The enclosing nature of nation-space denies agency to the emblematic citizens contained therein, whose happiness depends upon their "knowing their place." Eduarda Mansilla, for example, sends a message through the sermonizing narrator of *El médico de San Luis* that national happiness depends upon citizens who do not overreach their class status, gender, or provincial origins. It would seem that the exceptions to the rule are Sarmiento and Lucio V. Mansilla, the two writers I have analyzed who indirectly construct themselves as emblematic citizens within their own texts. Yet in both *Recuerdos de provincia* and *Una excursión a los indios ranqueles*, nation-space encloses *other* potential citizens, serving for the writer as a possible outlet to national leadership.

The examination of nation-space and the body through the idea of property would also provide new emphasis on the construction of the erotic body, for the notion raised another set of questions about where the "erotic" resides, and the relationship between sexuality, space, and ideas of property. While I have argued that feminine eroticism (which I believe was considered a threat to national order in the nineteenth century) sometimes appears in the literary narratives and in the Pueyrredón painting *La Siesta*, the sexual pleasure for women is always framed or contained by a sexualizing move that makes the pleasure a visual one for men: women's sexuality in these texts is about their construction as objects of property. In the narratives where female sexuality appears, it is always negatively inscribed: the bodies of women appear as the site of desire that brings ruin. As Sommer indicates, desire can also bringabout national unity in narrative. But making a distinction between the terms romantic, erotic, sexual, and sentimental demonstrates that while romantic women were seen as idealized citizens, erotic or sexual women were not. Women as emblematic citizens appeared in novels under the sign of the romantic: meaning that the gender shift I am tracking formed part of the move from romanticism to naturalism as well.

Positivism appeared early in Argentine narratives during the romantic period: Alberdi made his famous claim "Gobernar es poblar" in 1852. In the introduction to his *Bases*, the document that served as the outline for the Argentine constitution, Alberdi does not write about the Argentine self. The notion of American versus European identity is constructed around the question of property. Alberdi sees immigration as a way of solving not only the problems of the "uninhabited" [sic] country of Argentina, but as a means of resolving what he viewed as the specter of European socialism: "Llegarán aquellas sociedades [europeas] hasta un desquicio fundamental por cuestiones de propiedad, cuando tenemos a su alcance un quinto del globo terráqueo deshabitado?" ("Why should those societies arrive at a fundamental disagreement over questions of property, when we have at their reach a fifth of the uninhabited world?") (19). The comparison Alberdi is making depends upon a conception of the nation as property. Although romanticism continued in literary narratives until the late 1870s, some Argentine writers of the period were not assigning deep immutable qualities to land: instead they saw change as possible through the reproduction of Europeans on the land through the acquisition of property. The determinism of *Amalia* and *Facundo* gives way to the more evolutionary modes of thought contained in *Recuerdos de provincia* and *Una excursión a los indios ranqueles*.

Finally, as the result of some work done in response to questions about my rhetorical treatment of the indigenous tribes, I have become fascinated with the subject of how indigenous people appear in Argentine literature, and how they are constructed as "invaders" and "robbers" of white Argentine lands. Examining the subject of nation-space in regards to indigenous people raises the question of how (if ever) indigenous people are represented in Argentine literature as citizens. I have noted that white Argentines conveniently projected the Araucanian people as "invaders" in part because Araucanian kinship and economic networks extended into the southern part of Chile: the Araucanian tribes had migrated to Argentina following the Spanish invasion of Chile hundreds of years before. I am interested in how white Argentines understood these complex social formations, and how they were represented in narrative.

Moreover, I am interested in analyzing how indigenous nation-space was constructed by white Argentines and by foreign travelers (as far as I know there are no reliable nineteenth century accounts of indigenous narratives in Argentina). While ethnographic literature is scarce and unreliable in the nineteenth century, a study of travel writers (with Mansilla included) would be instructive. I have noted the homogenizing move towards indigenous people in nineteenth century Argentine literature: for that reason, Lucio V. Mansilla's text, with all its problems, remains valuable as one of the few works that attempted to study and document indigenous culture in nineteenth century Argentina.

In further studies of literary nation-space in Argentina, one limited to frontier narratives would be useful. The actual lands that, at any one time, were called the "frontera," were constantly shifting in the nineteenth century. How Argentine literary narratives conceived of the "frontier," and how the conception of these "wild" indigenous territories and their occupants changed after Roca's brutal invasion of the "desert," would also add considerably to my examination of ideas about citizenship, space and the nation. The literary narratives in the period between 1850 and 1880 are often focused on the fear and hatred of white Argentines towards the native people. When the "threat" of native attacks on those lands was removed by the Argentine military, what was the literary response? In my view, the concept of nation-space must register dramatic changes in the literature post 1880, when the territory that was once the object of so much desire and fear had been made available to white Argentines through the genocide of the native people of the pampas.

Bibliography

Adelman, Jeremy. "Constitutional Persuasions." *Republic of Capital: Buenos Aires and the Legal Transformation of the Atlantic World.* Stanford: Stanford University Press, 1998.

Aínsa, Fernando. "The Antinomies of Latin American Discourses of Identity and Their Fictional Representation." Trans. Amaryll Chanady. *Latin American Identity and Constructions of Difference.* Ed. Amaryll Chanady. Minneapolis: University of Minnesota Press, 1994. 1–25.

Alberdi, Juan Bautista. *Bases y puntos de partida para la organización política de la república argentina.* 1852. Buenos Aires: Editorial Plus Ultra, 1981.

Alonso, Carlos. "Oedipus in the Pampas: Lucio V. Mansilla's *Una excursión a los indios ranqueles.*" *Revista de estudios hispánicos.* 24.2 (1990) : 39–59.

Anderson, Benedict. *Imagined Communities: Reflections on the Origin and Spread of Nationalism.* New York: Verso, 1991.

Andrews, George Reid. *The Afro-Argentines of Buenos Aires: 1800–1900.* Madison: University of Wisconsin Press, 1980.

Austen, Jane. *Northanger Abbey.* 1818. London: Penguin, 1987.

Auza, Nestor Tomás. *Lucio V. Mansilla: La confederación.* Buenos Aires: Editorial Plus Ultra, 1978.

_____. *Periodismo y feminismo en la Argentina: 1830–1930.* Buenos Aires: Emecé Editores, 1988.

Avellaneda, Gertrudis Gómez de. *Sab.* 1841. Paris: Vertongen, 1920.

Bann, Stephen. *The Clothing of Clio: A Study of the Representation of History in Nineteenth-Century Britain and France.* Cambridge: Cambridge University Press, 1984.

_____. *The Inventions of History: Essays on the Representation of the Past.* Manchester: Manchester University Press, 1990.

Batticuore, Graciela. "Itinerarios Culturales. Dos Modelos de Mujer Intelectual en la Argentina del Siglo XIX." *Revista de Crítica Literaria Latinoamericana* 43–44 (1996): 163–180.

Berger, John. *Ways of Seeing.* 1972. London: British Broadcasting Corporation and Penguin Books, 1986.

Borim, Dário and Roberto Reis. "The Age of Suspicion: Mapping Sexualities in Hispanic Literary and Cultural Texts." *Bodies and Biases: Sexualities in Hispanic Cultures and Literatures*. Eds. David William Foster and Roberto Reis. Minneapolis: University of Minnesota Press, 1996.

Brennan, Timothy. "The National Longing for Form." *Nation and Narration*. Ed. Homi K. Bhaba. London: Routledge, 1990.

Bronfen, Elisabeth. *Over Her Dead Body: Death, Femininity, and the Aesthetic*. Manchester: Manchester University Press, 1992.

Brooks, Peter. *Body Work: Objects of Desire in Modern Narrative*. Cambridge, Mass: Harvard University Press, 1993.

Carlson, Marifran. ¡*Feminismo! The Woman's Movement in Argentina From its Beginnings to Eva Perón*. Chicago: Academy Chicago Publishers, 1988.

Chadwick, Whitney. "The Fine Art of Gentling: Horses, Women and Rosa Bonheur in Victorian England." *The Body Imaged: Human Form and Visual Culture Since the Renaissance*. Cambridge: Cambridge University Press, 1993, 89–107.

Colomina, Beatriz. Introduction. *Sexuality and Space*. Ed. Beatriz Colomina. Princeton Papers on Architecture. New York: Princeton Architectural Press, 1992.

Constitución de la Confederación Argentina. 1853. Rptd. in *Bases y puntos de partida para la organización política de la república argentina*. 1852. By Juan Bautista Alberdi. Buenos Aires: Editorial Plus Ultra, 1981.

De la Fuente, Ariel. "Facundo and Chacho in Songs and Stories: Caudillismo and Oral Culture in the XIX-Century Argentine Interior." Unpublished essay, 1998.

Dijsktra, Bram. *Idols of Peversity: Fantasies of Feminine Evil in Fin-de-Siècle Culture*. New York: Oxford University Press, 1986.

Duncan, Nancy. "Renegotiating Gender and Sexuality in Public and Private Places." *BodySpace: Destabilizing Geographies of Gender and Sexuality*. London: Routledge, 1996.

During, Simon. "Literature — Nationalism's Other? The Case for Revision." *Nation and Narration*. Ed. Homi K. Bhaba. London: Routledge, 1990. 138–153.

Echeverría, Esteban. *La cautiva*. 1837. *La cautiva. El matadero. Ojeada retrospectiva*. Ed. Carlos Dámaso Martínez. Buenos Aires: Centro Editor de América Latina, 1979.

_____. *Dogma Socialista*. 1846. Buenos Aires: Editorial Perrot, 1958.

_____. "El matadero." 1839. *La cautiva. El matadero. Ojeada retrospectiva*. Ed. Carlos Dámaso Martínez. Buenos Aires: Centro Editor de América Latina, 1979.

"Estado Sanitario." *Revista Médico-Quirurgica* 8.6. (1871) : 81–82.

Feijóo, María del Carmen. "La mujer en la historia argentina." *Todo es historia* 183 (1982): 8–16.

Fernández, Teodosio. Introduction. *Amalia*. By José Mármol. 1851, 1855. Madrid: Editorial Nacional, 1984.

"La Fiebre." *Revista Médico-Quirurgica* 8.7. (1871) : 118–119.

Foro de cultura y de la Nación. "Que significó en la Argentina de las últimas semanas la acción de la multitud?" *Clarín.com*. 27 January 2002. <www.clarin.com/suplementos/cultura/2002-01-26/foro.html>

Fortescue, William. *Alphonse de Lamartine: A Political Biography*. New York: St. Martin's Press, 1983.

Foster, David William. *The Argentine Generation of 1880: Ideology and Cultural Texts.* Columbia: University of Missouri Press, 1990.

_____. "Knowledge in Mansilla's *Una excursión a los indios ranqueles.*" *Revista Hispánica Moderna* 41.1 (1988) : 19–30.

Foucault, Michel. *Birth of the Clinic; an Archaeology of Medical Perception.* 1963. Trans. A.M. Sheridan Smith. New York: Vintage Books, 1973.

_____. *The History of Sexuality.* Vol. 1: An Introduction. 1978. New York: Vintage Books, 1990.

_____. *Surveiller et punir: Naissance de la prision.* Paris: Editions Gallimard, 1975.

Franco, Jean. *Plotting Women: Gender and Representation in Mexico.* New York: Columbia University Press, 1989.

_____. *Spanish American Literature Since Independence.* London: Ernest Benn, 1973.

Frederick, Bonnie. "Reading the Warning: the Reader and the Image of the Captive Woman." *Chasqui* 18.1 (1989) : 3–11.

Frisa, Manuel. On-line posting. 24 January 2002. Foro de cultura y de la Nación. "Que significó en la Argentina de las últimas semanas la acción de la multitud?" *Clarín.com.* 27 January 2002. <www.clarin.com/suplementos/ cultura/2002-01-26/foro.html>

Galindez, Bartólomo. Prólogo. *La conquista del desierto.* 1879. By Remigio Lupo. Buenos Aires. Editorial Freeland, 1968.

Garrels, Elizabeth. "Sarmiento and the Woman Question: From 1839 to the *Facundo.*" *Sarmiento: Author of a Nation.* Eds. Tulio Halperín Donghi, Iván Jaksíc, Gwen Kirkpatrick, and Francine Masiello. Berkeley: University of California Press, 1994.

Gates, Henry Louis. "Introduction: Writing 'Race' and the Difference it Makes." *"Race," Writing, and Difference.* Ed. Henry Louis Gates, Jr. Chicago: The University of Chicago Press, 1986. 1–20.

Geirola, Gustavo. "Eroticism and Homoeroticism in Martín Fierro." Trans. Melissa A. Lockhart. *Bodies and Biases: Sexualities in Hispanic Cultures and Literatures.* Eds. David William Foster and Roberto Reis. Minneapolis: University of Minnesota Press, 1996.

Goldsmith, Oliver. *The Vicar of Wakefield.* 1766. New York: E.P. Dutton, 1904.

González Echevarría, Roberto. *Myth and Archive: A Theory of Latin American Narrative.* New York: Cambridge University Press, 1990.

Gramuglio, María Teresa and Beatriz Sarlo. "José Hernandez." *La literatura gauchesca.* Vol. 6 of *Cuadernos de literatura argentina.* Buenos Aires: Centro Editor de América Latina, 1985.

Greenberg, Janet. "Toward a History of Women's Periodicals in Latin America, 18th–20th Centuries: A Working Bibliography." *Women, Culture, and Politics in Latin America.* Ed. Seminar on Feminism and Culture in Latin America. Berkeley: University of California Press, 1990.

Guerra, Rosa. *Lucía Miranda.* 1860. Buenos Aires: Universidad de Buenos Aires, Departamento Editorial, 1956.

Guy, Donna. "Mothers Alive and Dead: Multiple Concepts of Mothering in Buenos Aires." *Sex and Sexuality in Latin America.* Eds. Daniel Balderston and Donna Guy. New York: New York University Press, 1997.

_____. *Sex and Danger in Buenos Aires: Prostitution, Family, and Nation in Argentina*. Lincoln: University of Nebraska Press, 1991.

Halperín Donghi, Tulio. "Lamartine en Sarmiento: *Les Confidences* y la inspiración de *Recuerdos de provincia*." *Filología* 20.2 (1985) : 177–189.

_____. *Una nación para el desierto argentino*. Buenos Aires: Centro Editor de América Latina, 1982.

_____. *Proyecto y construcción de una nación (1846–1880)*. Buenos Aires: Ariel Historia, 1995.

Hernández, José. *El gaucho Martín Fierro. La vuelta de Martín Fierro*. Ed. Luis Sáinz de Medrano. Madrid: Ediciones Cátedra, 1979.

Hopkins, Cecilia. Review of *Ganado en pie*. *Página 12*, 28 September 2000, 29.

Hulme, Peter. *Colonial Encounters: Europe and the Native Caribbean 1492–1797*. New York: Routledge, 1992.

Iglesia, Cristina. "Mejor se duerme en la pampa. Deseo y naturaleza en *Una excursión a los indios ranqueles* de Lucio V. Mansilla." *Revista Iberoamericana* 63.178–179 (1997) : 185–192.

_____. Prólogo. *El ajuar de la patria: ensayos críticos sobre Juana Manuela Gorriti*. Buenos Aires: Feminaria Editora, 1993.

Iglesia, Cristina, and Julio Schvartzman. *Cautivas y misioneros: Mitos blancos de la conquista*. Buenos Aires: Catálogos, 1987.

Isaacs, Jorge. *María*. Bogotá: Imprenta Gaitán, 1867.

Isaacson, José. "*Martín Fierro*: un siglo de crítica." *Martín Fierro: Cien años de crítica*. Ed. José Isaacson. Buenos Aires: Plus Ultra, 1986.

Kaplan, Marina. "The Latin American Romance in Sarmiento, Borges, Ribeyro, Cortázar, and Rulfo." *Sarmiento: Author of a Nation*. Eds. Tulio Halperín Donghi, Iván Jaksíc, Gwen Kirkpatrick, and Francine Masiello. Berkeley: University of California Press, 1994.

Kirkpatrick, Susan. *Las Románticas: Women Writers and Subjectivity in Spain 1835–1850*. Berkeley: University of California Press, 1989.

Lamartine, Alphonse de. *Les Confidences*. Paris: Michel Lévy Frères, 1860.

Leguizamón, Martiniano. *La leyenda de Lucía Miranda*. Córdoba: Bautista Cubas, 1919.

Lewis, Marvin A. *Afro-Argentine Discourse: Another Dimension of the Black Diaspora*. Columbia: University of Missouri Press, 1996.

Lichtblau, Myron. *The Argentine Novel in the Nineteenth Century*. New York: Hispanic Institute, 1959.

Ludmer, Josefina. *El género gauchesco: Un tratado sobre la patria*. Buenos Aires: Editorial Sudamericana, 1988.

Luna, Felix. *Buenos Aires y el país*. Buenos Aires: Editorial Sudamericana, 1985.

Lynch, John. *Massacre in the Pampas, 1872: Britain and Argentina in the Age of Migration*. Norman: University of Oklahoma Press, 1988.

Maglioni, Luis C. Apéndice. *Conferencias sobre Higiene Pública*. By Dr. Guillermo Rawson. Ed. Luis C. Maglioni. Paris: Donnamette & Hatte, 1876.

Malosetti Costa, Laura. "Los desnudos de Prilidiano Pueyrredón como punto de tensión entre lo público y lo privado." *Las artes entre lo público y lo privado: Proceedings of the VI Jornadas de Teoría e Historia de las Artes, Universidad de*

Buenos Aires, September 12–15, 1995. Buenos Aires: Centro Argentino de Investigadores de Artes, 1995.

_____. *El rapto de cautivas blancas: un aspecto erótico de la barbarie en la plástica rioplatense del siglo XIX.* Serie Hipótesis y Discusiones 4. Buenos Aires: Filosofía y Letras, 1994.

"El manantial de vida." *Revista Médico-Quirurgica* 8.6. (1871) : 86–88.

Mansilla, Lucio V. *Una excursión a los indios ranqueles.* 1870. Caracas: Biblioteca Ayacucho, 1984.

_____. *An Expedition to the Ranquel Indians.* 1870. Trans. Mark McCaffrey. Austin: University of Texas Press, 1997.

_____. "Por qué...?" *Horror al vacío y otras charlas.* Ed. Cristina Iglesia. Buenos Aires: Editorial Biblos, 2000.

Mansilla de García, Eduarda. *Lucía Miranda.* 1860. Buenos Aires: J.C. Rovira, 1931.

_____. *El médico de San Luis.* 1860. Buenos Aires: Editorial Universitaria de Buenos Aires, 1962.

_____. "El ramito de romero." 1868. *Las escritoras: 1840–1940.* Ed. Elida Ruiz. Buenos Aires: Centro Editor de América Latina, 1980.

Marmier, Xavier. *Buenos Aires y Montevideo en 1850.* 1851. Trans. José Luis Busaniche. Buenos Aires: El Ateneo, 1948.

Mármol, José. *Amalia.* 1851, 1855. Madrid: Editorial Nacional, 1984.

Mártinez-Alier, Verena. *Marriage, Class and Colour in Nineteenth Century Cuba: A Study of Racial Attitudes and Sexual Values in a Slave Society.* Ann Arbor: University of Michigan Press, 1989.

Masiello, Francine. *Between Civilization and Barbarism: Women, Nation and Literary Culture in Modern Argentina.* Lincoln: University of Nebraska Press, 1992.

_____. "Lost in Translation: Eduarda Mansilla de García on Politics, Gender, and War." *Reinterpreting the Spanish American Essay.* Ed. Doris Meyer. Austin: University of Texas Press, 1994.

_____. Introducción. *La mujer y el espacio público: el periodismo femenino en la Argentina del siglo XIX.* Ed. Francine Masiello. Buenos Aires: Feminaria Editora, 1994.

Massey, Doreen. *Space, Place and Gender.* Cambridge: Polity Press, 1994.

Mathieu-Higginbotham, Corina. "El concepto de 'civilización y barbarie' en *Una excursion a los indios ranqueles.*" *Hispanofila* 89 (1987) : 81–99.

Mattos, Pedro A. "Hijiene pública." *Revista Médica- quirúrgica* (1870) : 346–350.

McCaffrey, Mark. Introduction. *An Expedition to the Ranquel Indians.* By Lucio V. Mansilla. Trans. Mark McCaffrey. Austin: University of Texas Press, 1997.

Michie, Helena. *The Flesh Made Word: Female Figures and Women's Bodies.* New York: Oxford University Press, 1987.

Miller, Nancy K. "Cultural Memory and the Art of the Novel: Gender and Narrative in Eighteenth-century France." *Textuality and Sexuality.* Eds. Judith Still and Michael Worton. Manchester: Manchester University Press, 1993. 70–87.

Mitre, Bartolomé. "Carta de Bartolomé Mitre a José Hernández." 14 April 1879. *Lewunmann, Borges, Martinez Estrada: Martín Fierro y su crítica.* Eds. María Teresa Gramuglio and Beatriz Sarlo. Buenos Aires: Centro Editor de América Latina, 1980.

Molloy, Sylvia. "The Unquiet Self: Mnemonic Strategies in Sarmiento's Autobiographies." *Sarmiento: Author of a Nation*. Eds. Tulio Halperín Donghi, Iván Jaksíc, Gwen Kirkpatrick, and Francine Masiello. Berkeley: University of California Press, 1994.

Montero, María Luisa. Lucio V. Mansilla y sus bibliotecas." *Boletín de la Academia Argentina de Letras*. 219–220 (1991) : 103–128.

Morphy, Howard. "Colonialism, History and the Construction of Place: The Politics of Landscape in Northern Australia." Ed. Barbara Bender. *Landscape: Politics and Perspectives*. Providence, R.I.: Berg Publishers, 1993. 202–234.

Nead, Lynda. *The Female Nude: Art, Obscenity and Sexuality*. New York: Routledge, 1992.

"Observaciones." *La Primavera*. 15 Oct. 1863, 31.

Onega, Gladys S. *La inmigración y la literatura argentina: 1880–1910*. Buenos Aires: Galerna, 1969.

Pacheco, Carlos. Review of *Ganado en pie*. *La Nación Line*. 17 April 2001. <http://www.lanacion.com.ar/01/04/27/ds_300791.asp>

Pagés Larraya, Antonio. "Eduarda Mansilla." *El médico de San Luis*. By Eduarda Mansilla. Buenos Aires: Editorial Universitaria de Buenos Aires, 1962.

Patmore, Coventry. "The Angel in the House." 1854. *The Poems of Coventry Patmore*. Ed. Frederick Page. London: Oxford University Press, 1949.

Piglia, Ricardo. "Sarmiento the Writer." *Sarmiento: Author of a Nation*. Eds. Tulio Halperín Donghi, Iván Jaksíc, Gwen Kirkpatrick, and Francine Masiello. Berkeley: University of California Press, 1994.

Pratt, Mary Louise. "Women, Literature, and National Brotherhood." *Women, Culture, and Politics in Latin America*. Ed. Seminar on Feminism and Culture in Latin America. Berkeley: University of California Press, 1990.

Prieto, Adolfo. *La literatura autobiográfica argentina*. Buenos Aires: Centro Editor de América Latina, 1996.

Puccia, Enrique H. *Breve historia del carnaval porteño*. Buenos Aires: Municipalidad de la Ciudad de Buenos Aires, 1974

Pueyrredón, Prilidiano. *Manuela de Rosas y Ezcurra*. 1851. Museo Nacional de Bellas Artes, Buenos Aires. Slide 22.

_____. *La Siesta*. 1865. Colección Blanquier. Reproduced from *Prilidiano Pueyrredón* by Jorge Romero Brest. Vol. 1, no. 2 of *Argentina en el Arte*. Buenos Aires: Viscontea Editora, 1966. Page 24.

Rama, Angel. *Los gauchipolíticos rioplatenses*. Buenos Aires: Centro Editor de América Latina, 1982.

Ramos, Julio. "Entre otros: *Una excursión a los indios ranqueles*." *Filología* 21.1 (1987) : 143–171.

Rawson, Guillermo. *Conferencias sobre higiene pública*. Ed. Luis C. Maglioni. Paris: Donnamette & Hatte, 1876.

Reid, Roddey. *Families in Jeopardy: Regulating the Social Body in France, 1750–1910*. Stanford, CA: Stanford University Press, 1993.

Renan, Ernest. "What Is a Nation?" Trans. Martin Thom. *Nation and Narration*. Ed. Homi K. Bhaba. London: Routledge, 1990. 8–22.

Ribera, Adolfo Luis. *El retrato en Buenos Aires: 1580–1870*. Buenos Aires: Universidad de Buenos Aires, 1982.

Rock, David. *Argentina 1516–1987: From Spanish Colonization to Alfonsín*. Berkeley: University of California Press, 1987.

Rodríguez Molas, Ricardo. *Historia social del gaucho*. Buenos Aires: Centro Editor de América Latina, 1982.

_____. "Sexo y matrimonio en la sociedad tradicional." *Todo es Historia* 186 (1982) : 9–43.

Rojas, Ricardo. *Historia de la literatura argentina*. Buenos Aires: Guillermo Kraft, 1957.

_____. "José Hernández, último payador." *La literatura argentina*. Vol. 9. Buenos Aires: Librería "La Facultad," 1924. Rpt. in *Martín Fierro: Cien años de crítica*. Ed. José Isaacson. Buenos Aires: Editorial Plus Ultra, 1986, 91–102.

Romero Brest, Jorge. *Prilidiano Pueyrredón*. Vol. 1, no. 2 of *Argentina en el Arte*. Buenos Aires: Viscontea Editora, 1966.

Rosenberg, Charles E. "Catechisms of Health: The Body in the PreBellum Classroom." *Bulletin of the History of Medicine* 69 (1995) : 175–197.

Rousseau, Jean-Jacques. *Confessions*.

Sabato, Hilda and Luis Alberto Romero. *Los trabajadores de Buenos Aires: La experiencia del mercado: 1850–1880*. Buenos Aires: Editorial Sudamericana, 1992.

Sáinz de Medrano, Luis. Introducción. *El gaucho Martín Fierro. La vuelta de Martín Fierro*. Ed. Luis Sáinz de Medrano. Madrid: Ediciones Cátedra, 1979.

_____. "Literatura argentina: Eduarda Mansilla de García." *El Nacional*. 11 July 1879. Rptd. in *Las escritoras: 1840–1940*. Ed. Elida Ruiz. Buenos Aires: Centro Editor de América Latina, 1980.

Sarmiento, Domingo Faustino. *Facundo: Civilización y Barbarie*. Madrid: Alianza Editorial, 1970.

_____. *Recuerdos de provincia*. Buenos Aires: Editorial de Belgrano, 1981.

_____. *A Sarmiento Anthology*. Ed. Allison Williams Bunkley. Trans. Stuart Edgar Grummon. Princeton, NJ: Princeton University Press, 1948.

Sarmiento, Francisco. *Esterilidad en la muger*. Diss: Facultad de Ciencias Médicas, Universidad de Buenos Aires, 1879. Buenos Aires: Porvenir, 1879.

Saulquin, Susan. *La moda en la Argentina*. Buenos Aires: Emecé, 1992.

Scarlett, Elizabeth. *Under Construction: the Body in Spanish Novels*. Charlottesville: University of Virginia, 1994.

Schoo Lastra, Dionosio. *El indio del desierto: 1538–1879*. 1928. Buenos Aires: Ediciones Meridion, 1957.

Scobie, James R. *Argentina: a City and a Nation*. New York: Oxford University Press, 1971.

Sedgwick, Eve Kosofsky. *Between Men: English Literature and Male Homosocial Desire*. New York: Columbia University Press, 1985.

Seminar on Feminism and Latin American Culture. *Women, Politics and Culture in Latin America*. Berkeley: University of California Press, 1990.

Sharp, Joanne P. "Gendering Nationhood: A Feminist Engagement with National Identity." *BodySpace: Destabilizing Geographies of Gender and Sexuality*. London: Routledge, 1996.

Shumway, Nicolas. *The Invention of Argentina*. Berkeley: University of California Press, 1991.

Slatta, Richard W. *Comparing Cowboys and Frontiers*. Norman: University of Oklahoma Press, 1997.

_____. *The Gaucho and the Vanishing Frontier*. Lincoln: University of Nebraska Press, 1983.

Soja, Edward W. *Postmodern Geographies: The Reassertion of Space in Critical Social Theory*. New York: Verso, 1989.

Sommer, Doris. *Foundational Fictions: The National Romances of Latin America*. Berkeley: University of California Press, 1991.

Sosa de Newton, Lily. *Las argentinas de ayer a hoy*. Buenos Aires: Zanetti, 1967.

Sosnowski, Saul. Prologue. *Una excursión a los indios ranqueles*. By Lucio V. Mansilla. Caracas: Biblioteca Ayacucho, 1984. ix–xxvi.

Stern, Mirta. "*Una excursión a los indios ranqueles*: espacio textual y ficción topográfica." *Filología* 20 (1985) : 117–138.

Subieta, Pablo. "*Martín Fierro*" (3er artículo). *Las Provincias*. 8 October 1881. Rpt. in Martín Fierro: *Cien años de crítica*. Ed. José Isaacson. Buenos Aires: Editorial Plus Ultra, 1986, 35–38.

_____. "*Martín Fierro*" (4to artículo). *Las Provincias*. 12 October 1881. Rpt. in Martín Fierro: *Cien años de crítica*. Ed. José Isaacson. Buenos Aires: Editorial Plus Ultra, 1986, 39–41.

_____. "El poeta Argentino." *Las Provincias*. 12 October 1881. Rpt. in Martín Fierro: *Cien años de crítica*. Ed. José Isaacson. Buenos Aires: Editorial Plus Ultra, 1986, 42–44.

Tomkins, Jane. "Indians." *Race, Writing, and Difference*. Ed. Henry Louis Gates, Jr. Chicago: University of Chicago Press, 1986. 59–77.

Trinh, T. Minh-Ha. *Women, Native, Other*. Bloomington: Indiana University Press, 1986.

Ubieto, Antonio, et al. *Introducción a la historia de España*. Barcelona: Editorial Teide, 1977.

Urban, Greg and Joel Sherzer. "Introduction: Indians, Nation-States, and Culture." *Nation-States and Indians in Latin America*. Eds. Greg Urban and Joel Sherzer. Austin: University of Texas Press, 1991.

Valis, Nöel. "The Language of Treasure: Carolina Coronado, Casta Esteban, and Marina Romero." *In the Feminine Mode: Essays on Hispanic Women Writers*. Eds. Noël Valis and Carol Maier. Cranbury, N.J.: Associated University Presses, 1990.

Villaverde, Cirilio. *Cecilia Valdés*. 1839, 1882. Mexico City: Editorial Porrúa, 1986.

Viñas, David. *Literatura argentina y realidad política*. Buenos Aires: Jorge Alvarez Editor, 1964.

West, Regina. "The Metonymy of Fashion." *Tailoring the Nation: Fashion Narratives of Nineteenth Century Argentina*. Diss. University of California at Berkeley, 1997. Ann Arbor: UMI, 1997.

Index